LIBRARY OF HEBREW BIBLE/ OLD TESTAMENT STUDIES

723

Formerly Journal for the Study of the Old Testament Supplement Series

Editors
Laura Quick, Oxford University, UK
Jacqueline Vayntrub, Yale University, USA

Founding Editors
David J. A. Clines, Philip R. Davies and David M. Gunn

Editorial Board
Sonja Ammann, Alan Cooper, Steed Davidson, Susan Gillingham,
Rachelle Gilmour, John Goldingay, Rhiannon Graybill, Anne Katrine Gudme,
Norman K. Gottwald, James E. Harding, John Jarick, Tracy Lemos,
Carol Meyers, Eva Mroczek, Daniel L. Smith-Christopher,
Francesca Stavrakopoulou, James W. Watts

THE CONFLICT BETWEEN FAITH AND EXPERIENCE, AND THE SHAPE OF PSALMS 73–83

Stephen J. Smith

LONDON • NEW YORK • OXFORD • NEW DELHI • SYDNEY

T&T CLARK
Bloomsbury Publishing Plc
50 Bedford Square, London, WC1B 3DP, UK
1385 Broadway, New York, NY 10018, USA
29 Earlsfort Terrace, Dublin 2, Ireland

BLOOMSBURY, T&T CLARK and the T&T Clark logo are trademarks of
Bloomsbury Publishing Plc

First published in Great Britain 2022
Paperback edition published 2024

Copyright © Stephen J. Smith, 2022, 2024

Stephen J. Smith has asserted his right under the Copyright, Designs and Patents Act, 1988, to be identified as Author of this work.

For legal purposes the Acknowledgments on p. ix constitute an extension of this copyright page.

All rights reserved. No part of this publication may be reproduced or transmitted in any form or by any means, electronic or mechanical, including photocopying, recording, or any information storage or retrieval system, without prior permission in writing from the publishers.

Bloomsbury Publishing Plc does not have any control over, or responsibility for, any third-party websites referred to or in this book. All internet addresses given in this book were correct at the time of going to press. The author and publisher regret any inconvenience caused if addresses have changed or sites have ceased to exist, but can accept no responsibility for any such changes.

A catalogue record for this book is available from the British Library.

Library of Congress Control Number: 2022933777

ISBN: HB: 978-0-5677-0273-9
PB: 978-0-5677-0276-0
ePDF: 978-0-5677-0274-6

Series: Library of Hebrew Bible/Old Testament Studies, volume 723
ISSN 2513-8758

Typeset by Newgen KnowledgeWorks Pvt. Ltd., Chennai, India

To find out more about our authors and books visit www.bloomsbury.com and sign up for our newsletters.

For my wife, Briana

CONTENTS

List of Tables	viii
Acknowledgments	ix
List of Abbreviations	xi

Chapter 1
INTRODUCTION — 1

Chapter 2
THE CURRENT STATE OF SCHOLARSHIP — 39

Chapter 3
PSALM 73: "GOD IS GOOD TO ISRAEL"—DESPITE CONFLICTING EVIDENCE — 71

Chapter 4
PSALMS 74–76: YAHWEH IS ZION'S GREAT KING—DESPITE CONFLICTING EVIDENCE — 81

Chapter 5
PSALMS 77–78: THE LORD IS GRACIOUS AND COMPASSIONATE—DESPITE CONFLICTING EVIDENCE — 103

Chapter 6
THE LITERARY UNITY OF PSALMS 73–78 — 125

Chapter 7
PSALMS 80–81: GOD WILL HEAR AND DELIVER—DESPITE CONFLICTING EVIDENCE — 143

Chapter 8
THE LITERARY UNITY OF PSALMS 79–82 AND THE SHAPE AND MESSAGE OF PSALMS 73–82 — 159

Chapter 9
CONCLUSION — 185

Bibliography	189
General Index	199
Index of Biblical References	203

TABLES

4.1	Analogous Literary Progression of Psalm 73 and Psalms 74–76	89
4.2	Lexical Parallels between Psalms 73:4–15 and 18–28	90
4.3	Parallels between Psalm 74 and Psalms 75–76	92
4.4	The Semantic Relationship between Psalm 73 and Psalms 74–76	99
5.1	Analogous Literary Progression of Psalm 73 and Psalms 77–78	111
5.2	Parallels between Psalm 77 and Psalm 78	112
5.3	The Semantic Relationship between Psalm 73 and Psalms 77–78	119
6.1	The Literary Relationship between Psalm 73 and the Unit of Psalms 74–78	135
7.1	Analogous Literary Progression of Psalm 73 and Psalms 80–81	149
7.2	Parallels between Psalm 80 and Psalm 81	151
7.3	The Semantic Relationship between Psalm 73 and Psalms 80–81	154
8.1	Analogous Literary Progression of Psalm 73 and Psalms 79/82	166
8.2	Parallels between Psalm 79 and Psalm 82	168
8.3	The Semantic Relationship between Psalm 73 and Psalms 79/82	170
C.1	The Shape and Message of Psalms 73–82	188

ACKNOWLEDGMENTS

I am indebted to many for constant support and encouragement during the long process that this work represents. This study reflects the influence and investment of many past professors, both at Reformed Seminary and Southern Seminary. It has been a blessing and a privilege to learn from so many excellent pastor-scholars at these institutions.

Special thanks are due to my advisor, Duane A. Garrett. He constantly pushed me to become a clearer and more effective writer throughout this process, and gave insightful and timely feedback at every step. I would also like to thank a number of scholars for their correspondence and for generously sharing their work with me: David Howard, Adam Hensley, William Yarchin, David Willgren, Alma Brodersen, and Peter Gentry. This work is stronger because of them.

I am also grateful to my parents Don and Cindy Smith, extended family members, and the students and staff at the Sovereign Grace Pastors College, especially Jeff Purswell, Melissa Goins, Gary Riccuci, and Paul Medler. They constantly encouraged and supported me throughout this long, and often difficult, process. This work bears the imprint of their support. Thanks are also due to Brad Harmon. Our many "long runs" helped clarify my thinking and provided needed refreshment for completing this project.

Finally, I am most indebted and grateful to my wife, Briana. She has sacrificed tremendously so that this book could see the light of day. Completing this project would have been impossible apart from her steadfast love, patience, and constant encouragement.

Stephen J. Smith
Madison, Mississippi
February 2022

ABBREVIATIONS

AOAT	Alter Orient und Altes Testament
ATANT	Abhandlungen zur Theologie des Alten und Neuen Testaments
BAR	*Biblical Archaeology Review*
BASOR	*Bulletin of the American Schools of Oriental Research*
BBB	Bonner Biblische Beiträge
BETL	Bibliotheca Ephemeridum Theologicarum Lovaniensium
Bib	*Biblica*
BN	*Biblische Notizen*
BSac	*Bibliotheca Sacra*
BZAW	Beihefte zur Zeitschrift für die alttestamentliche Wissenschaft
CahRB	Cahiers de la Revue biblique
CBQ	*Catholic Biblical Quarterly*
DCH	The Dictionary of Classical Hebrew
DSS	Dead Sea Scrolls
FAT	Forschungen zum Alten Testament
FOTL	The Forms of the Old Testament Literature
HAR	*Hebrew Annual Review*
HBS	Herders Biblische Studien
HTKAT	Herders Theologischer Kommentar zum Alten Testament
HTR	*Harvard Theological Review*
HUCA	*Hebrew Union College Annual*
ICC	International Critical Commentary
Int	*Interpretation*
JANESCU	*Journal of the Ancient Near Eastern Society of Columbia University*
JBL	*Journal of Biblical Literature*
JETS	*Journal of the Evangelical Theological Society*
JSOT	*Journal for the Study of the Old Testament*
JSOTSup	Journal for the Study of the Old Testament Supplement
JTS	*Journal of Theological Studies*
LHBOTS	Library of Hebrew Bible/Old Testament Studies
LSAWS	Linguistic Studies in Ancient West Semitic
LXX	Septuagint
MT	Masoretic Text
NCBC	New Cambridge Bible Commentary
NET	New English Translation
NIBCOT	New International Bible Commentary on the Old Testament
NICOT	New International Commentary on the Old Testament
NovT	*Novum Testamentum*
OTL	Old Testament Library

RB	*Revue Biblique*
SBLABib	Society of Biblical Literature Academia Biblica
SBLDS	Society of Biblical Literature Dissertation Series
SBLSCS	Society of Biblical Literature Septuagint and Cognate Studies
SJT	*Scottish Journal of Theology*
STDJ	Studies on the Texts of the Desert of Judah
TynBul	*Tyndale Bulletin*
TZ	*Theologische Zeitschrift*
VT	*Vetus Testamentum*
VTSup	Supplements to Vetus Testamentum
WBC	Word Biblical Commentary
ZAW	*Zeitschrift für die Alttestamentliche Wissenschaft*

Chapter 1

INTRODUCTION

Psalterexegese or editorial criticism is a major interest of modern-day Psalms studies.[1] This approach attempts to identify deliberate design in the Hebrew Psalter and determine its interpretive significance.[2] Its current prominence in Psalms studies can be traced to Brevard Childs's *Introduction to the Old Testament as Scripture*.[3] But its major catalyst was the work of one of Childs's students at Yale, Gerald Wilson. Wilson's 1985 study *The Editing of the Hebrew Psalter* sparked an interest in editorial criticism that shows no signs of waning any time soon.[4]

---

1. I use these two designations interchangeably in this study. The latter comes from J. A. Grant, "Editorial Criticism," in *Dictionary of the Old Testament: Wisdom, Poetry, & Writings*, ed. Tremper Longman III and Peter Enns (Downers Grove, IL: IVP Academic, 2008), 149–56.

2. See Grant, "Editorial Criticism."

3. Brevard S. Childs, *Introduction to the Old Testament as Scripture* (Philadelphia, PA: Fortress Press, 1979), 512–14. It should be noted that attempts to read the MT Psalter as, in some sense, a book have a long history. See David C. Mitchell, *The Message of the Psalter: An Eschatological Programme in the Book of Psalms*, JSOTSup 252 (Sheffield: Sheffield Academic Press, 1997), 15–65.

4. For the most up-to-date survey of the field, see David M. Howard Jr., "Reading the Psalter as a Unified Book: Recent Trends," in *Reading the Psalms Theologically*, ed. David M. Howard, Jr. and Andrew J. Schmutzer, forthcoming. For studies critical of *Psalterexegese*, see R. N. Whybray, *Reading the Psalms as a Book*, JSOTSup 222 (Sheffield: Sheffield Academic Press, 1996); Erhard S. Gerstenberger, "Der Psalter als Buch und als Sammlung," in *Neue Wege Der PsalmenForschung*, ed. Klaus Seybold and Erich Zenger, HBS 1 (Freiburg: Herder, 1994), 3–13; David Willgren, *The Formation of the "Book" of Psalms*, FAT II. Reihe 88 (Tübingen: Mohr Siebeck, 2016); David Willgren, "Did David Lay Down His Crown? Reframing Issues of Deliberate Juxtaposition and Interpretive Contexts in the 'Book' of Psalms with Psalm 147 as a Case in Point," in *Functions of Psalms and Prayers in the Late Second Temple Period*, ed. Mika S. Pajunen and Jeremy Penner, BZAW 486 (Berlin: De Gruyter, 2017), 212–28; David Willgren, "A Teleological Fallacy in Psalms Studies? Decentralizing the 'Masoretic' Psalms Sequence in the Formation of the 'Book' of Psalms," in *Intertextualität und die Entstehung des Psalters: Methodische Reflexionen— Theologiegeschichtliche Perspektiven*, ed. Alma Brodersen, Friederike Neumann, and David

The present study seeks to contribute to the method and results of *Psalterexegese* by offering a primarily synchronic editorial-critical investigation of Psalms 73–83. I make a case that this psalm collection has a deliberate design that reflects a sustained focus on addressing, and resolving, a multidimensional collision between "faith" (i.e., various core Israelite beliefs about God) and "experience" (the individual/community's current experience of God) that was precipitated by God's prolonged absence in the Temple's destruction (*c.* 586/587 BCE).[5] Further, I contend that the collection's design tacitly implies a singular theological message: God is *still* good to Israel—despite the conflicting evidence that this crisis appeared to represent.

The present chapter focuses on the important issue of method in editorial criticism. Here I discuss a number of key methodological issues and outline the approach I take to Psalms 73–83 in the study's main analytic chapters (Chapters 3–8). In Chapter 2 I situate the present work within the context of editorial-critical scholarship on these psalms. That literature survey highlights a number of problem areas that have arisen in the study of these psalms since Wilson's seminal dissertation. The nature of the issues involved points to the need for the fresh analysis offered here. Chapters 3–8 are the heart of this study: a detailed editorial-critical investigation of Psalms 73–83. The collective argument emerging from these chapters is summarized in the thesis outlined above. The final chapter draws together the study's conclusions and traces out some of their major implications.

Methodology

The issue of method in editorial criticism is crucial. The methods scholars choose (or do not choose) have a determinative impact on the conclusions they reach about the nature and extent of the design present in the portion of the MT Psalter under consideration (or the MT Psalter as a whole). In what follows I discuss the most significant methodological issues that have a bearing upon the present study.

Willgren, FAT II 114 (Tübingen: Mohr Siebeck, 2020), 33–50; David Willgren, "What Could We Agree On? Outlining Five Fundaments in the Research of the 'Book' of Psalms," in *The Formation of the Hebrew Psalter: The Book of Psalms between Ancient Versions, Material Transmission and Canonical Exegesis. Erich Zenger in Memoriam*, ed. Gianni Barbiero, Marco Pavan, and Johannes Schnocks, FAT II 114 (Tübingen: Mohr Siebeck, forthcoming); Alma Brodersen, *The End of the Psalter: Psalms 146–150 in the Masoretic Text, the Dead Sea Scrolls, and the Septuagint*, BZAW 505 (Berlin: De Gruyter, 2017).

5. The expression "collision between faith and experience" was inspired by Craig C. Broyles, *The Conflict of Faith and Experience in the Psalms: A Form-Critical and Theological Study*, JSOTSup 52 (Sheffield: Sheffield Academic Press, 1989).

The Scope of the Analysis

The first issue here concerns the rationale for the scope of analysis: why *these* eleven psalms (Pss 73–83)? Commenting on Psalms 120–134, William Yarchin recently observed that "we can reliably speak of a discrete subcollection textual unit by virtue of the superscripts at the beginning of each of those fifteen psalms [i.e., שיר המעלות], found in the very earliest manuscripts from the Judean Desert."[6] Similarly, the common "author" designation לאסף heading Psalms 73–83 formally identifies these eleven consecutive psalms as a discrete subcollection.[7] Supporting this claim is the observation that לאסף appears in our earliest witnesses to these psalms, as can be seen from their presence in the LXX (see τῷ Ασαφ heading Pss 72–82) and the relevant DSS that are not too fragmentary (see לאסף in Ps 82:1 and 83:1 of Mas1e). At the very least, the designation לאסף demarcates these eleven consecutive psalms as a discrete unit for study on a purely formal level.[8] I argue their *literary* unity at length in the main analytic chapters of this study.[9]

---

6. William Yarchin, "Why the Future of Canonical Hebrew Psalter Exegesis Includes Abandoning Its Own Premise," in Barbiero, Pavan and Schnocks, *The Formation of the Hebrew Psalter*. I should note that, as the title indicates, Yarchin's essay is critical of *Psalterexegese*.

7. I say "author designation" because, as will become clear, I believe that at least some of these psalms (e.g., Pss 74 and 79) stem from the exilic/postexilic period, possibly from an Asaphite guild (see Ezra 2:41; Neh 7:44). And, as will also become clear, I agree with Beat Weber that the collection's final form stems from that period as well. See Beat Weber, "Der Asaph Psalter—eine Skizze," in *Prophetie und Psalmen. Festschrift für Klaus Seybold zum 65. Geburtstag*, AOAT 280, ed. B. Huwyler, H. P. Mathys, and B. Weber (Münster: Ugarit-Verlag, 2001), 135–9. I should note that Weber considers Ps 79 to be the only truly exilic psalm in the collection. See the discussion of Weber's views in Chapter 2.

8. I am not claiming that לאסף necessarily reveals that these eleven psalms were once an independent collection, though it certainly may. This claim is commonly made and may be correct. But it cannot be demonstrated from the manuscript data. The point here is that, at the very least, לאסף formally sets these psalms apart on a synchronic level. The standard view in Psalms studies has been that Pss 73–83 *were* once an independent collection. David Willgren expresses a contrary view, arguing that such "author" designations "would not necessarily indicate previously independent collections of psalms since these designations … were added over time, and since the Dead Sea 'psalms' scrolls configured psalms in quite different ways, indicating that the contours of a collection do not need to overlap with the borders of a sequence of similarly designated psalms." Willgren, *The Formation of the "Book" of Psalms*, 178.

9. Of course, I am not the first to detect literary unity between these psalms. See, for example, Weber, "Der Asaph Psalter—eine Skizze," 118–27; Christine Dannette Brown Jones, "The Psalms of Asaph: A Study of the Function of a Psalm Collection" (PhD diss., Baylor University, 2009), 143–75; Michael D. Goulder, *The Psalms of Asaph and the Pentateuch*, LHBOTS 233 (Sheffield: Sheffield Academic Press, 1996), 15–36. What is unique is the nature of the literary unity I am arguing for in this study.

The Text of Psalms 73–83

To state the obvious, none of the original autographs of these psalms have survived from antiquity. Which textual witness (or witnes*es*), then, should be used as the basis for an editorial-critical study of this subcollection? In this study, I give primacy to Codex Leningradensis (Saint Petersburg MS B19^A), the oldest complete Hebrew manuscript of the Hebrew Bible.[10] Such prioritization of the Hebrew Masoretic Psalter (MT-150) has, in fact, been the standard practice in the field of *Psalterexegese* since Wilson's seminal study. This practice, however, is currently being called into question. Given the growing number of voices raising objections, it is necessary to consider the current discussion on this matter. At its center are the texts from the Judean Desert.

Prior to the discovery of the DSS, the textual data for the book of Psalms did not vary widely. But with their discovery this picture changed dramatically. Eva Mroczek explains,

> The picture [at Qumran] we have … is of a number of psalm collections, and collections containing psalms, that likely had very different genres and purposes. They are not copies of the same documents. They range from previously unknown works containing one psalm to fragments of single psalms, to collections of previously known psalms in previously unknown orders. *In no case do they represent the same content, order, or scope as our book of Psalms.* (emphasis added)[11]

Consequently, she concludes, prior to the first century the "book" of Psalms "can no longer be thought of as a fixed book, but an indeterminate collection without a stable order, inventory, or boundaries."[12]

Mroczek's conclusion draws upon the research of an important article by Mika S. Pajunen.[13] Pajunen's major contention is that using the manuscripts from Qumran to support the existence of an authoritative "book" of Psalms with clear boundaries, as is commonly done, is "based upon largely non-existing evidence"

---

10. Hereafter MS B19^A. MS B19^A was written in 1008–1010 CE. Currently the only complete scholarly edition is Biblia Hebraica Stuttgartensia (BHS), a diplomatic edition of MS B19^A. Technically speaking, BHS is not an *identical* reproduction of Codex Leningradensis. As William Yarchin notes, Leningradensis contains 149 psalms, whereas BHS presents 150. The discrepancy relates to Pss 114–115, which form a single composition in Leningradensis. As Yarchin notes, BHS consequently counts the final psalm number as both 150 (in Arabic enumeration) and 149 (in Hebrew enumeration). See William Yarchin, "Is There an Authoritative Shape for the Hebrew Book of Psalms?," *RB* 215 (2015): 358–9.

11. Eva Mroczek, *The Literary Imagination in Jewish Antiquity* (Oxford: Oxford University Press, 2016), 26.

12. Ibid., 32.

13. Mika S. Pajunen, "Perspectives on the Existence of a Particular Authoritative Book of Psalms in the Late Second Temple Period," *JSOT* 39 (2014): 139–63.

(141). He seeks to demonstrate this claim by considering the problematic nature of the evidence from two perspectives.

Pajunen first argues that the high number of "so-called Psalms manuscripts" found at Qumran (counted between 35 and 39) is a "statistical illusion" (140). He points out how little of the MT Psalter is actually preserved, and that what *is* preserved reveals significant paratextual variance (i.e., there is no single order of psalms, and the order is frequently at odds with the MT).[14] Further, he argues that the common practice of counting psalms manuscripts like those preserving portions of Isaiah or Deuteronomy (i.e., as evidence for the entire "book") is invalid. In his view, scholars have failed to recognize "the difference between a more or less unified, but nevertheless clearly definable book, and a collection of more than one composition."[15]

More specifically, Pajunen points out that, unlike Deuteronomy or Isaiah, the psalms manuscripts are compositions arranged in collections of different sizes and for various purposes. Consequently, a fragment of the former two books is likely to reflect the entire book, while a fragment of the latter is different. Fragments of *parts* of the MT Psalter cannot therefore be used as evidence for the *entire* MT Psalter. Thus, Pajunen considers the actual evidence for an MT Psalter at Qumran (and its importance/authority there) to be minimal at best.

But what about evidence for an authoritative "book" of Psalms during the Qumran period, particularly at Qumran (i.e., where the statistics used as evidence come from)? Here Pajunen points out that there are no explicit references to a book of Psalms in the manuscripts at Qumran, and so no evidence of such a book during the Qumran period (149). Rather, we instead find evidence of authoritative Psalters. Though the (proto-)MT Psalter is chronologically the oldest preserved, the existence of 11QPs^a and the LXX Psalter shows that it was not considered "the one and only immutable canonical arrangement" (156). There was consequently not "one true Psalter" in the Qumran period (157). Further, he argues that it is anachronistic to label psalm collections not contained in the three "Psalters" mentioned above "non-canonical" or "apocryphal" (e.g., *The Psalms of Solomon*). From the standpoint of that period, Pajunen contends, these collections were not considered somehow secondary or less authoritative.[16]

Based upon the nature of the evidence summarized above, Pajunen concludes, "Therefore, each collection should be studied *individually and in the same way, regardless of whether it contains 'canonical' or 'non-canonical' psalms*. Only then can it be truly evaluated how a book of Psalms came to be included in the later canon of Scripture (emphasis added)."[17]

---

14. See the discussion on ibid., 141–6.
15. Ibid. See Pajunen's argument on ibid., 146–9.
16. Pajunen, "Perspectives on the Existence of a Particular Authoritative Book of Psalms in the Late Second Temple Period," 157–62.
17. Ibid., 163.

Neither Mroczek nor Pajunen, however, brings the manuscript evidence from the Judean Desert to bear directly upon editorial criticism, in particular the priority the discipline has given to the MT Psalter. David Willgren is the most noteworthy voice in this regard. In his monograph-length critique of *Psalterexegese*, Willgren draws extensively upon the "artifactual" evidence from the Judean Desert summarized above to make his case that the Psalter is an anthology—not the deliberately designed coherent whole of *Psalterexegese*.[18] For Willgren, scholars working in that field have based their conclusions about the "shape and shaping" of the Psalter too heavily upon a synchronic analysis of MT-150.

Entering into this discussion, Willgren's study argues that the "how?" (i.e., the diachronic growth of the collection) and "why?" (to what end psalms have been juxtaposed in the collection) questions related to the formation of the book of Psalms should be answered in much closer dialogue with diachronic considerations, the DSS in particular. In conjunction with other evidence, Willgren sees these manuscripts as posing a direct challenge to a number of the "assured results" of *Psalterexegese* (e.g., the organizing function of superscriptions; the prefatory function of Pss 1–2; and the concluding function of the "Final Hallel" [Pss 146–150]).[19] I return to Willgren's treatment of Psalms 146–150 in his monograph for illustrative purposes below.

In a recent essay Willgren further develops the challenge of the DSS, particularly the problem they pose for Masoretic priority.[20] Willgren argues that, in giving the Masoretic sequence primacy in its analysis, *Psalterexegese* commits a "teleological fallacy." This is a fallacy committed "when scholars extrapolate ideas of fixed, final forms of text backwards so that each succinct stage of formation that precedes the latter is constituted similarly."[21] According to Willgren, a better approach is to begin with the earliest manuscripts themselves: the DSS. What do we find when we turn to these scrolls? Willgren summarizes his position:

> Ultimately, I believe that imposing the notion of a fixed sequence of psalms to which all other scrolls can be related (or even derived) is quite contrary to what is actually seen throughout the Dead Sea Scrolls. The scrolls are not *variants* of a MT "Book" of Psalms. The Dead Sea psalms scrolls rather reveal *variance*, and this needs to be *situated more squarely within our methodology*.[22]

By "variance" Willgren is referring especially to the "far-reaching paratextual instability" he observes in the DSS. "Paratextual instability" has in view things like

---

18. Willgren, *The Formation of the "Book" of Psalms*. Willgren defines an anthology as "a compilation of independent texts, actively selected and organized in relation to some present needs, inviting readers to a platform of continuous dialogue." Ibid., 25.
19. Willgren, *The Formation of the "Book" of Psalms*, 110–30, 160–2, 172–95, 275–82.
20. Willgren, "A Teleological Fallacy in Psalms Studies?"
21. Ibid., 46.
22. Ibid., 41.

variance in superscriptions and psalm sequence, the nature of the material (i.e., we only find "pieces" of the 'book' of Psalms in the scrolls), the physical shape and layout of the manuscripts, and the function and use of the actual scroll.[23]

Willgren then suggests three questions that can help "tackle" the challenge posed by the DSS: (1) Are the relevant paratexts stable over time? (or at least similar to the MT?); (2) What kind of paratext is it? How can its function be understood?; and (3) How is the psalm used? Can support for the proposed reading be found in the ancient contexts (i.e., the Second Temple period)? Given its significance of Psalm 106 in proposals for the "shape" of the book of Psalms (e.g., it contains a "book" dividing doxology, a Hallelujah framework, and a הודו-phrase), Willgren then uses this psalm to illustrate how these questions "can assist an analysis of paratextual instability in the formation process."[24]

Regarding the first question, Willgren observes that Psalm 106 is not found in the DSS in a sequence agreeing with MT-150, and does not appear to have any paratextual function in the scrolls where it is apparently attested. In answering the second, Willgren focuses on the psalm's opening clause (v. 1) and concluding doxology (v. 48) in light of the paratextual role editorial critics frequently assign them. Willgren's analysis suggests that neither has a paratextual function beyond the psalm itself (such a function was at least not originally intended). As for the third question, Willgren considers how Psalm 106 is used in 1 Chronicles 16 and 4Q380, showing that neither is "aware of any book-dividing function."[25] According to Willgren, this test case of Psalm 106 illustrates his main point: starting from the earliest manuscripts themselves enables scholars to avoid the teleological fallacy, the inevitable result being the "decentralization" of the Masoretic sequence.

In addition to the example of Psalm 106, we can use Psalms 146–150 ("the Final Hallel") as a second test case. As mentioned above, editorial critics widely hold that Psalms 146–150 constitute a unit that forms a deliberate concluding doxology to the Psalter. The basis of this claim is the unity observed between these psalms in MT-150 (and the ties they share with Pss 1 and 2). However, both Willgren and Alma Brodersen have argued that matters are not so simple. Reaching similar conclusions, they contend that the evidence for this widely held view dissipates when scholars consider *all* of the material manuscript data for these psalms (i.e., DSS; MT-150; LXX).

Willgren devotes ch. 12 of his monograph to "the Final Hallel."[26] After taking a close look at each psalm, Willgren considers the "artifactual variations" observable in MT-150, the DSS, and the LXX. For example, Willgren notes that only one of the four DSS preserving these psalms has a sequence that agrees with MT-150 (i.e., Mas1f).[27] Another variation relates to Psalm 147. Willgren observes that

23. See the discussion on ibid., 38–41.
24. Willgren, "A Teleological Fallacy in Psalms Studies?" 42.
25. Ibid., 44.
26. Willgren, *The Formation of the "Book" of Psalms*, 244–83.
27. Ibid., 276.

the MT-150 sequence contains the *least* number of shared links out of the four sequences in which the psalm appears. According to Willgren, this observation challenges the use of lexical links to establish a sequential reading of these psalms, a common method found in editorial-critical studies of "the Final Hallel."

Based largely upon such "artifactual variations," Willgren concludes that the widely held view of Psalms 146–150 among editorial critics is "unconvincing." Taking the important textual evidence of the DSS and LXX into account, he argues, suggests that Psalms 146–150 are likely *not* an "intentional unified composition" meant to be read sequentially as a conclusion to the Psalter.[28]

Alma Brodersen, who devotes an entire monograph to Psalms 146–150, reaches similar conclusions based upon a much more thorough investigation of these psalms.[29] Foundational to Brodersen's methodology is her text-critical decision to treat the MT-150, the DSS, and the LXX Psalter as parallel sources.[30] She explains, "Rather than going beyond the preserved manuscripts and their editions to construct a more original text as the basis of my exegesis, or simply choosing MT as the only basis, I read the text forms separately."[31] In over 250 pages, Brodersen provides an in-depth analysis of each psalm as they appear in MT-150, the DSS, and the LXX Psalter, and compares them in terms of their content, sequence, and intertextuality.[32] In a recent essay presenting a condensed version of her argument, Brodersen summarizes her major finding:

> Die parallele Auslegung des masoretischen Texts, der Qumranschriften und der Septuaginta führt zu Entdeckungen, die bei einer Konzentration auf den masoretischen Text oder einen kritischen Urtext auf Basis des masoretischen Text verborgen bleiben ... Zumindest muss sich Psalterexegese ihrer Begrenzung auf den masoretischen Psalter als „den" Psalter stärker bewusst sein.[33]

What exactly is the major "discovery that remains hidden" when concentrating on MT-150 (or a hypothetical original based upon it)? In light of the popular view among editorial-critics noted above, Brodersen's conclusion is potentially quite significant: "Psalms 146–150 are originally separate texts. They were not originally written to end or frame the Psalter as a unit."[34] This conclusion rests upon a twofold foundation: (1) the many differences between the three oldest sources for Psalms

---

28. Ibid., 281.
29. Brodersen, *The End of the Psalter*. I do not mean to imply here that Willgren's analysis is not thorough. It is just not an entire monograph.
30. Ibid., 18–20.
31. Brodersen, *The End of the Psalter*, 19.
32. See the discussion below for Brodersen's definition of intertextuality.
33. Alma Brodersen, "Quellen und Intertextualität: Methodische Überlegungen zum Psalterende," in Brodersen, Neumann, and Willgren, *Intertextualität und die Entstehung des Psalters*, 21.
34. Brodersen, *The End of the Psalter*, 270.

146–150; and (2) Brodersen's intertextual analysis, which leads her to conclude that "Psalms 146–150 do not refer to one another … and share almost no reference texts."[35]

Material manuscript data of another kind presents an additional challenge to the primacy given to MS B19[A] here. William Yarchin has assembled an impressive collection of medieval Hebrew manuscripts, a database that "includes over 400 medieval Hebrew manuscripts housed in libraries and institutions worldwide, 200 manuscripts from the Cairo Genizah, and all the relevant incunabula."[36] Yarchin, who has studied these manuscripts extensively, explains that "TR-150" is only one of roughly 150 different "psalter" configurations in the medieval Hebrew manuscripts.[37] Yarchin's research potentially poses a challenge for the following reason: the *configuration* or *segmentation* of Psalms 73–83 is central to my thesis that the collection has a deliberate design.

The point of this discussion of the material manuscript data is not to affirm or deny the viewpoints/interpretations presented. It is simply to illustrate a single point: to maintain credibility, it has become clear that editorial criticism must be carried out in closer dialogue with the full range of material evidence for the Hebrew Psalter.[38] For this reason, in what follows I provide a rationale for my decision to use MS B19[A] as a base text in this study. Given the study's limited scope, I do so specifically with reference to the collection under consideration.

Five manuscripts from the Judean Desert (all but one from Qumran) contain portions of one or more of these psalms (4Q87; 6Q5; 11Q6; 11Q8; Mas1e).[39] Apart

---

35. Ibid.

36. Yarchin, "Is There an Authoritative Shape for the Hebrew Book of Psalms?," 359.

37. "TR-150" stands for Textus Receptus-150, the "150 Psalm psalter that is found in the Bomberg Rabbinic Bible [A.D. 1525]." Yarchin, "Is There an Authoritative Shape for the Hebrew Book of Psalms?," 358. As Yarchin points out, this is the base text of virtually all modern translations and the modern Hebrew Bible editions underlying them. Yarchin introduces the terminology "TR-150" (instead of the traditional "MT-150" or MT-150 Psalter) since the configuration (not content or order) of psalms in the medieval Hebrew manuscripts often differs from that of the MT-150 Psalter.

38. This is not to imply that previous research has utterly ignored the DSS and LXX. For example, see Adam D. Hensley, *Covenant Relationships and the Editing of the Hebrew Psalter*, LHBOTS 666 (London: Bloomsbury T&T Clark, 2018), 33–41; and Egbert Ballhorn, *Zum Telos des Psalters: Der Textzusammenhang des Vierten und Fünften Psalmenbuches (Ps 90 –150)*, BBB 138 (Berlin: Philo, 2004), 33–5. The point is simply that the work of Willgren, Brodersen, Yarchin, and others shows the need for greater engagement with this evidence in future studies.

39. 4Q87 contains fragments of Ps 76:10–77:1, Ps 78:6–7, 31–35, and Ps 81:2–3; 6Q5, which may not be a psalms manuscript, possibly contains Ps 78:36–37. Interestingly, if 6Q5

from minor differences in orthography, there are no textual differences between these manuscripts and MS B19ᴬ. There are no clear "paratextual" variations either. As noted earlier, the "author designation" לאסף appears in the manuscripts that are not too fragmentary (see לאסף in Ps 82:1 and 83:1 of Mas1e). In terms of the arrangement and segmentation of psalms, there is no clear evidence for a layout other than what we find in MS B19ᴬ.

On the other hand, we do find clear agreement with MS B19ᴬ. Both 11Q6 and Mas1e preserve joins in agreement with the sequence of Psalms 73-83 in that manuscript (Pss 77-78 and Pss 81-83, respectively), and 4Q87 probably also reflects agreement.[40] The sequence contained in 11Q8 may agree with MS B19ᴬ, but the state of the manuscript does not allow for a firm conclusion.[41] 6Q5, which appears to contain remnants of Psalm 78:36-37, is too fragmentary to be of any value for our purposes.

Thus, the relevant manuscripts from the Judean Desert do not provide direct evidence for the *exact* shape of Psalms 73-83 as attested in MS B19ᴬ. As we have seen, Psalms 73, 74, 79, and 80 are not explicitly attested, and those attested are preserved in a fragmentary nature. However, the fragmentary nature of the manuscripts also works the other way around; the absence of evidence is not necessarily the evidence of absence. This is important to remember since most of these manuscripts are too fragmentary or badly damaged to be reasonably reconstructed.[42] Consequently, since the relevant manuscripts from the Judean Desert (1) do not reveal any clear divergence from MS B19ᴬ in terms of content, sequence, or segmentation; and (2) *do* preserve clear joins in agreement with MS

---

is a psalms manuscript, it would be the only evidence from Qumran for a psalms manuscript written on papyrus. See Eva Jain, *Psalmen Oder Psalter: Materielle Rekonstruktion und inhaltliche Untersuchung der Psalmenhandschriften aus der Wüste Juda* STDJ 109 (Leiden: Brill, 2014), 151-2; 11Q6 preserves only Ps 77:18-78:1; 11Q8 has portions of Ps 78:5-12 and 81:4-9; and Mas1e contains Pss 81-83 in a fragmentary nature.

40. A helpful chart of the joins agreeing with the MT Psalter among the DSS can be found in Willgren, *The Formation of the "Book" of Psalms*, 106-8.

41. Jain, *Psalmen Oder Psalter*, 196.

42. For example, see Jain's comments on 11Q6 and 11Q87. Jain, *Psalmen Oder Psalter*, 104, 186. Further, Jain thinks that Mas1e (which largely corresponds to MT) may have been large enough to contain Pss 1-89: "Sie [i.e., Mas1e] beinhaltet 29 Zeilen pro Kolumne statt wie bisher angenommen 32 Zeilen Die Rekonstruktion der Handschrift ergab, dass sie vermutlich in 67 Kolumnen (inklusive Handlesheets) Ps 1,1-89,53 beinhaltete und eine Länge von ca. 7,4 m hatte." Jain, *Psalmen Oder Psalter*, 210. See the discussion on pp. 209-10. Regarding 11Q8, Jain explains that we cannot draw conclusions about deviations, rearrangements, or omissions compared to the MT because the distance between the fragments (reconstructed from MT) is too large and indeterminate. Consequently, she notes, the manuscript's scope, content, and function can no longer be determined. Though she does note it could have possibly contained the entire MT Psalter. Jain, *Psalmen Oder Psalter*, 196.

B19^A (e.g., Mas1e), they give no compelling reason *not* to use MS B19^A as a base text for analysis.

Positive warrant for this decision comes from the LXX Psalter, the oldest complete source of any kind for Psalms 73–83. This translation was likely completed no later than the second century BCE, which means it predates both the medieval manuscripts of these psalms and the relevant fragments from the Judean Desert.[43] This early date is important because the sequence and segmentation of Psalms 73–83 in MS B19^A are identical to that of the LXX Psalter. The LXX Psalter therefore demonstrates that MS B19^A preserves the oldest attested shape for Psalms 73–83.[44] However, neither the LXX nor its hypothetical Hebrew *Vorlage* was used as a base text because (1) the former is a translation, not a Hebrew text;[45] and (2) the reconstruction of the latter is an extremely complex undertaking fraught with difficulties.[46]

Yarchin's impressive research indicates that all medieval manuscripts agree with the sequence and content of Psalms 73–83 as preserved in MS B19^A. The only notable, but still minor, deviation is that twenty-seven manuscripts begin a new psalm at 78:38.[47] This difference in the segmentation of a single psalm, however,

---

43. None of the relevant DSS are earlier than the first century CE The only possible exception is Mas1e, which may date to the end of the last century BCE. For the dating of the LXX Psalter to the second century BCE, see Hensley, *Covenant Relationships and the Editing of the Hebrew Psalter*, p. 20 n.38 and Joachim Schaper, "The Septuagint Psalter" in *The Oxford Handbook of the Psalms*, ed. William P. Brown (Oxford: Oxford University Press, 2014), 174–5. The oldest complete LXX Psalter manuscripts are Codex Vaticanus and Codex Sinaiticus, both from the fourth century CE. Though questioned by some, there is a high level of agreement between the presumed *Vorlage* of the LXX and the MT. As Peter Gentry notes, most of the differences "arise from differences between source and target languages as codes of communication, corruptions within the textual transmission of the Greek version, and variants which are due to the translator and not genuinely textual." Peter J. Gentry, "The Text of the Old Testament," *JETS* 52 (2009): 38. For example, Gentry himself has demonstrated that the significant discrepancy in length between the Greek translation of Job and the MT (the former being one-sixth shorter) is not due to a different parent text but to translation technique. See P. J. Gentry, *The Asterisked Materials in the Greek Job*, SBLSCS 38 (Atlanta, GA: Scholars Press, 1995).

44. The only notable differences in the LXX are the superscriptions of Pss 80 (LXX 79; see ὑπὲρ το Ἀσσυρίου) and 76 (LXX 75; see πρὸς τὸν Ἀσσύριον). But these are best explained as interpretive additions to a *Vorlage* very similar to the MT, not as real variants. Hensley, *Covenant Relationships and the Editing of the Hebrew Psalter*, 39.

45. In this connection, see the comments in James Barr, *Comparative Philology and the Text of the Old Testament* (Winona Lake, IN: Eisenbrauns, 1987), 2.

46. On this point, see Emmanuel Tov, *The Text-Critical Use of the Septuagint in Biblical Research*, 3rd ed. (Winona Lake, IN: Eisenbrauns, 2015), 62–112.

47. Personal correspondence with William Yarchin. In a 2015 article, Yarchin gives as an example MS 4° 780 from the National Library of Israel in Jerusalem. See Yarchin, "Is There an Authoritative Shape for the Hebrew Book of Psalms?," 365. This example is of particular

is an insufficient reason for not using MS B19^A as a base text. These twenty-seven manuscripts represent an *extremely small* percentage of the large database Yarchin has compiled. By far, the vast majority of these manuscripts (as Yarchin himself observes) agree with the configuration of Psalm 78 in MS B19^A.

In addition to this last observation, two others suggest that the segmentation of Psalm 78 in the twenty-seven medieval manuscripts is a secondary creation. Negatively, no textual evidence exists for Psalm 78:38–72 as a discrete unit before the Middle Ages. Positively, there *is* clear textual support for the configuration of Psalm 78 in MS B19^A as the most ancient attested (i.e., the LXX Psalter). It is reasonable to conclude that the segmentation found in the twenty-seven medieval manuscripts does not reflect an alternative textual tradition but is a secondary creation, probably for liturgical purposes.[48] Based upon the extant manuscript data, then, it is reasonable to conclude that MS B19^A preserves the original shape of Psalm 78.

This discussion of the most important manuscript data for Psalms 73–83 reveals the *stability* of this collection in the textual tradition, in terms of its content, sequence, and segmentation. To borrow Willgren's terminology, we see both textual stability *and* paratextual stability.[49] The latter is particularly significant since there is a heavy paratextual focus (especially on psalm sequencing and [tacit] segmentation) in the main analytic chapters of this study (Chapters 3–8).

In conclusion, the textual evidence we have considered warrants (1) using the oldest complete Hebrew manuscript (MS B19^A) as a base text in this study, and (2) the language "final form" for the shape of the collection attested therein; as we have seen, there is no clear evidence that this collection ever had a substantially different shape in terms of its major textual and paratextual features.

A brief word needs to be said about both Psalm 50 and Psalm 83. Like Psalms 73–83, Psalm 50 (MT) also contains the "author" designation לאסף and shares a number of literary similarities with Psalms 73–83. For these reasons, analyses of Psalms 73–83 usually include Psalm 50. The assumption is that Psalm 50 was originally part of that collection but was separated when incorporated into the MT Psalter.

I have nevertheless chosen to exclude Psalm 50 for two reasons. First, *if* they have any diachronic significance, common heading and content may only reflect

---

interest because the copyist presents Ps 78:38 in the manner that the manuscript presents psalm incipits. Another example is the 1298 MS Venezia Biblioteca Marciana Or. 207 A. In this manuscript, a later hand assigned the number עח ("78") to Ps 78:38–72 (MS B19^A). However, in the thirteenth-century manuscript Parm. 2355 the number and spacing comes from the original scribe. I am indebted to personal correspondence with William Yarchin for these details.

48. I am indebted to William Yarchin for this suggestion (personal correspondence).

49. Thus, the first of Willgren's three questions noted earlier has been answered ("Are the relevant paratexts stable over time?"). The remaining two receive answers in the course of the study.

that Psalm 50 stems from the same *larger corpus* associated with the figure of Asaph/an Asaphite guild, not the same *subcollection*.[50] Second, and related, Psalm 50 never occurs in consecution with Psalms 73–83 in the textual tradition. So, while Psalm 50 *may* have been part of this subcollection, there is no concrete textual evidence that it ever *was*. For purposes of this study, therefore, I restrict my analysis to the eleven consecutive psalms bearing the "author" designation לאסף.

Regarding Psalm 83, it will become clear later that, in my view, Psalms 73–82 are a literary unit to which Psalm 83 may not belong. That is, while *formally* grouped with Psalms 73–82 by virtue of the designation לאסף, the literary unity detected in Psalms 73–82 may not extend to Psalm 83. But since there is no justification for separating Psalm 83 at the outset, the working assumption is that Psalm 83 *does* belong with Psalms 73–82 until (potential) evidence to the contrary surfaces in the course of the study. Thus, I will often refer to "Psalms 73–83" when making statements about the design or purpose of "the collection," even though it may turn out that such statements ultimately do not apply to Psalm 83.

A Synchronic Approach

This study fits primarily within synchronic *Psalterexegese*. It is mainly a synchronic literary analysis of Psalms 73–83. My goal is to make a plausible case that (1) the collection's final form has a deliberate, overarching, literary design, and (2) the design detected reflects a sustained focus on addressing *and* resolving the multifaceted theological crisis precipitated by God's prolonged absence in the temple's destruction in 586 BCE.[51]

It will become apparent that I think the results of my synchronic analysis may have implications for the collection's formation. They may provide a window into the *Sitz im Leben* of the collection's present configuration, suggesting that it resulted from a single creative act (not a diachronic process) in the wake of the Temple's destruction in 586/587 BCE.[52] If correct, this study would offer an

---

50. An analogy might help clarify my reasoning here. Imagine that 2,000 years in the future a piece of paper containing eleven songs from a single artist (Pss 73–83 in the analogy) and a separate piece containing a single song from that same artist (Ps 50 in the analogy) were discovered buried at the same location. Research then revealed that the eleven songs all came from the same album produced in 2021. It would be invalid to automatically assume that the single song on the separate piece of paper belonged to that same album, though it may have. Alternatively, it may have been written by the same artist twenty years earlier. In that case, the single song (i.e., Ps 50) would stem from the same artist (i.e., an Asaphite guild) but not the same "subcollection" of songs (i.e., Pss 73–83).

51. The "resolve" portion of this claim, as we shall see, is significant in light of previous studies. Not a few studies understand Pss 73–83 to be *addressing* the sixth-century crisis. But, to my knowledge, none propose that this collection provides its own, self-contained, resolution to it.

52. "Single creative act" does not mean that each psalm was (necessarily) *written* for its current location. See the discussion below.

alternative proposal to views suggesting that the present configuration came about in successive redactional stages.[53]

However, I do not regard knowledge of the collection's historical origins or growth as essential for achieving my main goal, namely, understanding the design of the collection's final form, its purpose, and the theological message(s) it communicates. This outlook distinguishes my approach from diachronic-oriented methods like those of Beat Weber and Judith Gärtner, whose views we consider in Chapter 2. I find such studies intriguing and agree with a number of their observations on the collection's shape. But, in my view, the reconstructions of the collection's growth that they propose (inferred from a synchronic analysis of the MT, not actual manuscript data) ultimately involve too much speculation to shed significant light on its design, message, and purpose.[54] Insight into the history of the collection's growth would be helpful in this regard. But I do not believe it is necessary, as will become clear in the pages that follow.

That said, the above comments do reveal that there is a sense in which my study of the collection's "shape" also concerns its "shaping." The claim that this collection has a *deliberate* design that reflects "a sustained focus on addressing and resolving" a singular theological crisis is a teleological claim; it assumes that at least one person was responsible for that design, and had an end in view when giving the collection *this* design rather than another. In this sense, the approach taken here may be called an "author-/editor-oriented approach."

This designation does not refer to an ability to somehow "get inside the head" of the author(s)/editor(s) or even reconstruct the original readers or first recipients of this collection. Though, as mentioned above, later I do make a suggestion about the latter. Neither does it reflect a lack of awareness of the reader's role in the interpretive process (e.g., adopting one method and not another; bringing preconceptions to the reading process, etc.). Rather, it means that my aim (however imperfectly attained) is to detect and understand the design that those responsible for the collection's present configuration created. And it means that I believe a reasonable means of achieving this goal is a close synchronic literary analysis.[55]

The approach envisioned here is similar to, but distinct from, Egbert Ballhorn's "implicit reading concept" (*impliziten Lesekonzept*).[56] This concept is a modification

---

53. In this connection, see the studies of Beat Weber and Judith Gärtner summarized in Chapter 2.

54. The following comments exemplify the types of reconstructions I have in mind: "In redactional terms, then, one should assume that the arch of composition from Psalms 74; 77; and 79 has been interrupted by the insertion of Psalms 75 and 76"; "the redactional additions in Psalm 76:9–10 and 74:18–21 probably go back to the same hand that inserted Psalms 75 and 76 in the context of the Asaph collection and, in this way, designed the compositional arch from Psalms 74–76." Judith Gärtner, "The Historical Psalms. A Study of Psalms 78; 105; 106; 135, and 136 as Key Hermeneutical Texts in the Psalter," *Hebrew Bible and Ancient Israel* 4 (2015): 381–2.

55. In this connection, see the analogy of the modern volume below.

56. Ballhorn, *Zum Telos des Psalters*, 22.

of Wolfgang Iser's "implied reader" construct. According to Iser, the process of reading is an active and creative one. Iser stressed that it is necessary to take into account both the text itself and the actions involved in responding to that text. He postulated that we can conceive of works of literature as having two poles, an "artistic" and "aesthetic." The former is the text as created by the author; the latter is "the realization accomplished by the reader."[57] Identifying a work of literature, Iser contends, lies halfway between these poles: "*the convergence of text and reader brings the literary work into existence*, and this convergence can never be precisely pinpointed, but must always remain virtual, as it is not to be identified either with the reality of the text or with the individual disposition of the reader (emphasis added)."[58] The act of reading thus "causes the literary work to unfold its inherently dynamic character."[59]

Ballhorn introduces the "implicit reading concept" in light of criticisms of the "implied reader" construct. On the one hand, some have noted that this construct is misleading in that it represents an anthropomorphic description. On the other, the terminology remains unclear as to whether it is an event on the part of the text or reader.[60] By speaking of the "implicit *reading concept*" Ballhorn seeks to more clearly separate the structure of the text from the diverse, though not arbitrary, reading processes that respond to the text.[61] Ballhorn's approach attempts to react to the structures that can be identified within the MT Psalter itself. The focus is not on the text's production or compositional history but the "end product as a total work of art" (*Endprodukt als Gesamtkunstwerk*) and the goal to which the text's composition is leading the reader.[62] Thus, Ballhorn's model is not focused on discerning authorial or editorial intent but the structures and "internal reference systems" (*internen Verweissystemen*) that can be identified in a text.[63]

The author-/editor-oriented approach taken here resembles Ballhorn's "implicit reading concept" in this way: it aims to allow structures that can be identified in the composition (i.e., Pss 73–83) to guide interpretation in the direction or goal that the composition is leading the reader/singer. However, I use the terminology "author-/editor-oriented" given the inescapable reality that behind that composition (and all its structures) is at least one person/community. Thus, even if the end result can only be considered *a* reading rather than *the* reading, inasmuch as I am reacting to the structures that characterize the collection's shape, I am of necessity reacting to the structures that at least one person *intended* to create. In these structures,

---

57. Wolfgang Iser, *The Implied Reader: Patterns of Communication in Prose from Bunyan to Beckett* (Baltimore, MD: Johns Hopkins University Press, 1974), 275.
58. Ibid.
59. Ibid.
60. Ballhorn, *Zum Telos des Psalters*, 22.
61. Ibid.
62. Ibid., 18.
63. Ibid.

then, we are being led not merely by "the composition" but by the "footprints," so to speak, of those that gave the collection its present shape.[64]

Thus, in my view, any approach that aims to allow the text itself to set the interpretive agenda simply cannot avoid making claims about "authorial" or "editorial" intent, whether they use such language or not. For this reason, while my focus is a synchronic literary analysis of the collection's "shape," "shaping" language (e.g., "editorial purpose"; "editorial concern"; "the editor[s]") will sometimes be used when describing that shape.

One further clarification about the designation "author-/editor-oriented" is necessary. In the study discussed above, Alma Brodersen focuses on two types of diachronic intertextual references in Psalms 146–150 often cited as evidence that these psalms were originally written as a unit to end or frame the Hebrew Psalter: (1) author-intended intertextual references between the psalms themselves (e.g., the author of Ps 150 refers to Ps 149), and (2) shared reference texts (e.g., Pss 146 and 150 refer to a common source text).[65] Her conclusion noted above that "Psalms 146–150 do not refer to one another … and share almost no reference texts" is a major pillar of her argument that these psalms were *not*, in fact, originally written for their current location.[66] Thus, Brodersen's concern is identifying various types of non-incidental diachronic links that originate with the authors of individual psalms.

Like Brodersen, my concern is to identify *non-incidental* literary correspondence between discrete psalms. And I do argue that one such relationship consists in a shared reference text.[67] But "author-oriented" in this study does *not* mean my aim is (1) to detect links that can be traced to the authors of individual psalms (i.e., the author of Ps 77 refers to Ps 78); or (2) to show that each, or even one, psalm was necessarily *written* for the collection under consideration, though any number could have been.

Rather, as I am using the term, "author-/editor-oriented" means only that my aim (whether successful or not) is to identify literary design that can be traced to those responsible for the configuration of the collection being examined—not merely the creative imagination of the modern reader. For my purposes, it is important *that* deliberate literary correspondence exists between psalms, not *how* it was created.[68] Suggestions I do make about the origin of correspondences I regard as highly tentative. As can be discerned from my comments above, in

---

64. I borrow the analogy of "footprints" from Nancy L. DeClaissé-Walford, *Reading from the Beginning: The Shaping of the Hebrew Psalter* (Macon, GA: Mercer University Press, 1997), vii.

65. See Brodersen, *The End of the Psalter*, 24–7.

66. Ibid., 270.

67. See the discussion of Pss 77 and 78 in Chapter 5.

68. Hensley points out that "scholars typically account for lexical and thematic 'links' between psalms in two ways: either they originated with the individual psalms and motivated their placement, or editors created them to bind psalms together—or some combination thereof." Hensley, *Covenant Relationships*, 69. Hensley himself thinks that links generally

my view attempts to trace connections between psalms, or the addition of entire psalms, to various redactional stages (1) involve too much speculation to be of significant value, and (2) are unnecessary for understanding the collection's literary structure, purpose, and theological message(s).

A modern analogue may help clarify the approach I am outlining here. A volume currently on my desk consists of twenty-nine discrete chapters.[69] Though subheadings are lacking (in both the table of contents and body of the book), close attention to the content and sequence of its essays reveals that the entire volume has a deliberate arrangement. And it divides into multiple subgroupings, each engaging an aspect of the singular topic the volume addresses. Some essays were composed specifically for the volume; others were created for an earlier, completely separate, context. The latter were deliberately selected for reuse in this volume, and now contribute to *its* overarching purpose. These essays now fit seamlessly into their new context, even though a comparison with their original form reveals that integration occasioned minor editorial updating. The evidence of such updating, however, is untraceable without the original composition.[70]

Whatever the volume's history (e.g., earlier iterations of the essays; the reuse of earlier essays; minor editorial updating, etc.), its present form is a coherent "text" with a deliberate structure (at both micro- and macro-levels) and sustained purpose. And while it may be helpful, knowing the history of the volume's formation/redaction is unnecessary for understanding its structure and purpose; a close consideration of its present shape will do.

In a similar way, whatever the history of the collection under investigation (e.g., the history of each psalm; the reuse of earlier psalms; editorial updating, etc.),

---

reflect editorial selection of psalms. The nature of the correspondence I discover between Pss 73–83, I would suggest, points to some combination of editorial selection and creation.

69. I am referring to Gary A. Rendsburg, *How the Bible Is Written* (Peabody, MA: Hendrickson, 2019).

70. One example comes from ch. 6 ("Alliteration in the Exodus Narrative"), which originally appeared under the same title in *Birkat Shalom: Studies in the Bible, Ancient Near Eastern Literature, and Postbiblical Judaism Presented to Shalom M. Paul on the Occasion of His Seventieth Birthday* (Winona Lake, IN: Eisenbrauns, 2008), ed. Chaim Cohen, Victor Avigdor Hurowitz, Avi M. Hurvitz, Yochanan Muffs, Baruch J. Schwartz, and Jeffrey H. Tigay, 83–100. The opening line of ch. 6 is as follows: "*We continue our examination* of alliteration in biblical prose in this chapter (emphasis added)." Rendsburg, *How the Bible Is Written*, 100. This statement clearly situates the essay within the larger context of the volume, and its proximate context more specifically (i.e., a group of essays on alliteration in biblical prose). However, a comparison with the original essay reveals this line to be a minor editorial update to integrate this essay seamlessly into its new context. Yet, without the original essay, such updating would be impossible to trace. This modern analogy reveals that extreme caution is necessary when speculating about (1) which aspects of a text are or are not later additions, and (2) what redactional "stage" portions of the text being analyzed stem from.

I am proposing that its final form is a literarily coherent "text" with a deliberate design and singular purpose. The discrete psalms are deliberately sequenced (i.e., it matters that Pss 75 and 76 *follow* Ps 74) and deliberately grouped (e.g., Pss 74–76; 77–78), even though grouping boundaries are not explicitly marked in extant manuscripts (analogous to the lack of subheadings in the modern volume).[71] These groupings are, however, *tacitly* indicated by a close consideration of the content and arrangement of the collection's psalms, as well as the literary correspondences they share (analogous to similar indicators in the modern volume). And each grouping, I contend, engages a different aspect of a singular topic (like the essay groups in the modern volume): a seeming contradiction within God himself brought on by his prolonged absence in the Temple's destruction.

Despite our inability to detect it, the collection's formation likely consisted of multiple forms of editorial activity: minor updating for integrative purposes, the selection of preexisting psalms/psalm sequences, the composition of new psalms/psalm sequences, the rearrangement of psalms, and so on. While it may be helpful to know this history, such knowledge is not necessary to gain a reasonable understanding of the structure, message, and purpose of its final form. As I hope to show, a close consideration of its literary shape is sufficient.

"Psalms Exegesis" and Psalterexegese

"Psalms exegesis" is prior to, and an essential precondition for, *Psalterexegese*. This is simply a consequence of the fact that, as Adam Hensley points out, "the Psalter explicitly represents itself as a collection of existing compositions, i.e., individual psalms."[72] This does not mean that there cannot *also* be a larger literary unity between a sequence or group of discrete compositions. It only means that editorial critics must be careful not to seek that unity at the expense of the individuality of each discrete composition/collection. At least in principle, *Psalterexegese* and "psalms exegesis" are not in competition; they are compatible.

---

71. In a recent discussion of "TR Pss 90-106" (for "TR," see n. 37 above), William Yarchin points out that such explicit indicators are present for these psalms in medieval manuscripts. For example, one presents TR 92+93, 96+97, and 98+99 as single psalms. As Yarchin notes, this provides material evidence for claiming that "premodern scripture communities and their scholars were discerning a psalm-unit with those particular textual boundaries." Yarchin, "Why the Future of Canonical Hebrew Psalter Exegesis Includes Abandoning Its Own Premise." The lack of such explicit indicators for the groupings I propose, however, does not weaken or negate my conclusions. While their presence would certainly support my conclusions, their absence does not negate them. As Yarchin himself notes, "the fact that no extant manuscript presents such a segmented unit does not deny the insights into the text's ... synchronic signification." Yarchin, "Why the Future of Canonical Hebrew Psalter Exegesis Includes Abandoning Its Own Premise."

72. Hensley, *Covenant Relationships and the Editing of the Hebrew Psalter*, 13.

Some scholars, however, are not so sure. Consider Hermann Spieckermann's comments in a recent article:

> The essay is a plea for ending the hunt for the message inscribed into the final shaping of the Psalter. … The Psalter is not in need of having its contents labeled with inadequate generalising terms. The complexity of the psalms does not favor this approach. Instead, the psalms are waiting to be appreciated as textual individuals and each psalm as part of its special position in a manageable cluster of texts.[73]

Spieckermann's comments here, and the article as a whole, are directed primarily at attempts to read the entire MT Psalter as a literary unity, not smaller collections such as Psalms 73–83.[74] Nevertheless, the aversion in these comments to reading discrete units (whether individual psalms or smaller collections) together as a literary unity, a unity which can be adequately summarized with "generalising terms," makes Spieckermann's article relevant for present purposes.

A concern to maintain the integrity of each individual psalm and smaller collection is valid and commendable. *Psalterexegese* has at times sought the "canonical" meaning at the expense of these discrete units. Some studies virtually ignore psalm boundaries, essentially "blending" groups of psalms together to create a single seamless "text."[75] Others respect psalm boundaries but advance theses about the "canonical meaning" that conflict with the meaning and/or purpose of one or more psalms in question.[76] I take it to be axiomatic that the "canonical meaning" will not contradict or otherwise do "violence" to the meaning of any one psalm in the sequence. Such an approach is rooted in the inherent nature of the Psalter itself, which, as noted above, "explicitly represents itself as a collection of existing compositions, i.e., individual psalms."

---

73. Hermann Spieckermann, "From the Psalter Back to the Psalms: Observations and Suggestions," *ZAW* 132 (2020): 21. Gerstenberger has expressed similar concerns. See Eric Zenger, "Psalmenexegese und Psalterexegese: Eine Forschungsskizze," in *The Composition of the Book of Psalms*, ed. Erich Zenger, BETL 238 (Leuven: Peeters, 2010), 25.

74. Indeed, Spiekermann explicitly cites Pss 73–83 in this regard. In his view, J. Gärtner and A. Klein have "demonstrated that the Asaph-collection is organised around Ps. 78." Spieckermann, "From the Psalter Back to the Psalms," 15. The analysis carried out later, however, suggests that this view is mistaken. Spiekermann is referring to the following two works here: Judith Gärtner, *Die Geschichtspsalmen: Eine Studie zu den Psalmen 78, 105, 135 und 136 als hermeneutische Schlüsseltexte im Psalter*, FAT 84 (Tübingen: Mohr Siebeck, 2012); Anja Klein, *Geschichte und Gebet. Die Rezeption der biblischen Geschichte in den Psalmen des Alten Testaments*, FAT 94 (Tübingen: Mohr Siebeck, 2014).

75. This approach is particularly characteristic of Robert Cole's *The Shape and Message of Book III (Psalms 73–89)*, JSOTSup 307 (Sheffield: Sheffield Academic Press, 2000). See Chapter 2.

76. See Chapter 2 for examples.

However, the reality is that *Psalterexegese as such* is not incompatible with "psalms exegesis." Like the earlier analogy of the modern volume, there is no reason in principle that a group of individual texts could not have been collected/written and organized to communicate an overarching message rooted in a unified editorial purpose—a message that could be summarized in a "generalising" way. The same holds true for individual collections like Psalms 73–83. A group of discrete texts, or discrete collections, can legitimately be read as a literary unity *and* their individuality respected. In fact, I hope to show that the literary unity of the collection under investigation comes into focus *precisely by* respecting the individuality of each psalm.

In light of this discussion, I will carry out "psalms exegesis" prior to *Psalterexegese* in the main analytic chapters of this study. Before investigating any potentially significant literary similarities between psalms (i.e., similarities reflecting deliberate design), I offer a brief but careful analysis of the psalms under consideration. This analysis is foundational for both identifying deliberate design and assessing its significance. And I hope to show that this procedure helps guard against making "a fruit purée" of the "wonderful pieces of fruit" that are the collection's individual psalms.[77]

Deliberate Design: Identification and Interpretation

But how should *Psalterexegese* proceed once the relevant psalms have been considered as "textual individuals"? A foundational distinction in this regard is between "indicators" and "significance." Before making claims about the significance of the shape of a group of psalms (no matter the size), interpreters should first identify *indicators* of deliberate design.[78] This practice aims to ensure that claims about significance are not driven by a priori interpretive assumptions (e.g., that deliberate design exists; the operation of a certain organizing principle, etc.) or cursory observations.[79]

77. Zenger, "Psalmenexegese und Psalterexegese: Eine Forschungsskizze," 24–5. I am indebted to the following essay for this reference: Nancy L. deClaissé-Walford, "The Canonical Approach to Scripture and the Editing of the Hebrew Psalter," in *The Shape and Shaping of the Book of Psalms: The Current State of Scholarship*, ed. Nancy L. deClaissé-Walford, Ancient Israel and its Literature 20 (Atlanta, GA: SBL Press, 2014), 9. Gerstenberger, who is critical of editorial criticism, apparently told Erich Zenger that "die Psalterexegese würde die Individualität der Psalmen missachten und sie ... mache aus den wunderschönen Einzelfrüchten der Psalmen missachten und sie ... mache aus den wunderschönen Einzelfrüchten der Psalmen ein 'Früchtemus.'" See DeClaissé-Walford, "The Canonical Approach to Scripture and the Editing of the Hebrew Psalter," 9.

78. Gerald H. Wilson, "The Shape of the Book of Psalms," *Int* 42 (1992): 129.

79. In this connection, see Willgren's critique of Zenger's case for the unity of Pss 146–150. Willgren, *The Formation of the "Book" of Psalms*, 276–7. Here Willgren points out (rightly in my view) that in Zenger's analysis *arguments* for intentional juxtaposition "are not always distinguished from *readings* proceeding such a notion." Willgren, *The Formation*

Wilson wisely stressed the importance of this distinction years ago:

> In dealing with these two questions of "indicators" and "significance," one must take care not to confuse them. The reason is that assumptions regarding the significance of the arrangement ... can influence what one takes to be indicators of shape.[80]

Wilson refers to this pitfall in another place as the "working hypothesis":

> Working hypotheses are a valid and useful means of research in the sciences where they can be tested repeatedly through experimentation in a controlled environment. They are, however, much more problematic in literary analysis where they can have the unfortunate effect of providing self-fulfilling prophecies. Especially in such a thematically diverse literature as the Psalms, a hypothesis set out beforehand can allow the researcher to see what supports the thesis and ignore what does not.[81]

According to Wilson, this pitfall is avoided by allowing "any sense of the structure that develops to derive from an intensive and thorough analysis of the psalms in question in terms of their linguistic, thematic, literary, and theological links and relationships."[82] Such a rigorous "bottom-up," inductive, approach is taken in this study.

To avoid collapsing these distinct issues into one interpretive move, the main analytic chapters of this study consistently first present evidence of deliberate design before turning to the question of significance. This procedure may feel overly rigid at times, but it has the advantage of being methodologically sound. The remainder of this chapter is essentially an unpacking of the approach I take to these related issues in this study.

A Method Centering on Parallelism

The primary method of identifying deliberate design in this study is *parallelism*. Adele Berlin defines parallelism as "the correspondence of one with thing with another."[83] She elaborates,

---

of the "Book" of Psalms, 275. That is to say, deliberate design is at times assumed to exist rather than argued, the result being that Zenger's case suffers.

80. Wilson, "The Shape of the Book of Psalms," 129.

81. Gerald H. Wilson, "Understanding the Purposeful Arrangement of Psalms in the Psalter," in *The Shape and Shaping of the Psalter*, ed. J. Clinton McCann, JSOTSup 159 (Sheffield: Sheffield Academic Press, 1993), 44. As an example of this misuse, Wilson points to John Walton's study of the Psalter. See J. H. Walton, "Psalms: A Cantata about the Davidic Covenant," *JETS* 34 (1991): 21–31.

82. Wilson, "Understanding the Purposeful Arrangement of Psalms in the Psalter," 48.

83. Adele Berlin, *The Dynamics of Biblical Parallelism* (Grand Rapids, MI: Eerdmans, 1994), 2.

Parallelism promotes the perception of a relationship between the elements of which parallelism is composed, and this relationship is one of correspondence. The nature of this correspondence varies, but in general it involves repetition or the substitution of things which are equivalent on one or more linguistic levels.[84]

The word "equivalent" in the last line captures the essence of Berlin's conception of parallelism: "My thesis is that parallel lines *are in some way linguistically equivalent*" (emphasis added).[85] This definition is helpful because, unlike earlier (narrower) definitions (e.g., Lowth), it is able to account for the broad range of equivalences that biblical parallelism involves. As Berlin demonstrates at length, the biblical authors exploited linguistic equivalence in a virtually endless number of ways. In her study, Berlin explores these ways under the categories of the grammatical, lexical, semantic, and phonological aspects of parallelism.

Berlin's definition is helpful in another way:

Once we admit smaller segments as being parallel—e.g., words, phrases, even sounds—though the lines to which they belong are not parallel, we raise the incidence of parallelism within a text. And if we do not restrict our search for linguistic equivalences to adjacent lines or sentences, but take a global view, finding equivalence anywhere within a text, we raise the incidence of parallelism still more. ... For instance, the device known as inclusion, in which the first and last lines of a text contain the same words or phrases, is actually a form of parallelism and should be recognized as such.[86]

Berlin's point is that biblical parallelism is not restricted to the level of the line but can operate at any level of the text. Thus, her definition is helpfully broad in two ways: it accounts for the fact that biblical parallelism (1) involves a broad range of linguistic equivalences; and (2) operates on a "global" level in texts.

Michael Snearly has recently applied Berlin's insights into biblical parallelism to methodology in *Psalterexegese*. He explains,

The second linguistic field [the first being text linguistics] that may lay a foundation from which to understand the Book of Psalms as a literary unity is poetics ... Berlin's restatement of parallelism opens an avenue for grounding the relationship between psalms in the field of poetics. If parallelism exists at higher literary levels than the line, then it could be possible to demonstrate that parallelism exists at the highest literary levels: groups of poems and books. And if it could be shown that parallelism exists at those highest levels,

---

84. Ibid.
85. Ibid., 90.
86. Ibid., 3.

then a case could be made that those highest levels were meant to be read as literature.[87]

Snearly is not claiming that deliberate parallels between psalms *must* exist because we find them on a global level within psalms. As his study exemplifies well, deliberate parallels between psalms *must be argued*, not simply assumed to exist. Rather, his point is that the operation of deliberate parallelism at the highest levels of individual texts provides a valid rationale from poetics for exploring whether such parallelism does, in fact, exist between them. This is an important methodological point: Berlin's insights into inner-psalm parallelism provide a methodological grounding point in poetics for an editorial-critical method that centers on inter-psalm parallelism.

Further validation of this method comes from general methodological observations made by Bruce Waltke. Waltke has rightly noted that, when developing methods for biblical study, scholars must keep in mind that "the inherent nature of any object to be studied dictates the best method for elucidating its properties."[88] Applied to *Psalterexegese*, this means that the inherent nature of poetic literature in general, and psalmic literature in particular, determines the best method(s) for identifying deliberate design.

It would be difficult to find a structuring device/organizing principle more constitutive of the "inherent nature" of psalmic literature than parallelism. Parallelism *pervades* this literature. In one form or another, to one degree or another, it operates within nearly every poetic line, between many, and frequently structures stanzas, strophes, and whole compositions. Snearly is, therefore, correct to conclude that parallelism is "the main 'ingredient' in poetic literature."[89] Parallelism thus emerges organically from the psalmic literature as a method of detecting deliberate design at the inter-psalm level.[90]

The methodological implications of these observations are clear: parallelism distinguishes itself as a valid and promising method of identifying deliberate design at the inter-psalm level. As between two lines of poetry, various forms of parallelism between proximate (and, sometimes, distant) *psalms* in this collection

---

87. Michael K. Snearly, *The Return of the King: Messianic Expectation in Book V of the Psalter*, LHBOTS 624 (New York: Bloomsbury, 2016), 46, 48.

88. Bruce K. Waltke, *An Old Testament Theology: An Exegetical, Canonical, and Thematic Approach* (Grand Rapids, MI: Zondervan, 2007), 79.

89. Snearly, *The Return of the King*, 46.

90. The obvious assumption is that parallelism would likely have been a "main ingredient" in *creating* literary unity at the inter-psalm level. This assumption is reasonable given (1) the central role of parallelism in the creation of individual psalms; and (2) it is a priori likely that the same basic literary devices used to create literary unity within psalms would be used when creating a similar type of unity between them. Ho makes a similar observation in his study: "If … design … does exist, it is highly plausible that poetic techniques at work in individual psalms are also expressed beyond a single psalm." Peter C. W. Ho, *The Design of the Psalter: A Macrostructural Analysis* (Eugene, OR: Pickwick, 2019), 4.

"promote the perception of a relationship," to use Berlin's words.[91] Making a case for the deliberate nature of this relationship and explaining its significance is the burden of this study.

Inter-Psalm Parallelism: A Closer Look Parallelism, then (as Berlin defines it), is the central method I use for detecting and justifying deliberate design in this collection. To anticipate the most significant application of this method, I argue that a parallel relationship between the opening Psalm 73 and various psalm sequences/pairings segments the collection into four distinct and deliberately arranged psalm groups: Psalms 74–76, 77–78, 79/82, and 80–81.[92] As will hopefully become clear, the striking nature of this relationship suggests intentionality. And I argue that recognition of this relationship is the key to unlocking the collection's overall design, major theological message, and overarching editorial purpose.

Other parallels, however, are also significant. Later I argue that the literary correspondence with Psalm 73 just described singles out various repetitions or links within the groupings outlined above as reflecting deliberate design (e.g., links between Ps 74 and both Pss 75–76). The types of parallels identified are well-established at the inner-psalm level, namely, lexical and thematic parallels. Both have also played a central role in *Psalterexegese* since Wilson's seminal study. It will be helpful to briefly define these two types given their importance in establishing a deliberate relationship between Psalm 73 and the psalm sequences/pairings outlined above.

Lexical correspondence can take the form of equivalent (or identical) words, roots, phrases, entire clauses, and so on. In *Psalterexegese* lexical equivalence is frequently discussed in terms of "keywords," which may be defined as "a word or root [that] is repeated meaningfully within a text or series of texts."[93] Many editorial critics give pride of place to this type of correspondence in their studies. For example, one such scholar isolates fourteen different lexica that collectively "bind ... together" Psalms 107–118.[94] Thus, like their inner-textual counterparts, editorial critics have argued that keywords observable at the intertextual level (i.e., between psalms) reflect literary unity between the psalms so linked.

Editorial critics have applied the term "keyword" to more than just individual words or forms. In David Howard's important study, key-word links consist of

---

91. For "distant parallelism," see below.

92. The slash dividing Ps 79 and 82 indicates that, though not sequential, these psalms are deliberately grouped together in the collection's design. See Chapters 7 and 8 for justification of this claim.

93. Shimon Bar-Efrat, *Narrative Art in the Bible* (New York: T&T Clark, 2004), 212. Some have rather stringent criteria for what constitutes a "keyword." For Snearly a keyword "represents at least 50% of the usage within Book V and/or 20% of the usage within the Psalter." Snearly, *The Return of the King*, 117. Such specific percentages, however, seem to me arbitrary and unnecessary. In this connection, see the discussion of criteria below.

94. Snearly, *The Return of the King*, 117.

single words,[95] whole clauses (e.g., הריעו ליהוה כל הארץ in Pss 98:4 and 100:1), entire verses (e.g., Pss 96:13 and 98:9),[96] and even "complexes of identical words and ideas" (e.g., Pss 95:6–7c and 100:3).[97] Similarly, in this study any type of *deliberate* lexical correspondence between psalms is considered a "key-word link." At the level of the individual psalm, a "keyword" is any word that is meaningfully repeated within that psalm.

Bruce Waltke observes that "themes are short topics that wind their way through a work and are usually identifiable by keywords/motifs."[98] Themes have a structuring and unifying function within texts. They "grant coherence and simplicity to what might seem on the surface disparate and divided,"[99] act as a "unifying and integrating principle,"[100] and can even function as a "determining factor in the overall composition of the book."[101] Notably, themes are not always apparent on the surface of the text. They must sometimes be "abstracted by interpretation."[102] This is important to keep in mind since different language can be used to describe one and the same theme. As already noted, motifs and keywords can help identify a text's themes.[103]

In *Psalterexegese* thematic correspondence manifests in "short topics" that one or more psalms of varying proximity share. It is often, though not always, "identifiable by keywords/motifs." Editorial critics have contended that shared themes can reflect literary unity between psalms. An oft-cited example is the

---

95. David M. Howard Jr., *The Structure of Psalms 93–100*, Biblical and Judaic Studies 5 (Winona Lake, IN: Eisenbrauns, 1997), 100.

96. These two verses differ in only one word. Compare לפני יהוה כי בא כי בא לשפט הארץ ישפט תבל בצדק ועמים באמונתו ("before the Lord, for he comes to judge the earth, he will judge the world in righteousness and the peoples in faithfulness") and לפני יהוה כי בא לשפט הארץ ישפט תבל בצדק ועמים במישרים ("before the Lord, for he comes to judge the earth, he will judge the world in righteousness and the peoples in uprightness").

97. "Come, let us worship and bow down; let us bless before the Lord, our Maker! For he is our God, and we are the people of his pasture, and the flock of his hand. This day, O that you would hear his voice! (באו נשתחוה ונכרעה נברכה לפני יהוה עשנו כי הוא אלהינו ואנחנו עם מרעיתו וצאן ידו היום אם בקלו תשמעו)" (Ps 95:6); "Know that the Lord, he is God. He is our maker (and) we are his, we are his people and the flock of his pasture (דעו כי יהוה הוא אלהים הוא עשנו ולא ולו אנחנו עמו וצאן מרעיתו)" (Ps 100:3).

98. Waltke, *An Old Testament Theology*, 90.

99. Ibid.

100. Shimon Bar-Efrat, "Some Observations on the Analysis of Structure in Biblical Narrative," *VT* 30 (1980): 169.

101. Ibid., 168–9. Bar-Efrat shows how the theme of "transference of leadership" in 1 Sam functions as "a determining factor in the overall composition of the book." Ibid.

102. Ibid., 169.

103. Robert Alter defines a motif as "a concrete image, sensory quality, action, or object [that] recurs. ... It has no meaning in itself without the defining context of the narrative." Robert Alter, *The Art of Biblical Narrative* (New York: Basic Books, 1981), 95.

theme of Yahweh's kingship that runs through Psalms 93–100. According to McKelvey, this theme "proves to be the primary conjunctive feature that binds Psalms 93–100 as a sub-group in Book IV."[104] Howard points out that this theme is reflected in these psalms by what he calls "thematic word links." He defines these as "themes elaborated via repeated words or lexemes ... found in any two psalms that show connections between the two."[105] Howard also observed other, lesser, themes binding these psalms together that are not reflected in common vocabulary and lexemes. Howard, therefore, distinguishes between two types of thematic links in his study: those reflected in common vocabulary and those that are not.

In this study, a thematic link is a short topic shared by two or more psalms that reflects deliberate design. It may or may not be identifiable by keywords and/or motifs. I will contend that both thematic and key-word links operate within Psalms 73–83 as others have observed them functioning elsewhere, namely, as indicators of literary unity between the psalms so linked.

It is important to point out that my aim is not simply to amass all parallels that may reflect intentionality. Rather, following Snearly and others, I present only what appears to be the most compelling evidence. This practice aims to guard against editorial criticism's version of "parallelomania," the tendency of some studies (e.g., Cole's *The Shape and Message of Psalms 73–83*) to amass "frivolous links ... that either overshadow the more plausible evidence or, worse, stand in the place of genuine evidence."[106] This practice also lays the most solid foundation possible for interpretation; the conclusions drawn are only as strong as the evidence (and, more fundamentally, the method) upon which they are based.

Incidental Language However, not every lexical or thematic correspondence between proximate psalms reflects intentionality. Indeed, there is much incidental language between psalms. Given this reality, some have understandably questioned whether literary similarities between psalms can provide a firm foundation for claims about deliberate design. Consider Willgren's following comments:

> Literary features such as themes, catch phrases, and recurring vocabulary, cannot be easily taken as intentional, since it is well known that recurring language is an intrinsic feature of poetry. Although it should not be excluded that such factors might have played a part as psalms were juxtaposed, it is questionable whether the observations made provide an adequate foundation for detecting large-scale purposes.[107]

---

104. Michael G. McKelvey, *Moses, David and the High Kingship of Yahweh: A Canonical Study of Book IV of the Psalter*, Gorgias Biblical Studies 55 (Piscataway, NJ: Gorgias Press, 2013), 263.
    105. Howard, *The Structure of Psalms 93–100*, 100.
    106. Snearly, *The Return of the King*, 19.
    107. Willgren, *The Formation of the "Book" of Psalms*, 15.

The assumption here seems to be that incidental language disqualifies, or at least devalues/minimizes, literary similarity as a reliable guide to deliberate design. Revisiting our earlier analogy, however, shows that there is no necessary reason why this should be the case. Imagine a hypothetical scenario in which archaeologists unearth the modern volume 2,000 years in the future. The largest portion containing the essays has been well preserved, but everything else has been lost (e.g., the cover, front matter, indices, etc.). Recalling that subheadings are lacking, how would our fictitious future scholars determine whether this volume had a deliberate design?

A moment's reflection reveals that central to this process would be the very types of literary similarity that Willgren doubts can serve as an "adequate foundation" for this task (e.g., recurring vocabulary, themes, motifs, catch phrases, etc.). Some links of this kind would stand out as prominent among the incidental connections. To give an actual example from the volume, the word "wordplay" shared by adjacent essays on the topic—the first incorporated from an earlier volume (with minor updating); the second written for the volume itself—is clear evidence of deliberate design or editorial intent: it reflects the larger topic of "wordplay" that explains the rationale for the (deliberate) juxtaposition of these essays.[108] For scholars studying this textual artifact, this keyword would be an important piece of evidence that these adjacent essays form a distinct, deliberately sequenced, grouping.

But *why* does this single word stand out among the incidental connections? The answer anticipates the discussion of criteria below. In this case, it is not the word's *sheer* frequency. Neither is it that the word is exclusive to these essays; it appears in others. It is the word's *concentration*. The word occurs more frequently at this particular location in the volume (i.e., these adjacent essays) *relative to others*. This is the chief explanation for the word's prominence and what gives it a key role in distinguishing the essays as a distinct grouping.

This fictitious future scenario illustrates that incidental language in no way disqualifies or devalues literary similarity as a reliable guide to deliberate design. It only reveals the need for criteria that can help determine when similarity likely reflects intentionality and when it is merely incidental.

Criteria The first thing that needs to be stressed here is that criteria are *necessary*. Willgren rightly observes that "a lack of solid methodological criteria makes proposed links difficult to assess."[109] The lack of sound and/or explicit criteria has, in fact, been a problem in editorial criticism at times. Alma Brodersen, for example, recently expressed frustration over the lack of criteria in studies focusing on Psalms 146-150.[110] Snearly pointed out a similar shortcoming in his study, observing that Robert Cole's *The Shape and Message of Psalms 73-89* "tends to see any similarity

---

108. See Rendsburg, *How the Bible Is Written*, 358–410.
109. Willgren, "What Could We Agree On?" In this connection, see the criteria Willgren lays out for identifying diachronic intertextual references between the "book" of Psalms and other texts. Willgren, *The Formation of the "Book" of Psalms*, 291.
110. Brodersen, *The End of the Psalter*, 24.

whatsoever as evidence of editorial significance."[111] Sound methodology, therefore, requires the explicit articulation of sound criteria for detecting deliberate design.

As already mentioned, not every instance of the parallels outlined above (or other kinds) reflects deliberate design. Not every *shared* word, for example, is a *key*word (i.e., one *meaningfully* repeated). Parallels must not simply be amassed; they must be evaluated to weed out incidental connections. Otherwise, the method will almost certainly slip into "rampant subjectivity."[112]

The presence of evaluative principles or criteria, however, does not mean the absence of subjectivity. Like every method, an element of subjectivity is unavoidable here as well. But this reality no more invalidates this method than any other. We can formulate solid principles and apply them consistently to remove as much subjectivity from the interpretive process as possible.

The goal in what follows is not to provide an exhaustive set of principles or criteria for identifying non-incidental links between psalms.[113] It is to outline the major ones I use to corroborate the design outlined earlier (which, as noted, is suggested on other grounds), namely, the deliberate parallel relationship between Psalm 73 and four psalm sequences/pairings that follow. There I noted that this literary correspondence singles out certain repetitions within each sequence/pairing as reflecting deliberate design. In Chapters 4–8, I apply the criteria/principles that follow to corroborate or provide deeper roots for the intentionality of those repetitions, thereby strengthening the claim that the proposed design is likely deliberate.

A foundational evaluative principle is the frequency criterion, which has a number of applications.[114] The first is *rarity*. The rarity of a word or theme can often suggest intentionality.[115] An example from the present study is the parallel למשאות/למשואות ("to ruins") (Pss 73:18 and 74:3), which Cole points out is a *dis legomenon* in the Hebrew Bible.[116] Here rarity (in conjunction with close proximity; see below) is one argument for intentionality, the deliberate juxtaposition of these adjacent psalms.

---

111. Snearly, *The Return of the King*, 19.

112. Grant, "Editorial Criticism," 153. Borrowing a principle from text criticism, Snearly has rightly observed that "evidence must be weighed, not counted" in editorial criticism as well. Snearly, *The Return of the King*, 19.

113. For criteria proposed in other studies, see the discussion in Ho, *The Design of the Psalter*, 52–4.

114. For an example of how this principle has been used at the inner-textual level, see Bar-Efrat, *Narrative Art in the Bible*, 212–15. For editorial-critical studies consistently employing some version of what I am calling "the frequency criterion," see Howard, *Psalms 93–100*; McKelvey, *Moses, David and the High Kingship of Yahweh*; Snearly, *The Return of the King*; Ho, *The Design of the Psalter*.

115. Brodersen cautions that this criterion "is to be used with caution as it may be due to a lack of sources." Brodersen, *The End of the Psalter*, 25n.150.

116. Cole, *The Shape and Message of Book III*, 236. The examples in this section are discussed in later chapters. I list them here simply for illustrative purposes.

This first application is rarity conceived of in a sort of "absolute" sense. Closely related but distinct is what might be called *relative* rarity. These are cases where a literary feature may not be rare in the Hebrew Bible, for instance, but *is* rare in the distinct unit of Psalms 73–83. One parallel I identify with this criterion (in conjunction with other considerations) is the common adjective רשע ("wicked"). It occurs over three hundred times in the Hebrew Bible, but infrequently in Psalms 73–83. This application qualifies the first in an important way: a word does not have to be rare in an "absolute" sense to reflect intentionality; common words, themes, and so on that are rare in a relative sense can suggest intent.

A third application is the *concentration* criterion. Features clustering more heavily in proximate psalms relative to the surrounding environment (i.e., other psalms and sequences of psalms) often suggest intentionality. This principle was touched on earlier in the case of the analogy of the modern volume. There we saw that the clustering of the word "wordplay" in adjacent essays is one indicator of intentionality; it reflects the deliberate grouping/sequencing of the adjacent essays.

Similarly, the concentration of a literary feature (or features) (e.g., keywords or themes) in a group of psalms relative to others can suggest intentionality. The reader should recall in this connection the theme of Yahweh's kingship that runs through Psalms 93–100. Snearly consistently applies this principle on a larger scale in his study, which "moves beyond demonstrating similarities among proximate psalms to showing that those similarities *do not occur with the same frequency in other parts of the Psalter*" (emphasis added).[117] To use an example from the present study, the concentration of various literary features in Psalms 74–76 relative to the rest of the collection (e.g., the noun שם and the larger theme of God's kingship it reflects [74:7, 10, 18, 21; 75:2; 76:2, 4]) is one piece of evidence suggesting that this sequence is a deliberate and distinct grouping.

In addition to frequency, there is *distinctiveness*. Literary correspondence or parallelism that is particularly distinctive in nature/unique can point to deliberate design. The chief example from the present study is the literary correspondence outlined above between Psalm 73 and the psalm sequences/pairings of Psalms 74–76, 77–78, 79/82, and 80–81. That each grouping resembles very distinctive aspects of Psalm 73 (see Chapters 3–8) suggests intentionality.

A third principle relates to the *amount* of potential non-incidental similarity. A high amount of lexical overlap alone (or some other kind) does not necessarily establish the presence of deliberate design. A high amount of seemingly incidental links is not a firm foundation for anchoring intent. But a high amount of non-incidental parallelism *is* (i.e., parallels considered likely intentional based upon solid criteria). Amount (of non-incidental parallelism) is not a necessary condition for grounding claims to intentionality, but it is a sufficient one.

---

117. Snearly, *The Return of the King*, 19. Snearly points out that such evidence is what led to the identification of the Elohistic Psalter.

Location can also suggest intentionality. One application of this principle relates to instances of "distant parallelism." As an established and inherent feature of certain types of inner-psalm parallelism (e.g., inclusion), distant parallelism can help corroborate deliberate design. I say "corroborate" and not "identify" here because a heightened degree of subjectivity is involved with potential instances of distant parallelism. In this study, therefore, distant parallelism is only applied in a corroborative way. I only cite it as potential evidence if other criteria are met.

This approach can be illustrated from Snearly's study. Snearly cites as an example of distant parallelism the summons הדו ליהוה כי טוב כי לעולם חסדו ("Give thanks the Lord, for he is good, for his steadfast love endures forever!") in Psalm 107:1 and Psalm 118:29. Analogous to inner-textual inclusion, these verses occur at the opening and closing boundary of a psalm respectively. Given that, according to Snearly, what I am calling the "concentration criterion" identifies the intervening psalms (i.e., Pss 107–18) as a distinct grouping, the presence of identical verses at these extremity locations is noteworthy—inclusion is a well-documented bracketing device at the inner-textual level. In cases like this, location can play an important role in corroborating deliberate design. Here, it substantiates Snearly's claim that Psalms 107–118 are a distinct grouping.

Location can suggest intentionality in other ways. This is true of cases where the parallel feature (e.g., a keyword) is located at a structurally prominent location in one or more of the linked psalms. For example, in Chapter 5 we will see that both Psalms 77 and 78 contain allusions (reflected in the same terminology) to the foundational Israelite credo of Exodus 34:6–7. One argument that this intertextual reference reflects the deliberate juxtaposition of these psalms (in addition to both psalms alluding to the same text) is that it occurs in a structurally prominent location in each psalm.

This last observation points to another way that location can corroborate intentionality, namely, if a parallel feature occupies a central "location" in the message, argument, rhetorical strategy, and so on, of one or more of the linked psalms. As we shall see, the aforementioned parallel between Psalms 77 and 78 meets this criterion as well.

Another application of the "location" principle is *close proximity*. Close proximity is not a necessary criterion for intentionality; *distant* parallelism is a well-established technique at the inner-textual level. But close proximity can corroborate intentionality in certain cases. An example from Chapter 5 is the noun מועד ("appointed time/place") occurring in Psalms 74 and 75 (74:4, 8; 75:3). In addition to its rarity (it only appears in five total psalms in the MT Psalter), the noun's only two occurrences in Psalms 73–83 come in *adjacent* psalms (Pss 74 and 75). Here close proximity suggests intentionality. Or at least it warrants and invites a search for further corroboration. In Chapter 5 I argue that such evidence does, in fact, exist. The "close proximity" principle would also apply to the *dis legomenon* למשאות/למשואות ("to ruins") (see 74:3 and 73:18) mentioned above.

A principle that arises from the preceding one is that the likelihood of a parallel's intentionality increases if it meets *multiple criteria*. For example, in Chapter 6 I argue that the phrase הר ציון ("Mt. Zion") in Psalms 74:2 and 78:68 is one component of an inclusion that brackets Psalms 74–78. Applications of three or four criteria converge to suggest that this phrase reflects deliberate design: (1) "location"; it appears at the extremity locations of a psalm sequence identified as deliberate and distinct on other grounds (see the cumulative argument of Chapters 4–6); (2) relative rarity; the exact phrase only appears elsewhere in the MT Psalter in two other psalms (see 48:3, 12; 125:1), though the plural הררי ציון ("mountains of Zion") appears in 133:3; and (3) "amount"; it is not an isolated key-word link but occurs in a cluster of other keywords at these extremity locations.

Other important principles include the following: (1) the parallel is a keyword in one or more of the linked psalms; (2) the parallel consists of the exact (or nearly exact) repetition of uncommon (either in an absolute or relative sense) phrases or clauses; (3) the parallel consists of a shared reference text (i.e., both psalms clearly allude to the same text); (4) the parallel consists of a striking structural correspondence between the linked psalms;[118] and (5) symmetry in the collection's design.[119]

These are the foundational principles/criteria I use in this study. If their reasonableness is not immediately apparent, I hope that it will become so throughout the course of the study. Every parallel considered "intentional" (i.e., appearing to reflect a deliberate literary relationship between the psalms so linked) meets at least one of the above criteria. As mentioned earlier, these principles/criteria are used to corroborate a deliberate parallel relationship I detect on other grounds between Psalm 73 and multiple psalm sequences/pairings that follow. Thus, their application provides another line of evidence suggesting that this relationship is, in fact, deliberate. "Suggesting" rather than "proving" is intentional here; proof is too lofty of a goal in literary analysis. My goal is more modest. I aim to *make a case* for deliberate design through multiple lines of evidence and applying sound criteria.

Two further points under this heading are in order. The first relates to "weighing" parallels: even significant parallels (i.e., those appearing to reflect intentionality) must be "weighed." Some significant parallels are more valuable than others for bringing into focus the distinctive contours of the collection's design and/or understanding its significance. For example, we will see in Chapter 5 that Psalms 77 and 78 contain many links that appear to reflect their deliberate juxtaposition. But some are more important for establishing the rationale behind it. Similarly, in Chapter 8 the parallels that Psalm 80 shares particularly with 81:14–17 stand out among other intentional links to confirm the rationale behind Psalm 81's placement.

---

118. See the discussion of Pss 77 and 78 in Chapter 5 for an example of this type of parallel.

119. For instance, I argue that the collection's psalm groups closely resemble one another in terms of their content, message, and structure. Such symmetry corroborates intentionality. See Chapters 6 and 8.

Second, while I do not use the larger MT Psalter as a *literary* context for Psalms 73–83 in this study (i.e., my literary analysis is restricted to Pss 73–83), I do use it (along with the Hebrew Bible as whole) as the primary *linguistic* context for applying the above criteria.[120] These 150 texts provide a sufficient database for reasonably grounding the claims about intentionality I make in later chapters.

Deliberate Design and Structure

It is probably clear by now that a fundamental assumption of this study is that establishing the collection's structure is vital for understanding the nature and purpose of its design. When speaking of the collection's structure in this study, I have two specifics in mind. The first is the number and boundaries of the collection's literary units. I have already indicated that one such unit is the psalm group, a distinct literary unit consisting of multiple individual psalms.

Regardless of whether the term is used, the concept of the "psalm group" has become a common and important one in *Psalterexegese*. It will also factor significantly in this study. In his important 2004 study, Jamie Grant provided the following helpful observations on the concept:

> As well as looking for linking, the reader should also look for indicators of editorial separation of groups of psalms from their setting. The whole idea of a psalm grouping implies both a conjunctive and disjunctive literary function. On the one hand, the idea of a "psalm grouping" implies a degree of connection between the psalms within that grouping, and, logically it in turn implies a degree of separation from the other neighboring psalms which are not part of this psalm grouping.[121]

Grant is pointing out that the concept of a psalm group is a function of literary continuity *and* discontinuity. When Grant published his study in 2004, he lamented the lack of attention studies had given to the latter:

> To date psalm groupings have been defined largely by focusing on the factors that link the psalms under examination. Little consideration has been paid to the factors that separate a group of psalms from its near neighbors. This seems to be a methodological weakness and clearer definition must be given to this important factor within the canonical approach.[122]

---

120. I realize that the two contexts can be related. However, I attempt to refrain from making appeals to linguistic evidence that are dependent upon the literary location of Pss 73–83 in the MT Psalter.

121. Jamie A. Grant, *The King as Exemplar: The Function of Deuteronomy's Kingship Law in the Shaping of the Book of Psalms*, SBLABib 17 (Atlanta, GA: SBL Press, 2004), 226.

122. Ibid.

It is a happy development that scholars have given greater attention to literary discontinuity or "indicators of editorial separation" since Grant penned these words. Still, neglect persists. One way I hope to contribute to the understanding of this collection's design is by drawing attention to what I believe is overlooked evidence of literary discontinuity within it.

There is no consensus over the number or boundaries of the psalm groups represented in Psalms 73–83.[123] We have already noted the basic reason for this: the boundaries of these groupings are not explicitly marked in extant manuscripts. As Grant's comments above reflect, this means that scholars must rely upon tacit indicators or, to use Willgren's terms, paratextual features (e.g., lexical links; psalm sequence, superscriptions) to locate these boundaries. The structuration a scholar proposes depends upon which paratextual features are deemed significant (or more/most significant) for structural purposes, which are even recognized in the first place (or overlooked), and how such features are interpreted.

So, for example, an emphasis upon issues of genre (Ho) and form-critical observations (Millard) leads some to divide the collection into two parallel halves (i.e., Pss 73–78; 79–83). The analysis of another scholar (Boadt), who argues that a technique called "paneling" unites Psalms 73–78, seems to confirm at least the first part of this structuration. However, highlighting different features leads to an alternative structuration that cuts directly across this one. Based upon a perceived focus on the "messianic features" of Joseph and Jacob in Psalms 77–83, one scholar contends that *these* psalms form an editorially intended literary unit (Robertson).

There are even tensions within the structuration of a single scholar. Hossfeld and Zenger, for instance, argue that considerable literary correspondence reveals that Psalms 77–79 are a tightly knit grouping, implying that Psalm 79 *concludes* a psalm grouping. At the same time, however, detection of what they believe is an editorially intended thematic-theological progression in Psalms 79–82 (a "compositional arc") identifies these psalms as a unit, implying that Psalm 79 *begins* a unit.[124]

Such a lack of consensus over the collection's structure matters for the following reason: there is a close relationship between structure and *meaning*. "If we know *how* texts means," explains Adele Berlin, "we are in a better position to discover *what* a particular text means."[125] Along the same lines, Peter Gentry notes, "Perhaps as much as 50 percent of the 'meaning' of a text is communicated by the literary forms and micro- and macrostructures (i.e., arrangement) of the constituent parts, and only 50 percent by the actual words or statements in the text or the

---

123. See Chapter 2.

124. It is theoretically possible that Ps 79 is something of a "Janus psalm." But these scholars make no such argument.

125. Adele Berlin, *Poetics and Interpretation of Biblical Narrative* (Winona Lake, IN: Eisenbrauns, 1983), 17. I am indebted to Gentry's study cited in the next note for this quotation.

assembly of the texts that make up the larger work."[126] Specific percentages aside, Gentry's point stands: a text's structure or form is not disposable "packaging" *for* its meaning; it is an indispensable and central aspect *of* its meaning.

It follows that decisions regarding grouping boundaries will significantly impact one's conception of the collection's design. For example, a markedly different theological message arises depending upon whether the collection's laments (e.g., Pss 74, 77, 79–80) or (more or less) hopeful intervening psalms (e.g., Pss 75–76; 78, 81–82) begin psalm groups. Does Psalm 74, for instance, begin a grouping on a note of desperation that reaches a hopeful conclusion in Psalms 75–76? Or do both Psalms 75 and 76 begin a grouping on a note of hope that reaches a desperate conclusion in Psalm 77? Or maybe some combination of the two is correct?

More fundamentally, it matters significantly if the collection even segments into clearly definable groupings. We will see that some, such as Robert Cole and Christine Jones, perceive a far less definable structure than the scholars referred to above. For these scholars, the collection progresses rather fluidly in a narrative-like linear "flow," oscillating back and forth between waves of lament/despair (e.g., Ps 74) and waves of hope (e.g., Pss 75–76). Cole even detects a discernable "plot," "characters," and "dialogue" in these psalms.

These last observations raise the second issue I have in mind when referring to the collection's structure, the organizing principle(s) used to sequence its psalms.[127] The analyses of the scholars just mentioned, Cole and Jones, clearly assume that a linear narrative-like organizing principle governs psalm sequencing, though such is not explicitly stated in their studies.[128] This is the view, widely held since Wilson's seminal study, that some sort of linear "plot development" or "storyline" is at work in the progression from one psalm (or group of psalms) to the next.[129]

---

126. Peter J. Gentry, "The Literary Macrostructures of the Book of Isaiah and Authorial Intent," in *Bind Up the Testimony: Explorations in the Genesis of the Book of Isaiah*, ed. Daniel I. Block and Richard L. Schultz (Peabody, MA: Hendrickson, 2015), 227.

127. For a helpful, though dated, discussion of the role that sequence has played in *Psalterexegese*, see Harry P. Nasuti, "The Interpretive Significance of Sequence and Selection in the Book of Psalms," in *The Book of Psalms: Composition & Reception*, ed. Peter W. Flint and Patrick D. Miller, VTSup XCIX (Leiden: Brill, 2005), 316–21.

128. See the discussion of their studies in Chapter 2.

129. As is well-known, it has become popular to use the language of "metanarrative" to describe the MT Psalter's macrostructure since Wilson's seminal work. See deClaissé-Walford, "The Canonical Approach to Scripture and the Editing of the Hebrew Psalter." This interpretation focuses on "seam" psalms such as Pss 2, 72, and 89, arguing that they chart the trajectory of the rise and fall of the Davidic monarchy. Books IV and V respond to this failure by pointing readers away from human kingship to Divine kingship as the basis for hope (Pss 93–100). For one of the most recent, and sophisticated, arguments that the MT Psalter should be read as a narrative, see Snearly, *The Return of the King*, 80–5. Here Snearly draws upon modern narrative theory, arguing that the MT Psalter should be read as a "multiple-focus narrative."

Peter Ho's study provides an even more recent example of this approach: "The hope awakened at the temple (73:17–28) is *quickly quashed* by descriptions of the temple *a few verses later* (74:3-4) (emphasis added)."[130] Like similar statements in the studies of Cole, Jones, and others, this statement is not a mere description of adjacent texts; it is an *interpretation* of their relationship that rests upon the assumption of a linear narrative-like organizing principle at work in psalm sequencing.

Whether made consciously or not, decisions on this second structural issue also significantly impact one's conception of the collection's design. To stick with the above example, we will see later that the adoption of a linear narrative-like organizing principle naturally leads its proponents to detect no definitive resolution to the collection's laments (e.g., Ps 74); lament simply "resumes" "after" the intervening hopeful psalms such as Psalms 75 and 76 (i.e., Ps 77). The organizing principle adopted thus strongly influences the emerging message: the hope reflected in the collection is significantly "tempered" or muted by the "continuous" cry of lament.

The salient point arising from the above discussion is this: structure matters; decisions about the boundaries of psalm groups and the organizing principle(s) at work within (and between) them have a determinative influence upon the meaning one attaches to the collection's present shape (e.g., its theological message[s], editorial purpose[s], etc.).

Two Overlooked Paratextual Features

A central argument running though this study is that previous analyses have largely overlooked the two most important paratextual features related to the collection's design, and consequently central components of its message and purpose. It will be helpful to briefly sketch these features here at the outset of the study.

The first has already been touched on above: the deliberate parallel relationship between the opening Psalm 73 and following psalm sequences/pairings: Psalms 74–76, 77–78, 79/82, and 80–81. As I argue at length later, each of these sequences strikingly mirrors the same distinctive aspects of Psalm 73 on an inter-psalm level. This literary correspondence has gone virtually undetected in previous studies, though both Joseph Jensen and J. Clinton McCann have put their finger on aspects of it.[131] At the very least, it has not received a prominent place in discussions of the

---

130. Ho, *The Design of the Psalter*, 98. It should be noted that Ho sees other structuring principles at work in these psalms as well. See Chapter 2.

131. Regarding Ps 73–76, Jensen observes: "Ps 74 relates to Ps 73:1–16 and Ps 76 to 73:18–28, with Ps 75 corresponding to the revelatory experience in 73:17." Joseph E. Jensen, "Psalm 75: Its Poetic Context and Structure," *CBQ* 63 (2001): 419. Relatedly, McCann comments: "Psalm 73, with its movement from lament to hope, sets the tone for the whole of Book III." J. Clinton McCann, "Books I–III and the Editorial Purpose of the Hebrew Psalter," in *The Shape and Shaping of the Psalter*, 96–7. My analysis, however, suggests that neither study has fully grasped the nature or implications of the correspondence between Ps 73 and the psalms that follow.

collection's design. I will attempt to show that it should take center stage in these discussions.

The details of, and evidence for, this relationship will become apparent as the study progresses. The important point here is this: recognition of this relationship, I contend, throws the boundaries of the collection's four psalm groups into sharp relief, and isolates Psalm 73 at its head as a separate literary unit. Recognition of this correspondence, therefore, emerges as the key that unlocks the collection's macrostructure. And, given the close relationship between structure and meaning, I will argue that this correspondence is also the key to discerning the collection's major theological message and overarching purpose.

The second paratextual feature relates to the organizing principle used to sequence Psalms 73–83. The main analytic chapters of this study identify a single organizing principle used in the sequencing of this collection's psalms. The principle that emerges, I contend, is rooted in parallelism, the recursive technique Peter Gentry has labeled "progressive repetition." Gentry explains,

> Normally, a Hebrew author begins a discourse on a topic, develops it from a particular angle, and then ends that conversation. Next, he begins another conversation, taking up the same topic again and considering it from a different perspective. When we hear these two discourses on the same topic in succession, they function like the left and right speakers of a stereo system. ... When we hear the two together the effect is a sound that is in stereo instead of being one-dimensional.[132]

Gentry observes that this approach to literature is the basis of parallel lines and inverted parallel patterns such as chiasmus/concentric structures.[133] "Progressive repetition" is an apt label because the same topic is taken up multiple times ("repetition") but developed in different ways or from different perspectives when repeated ("progressive").[134]

This approach to literature, I contend, governs the relationship between Psalm 73 and the four psalm groups that it parallels, as well as the relationship between the groupings themselves. It also structures what I argue are the two major units or "halves" of this collection (Pss 74–78 and 79–82).[135] As will become clear, it is my

---

132. Gentry, "The Literary Macrostructures of the Book of Isaiah and Authorial Intent," 230.

133. Ibid., 231–2.

134. Peter J. Gentry, *How to Read & Understand the Biblical Prophets* (Wheaton, IL: Crossway, 2017), 41.

135. My analysis of Pss 73–83, therefore, reveals three levels of structure beyond the individual psalm: (1) the psalm group(ing) (Pss 74–76; 77–78; 80–81; 79/82), composed of multiple individual psalms; (2) the unit (74–78; 79–82), composed of multiple psalm groups (Pss 74–76, 77–78; Pss 79/82; 80–81); and (3) the collection (Pss 73–83), composed of multiple units (74–78; 79–82). Thus, psalms grouped on a higher level (i.e., the unit [e.g., Pss 74–78]) may be divided on a lower one (e.g., the psalm group [Pss 74–76; 77–78]). There

belief that oversight of progressive repetition as the collection's primary organizing principle has distorted (albeit unintentionally) its structure and, as a consequence, its central message and purpose. Conversely, I hope to show that recognition of its operation leads to fresh insights in these areas.

is an analogy here with the Hebrew accent system. On one level, all of the words in a verse are grouped together (e.g., the level of the Soph Pasuq). But on a lower level, these same words are separated (e.g., the level of the Athnach).

Chapter 2

THE CURRENT STATE OF SCHOLARSHIP

This chapter situates the present work within the context of editorial-critical scholarship on Psalms 73–83 since Wilson's seminal dissertation. I first consider the most important studies/perspectives on this collection, in terms of both their approach and conclusions. I then draw attention to various problem areas arising from this literature survey that reveal the need for a fresh appraisal. The survey is representative, not exhaustive, and is arranged by author. It includes works of varying scopes, as these psalms receive treatment in studies on Psalms 73–83, Book III of the MT Psalter (Pss 73–89), and the MT Psalter as a whole.

Gerald Wilson

Wilson's most substantial comments on Psalms 73–83 do not appear in his seminal dissertation but in a later essay.[1] Here he argues that Book III is part of a segment of the MT Psalter (i.e., Books I–III) that forms a response to the "agony and loss in the exilic community."[2] He points to Psalms 74 and 89 as psalms that "leave us no choice" but to acknowledge this fact. Within Book III itself, Wilson suggests that Psalm 73 was added to the book's opening "seam" during the final stage of the Psalter's redaction.[3] He claims that this psalm stands outside of the "bookends" of Psalms 74 and 89—which have a more "angry and demanding tone"—and "offers a contrasting way forward in response to the loss of exile."[4] Wilson's overall assessment of Book III is surprisingly positive: "The psalms of the third book offer

---

1. See Gerald H. Wilson, "The Structure of the Psalter," in *Interpreting the Psalms: Issues and Approaches*, ed. David Firth and Phillip S. Johnston (Downers Grove, IL: IVP, 2005), 235–40.

2. Ibid., 235. Wilson notes here his belief that both Books I–III and IV–V are responses to the agony of the exile. In the Psalter's final redaction, the viewpoint of the latter two books takes precedence.

3. Ibid., 239. He points out that the Qumran evidence is consistent with this observation. Ps 73 is only one of nineteen canonical psalms from Pss 2–89 for which there is no manuscript evidence. Ibid., 239n. 18.

4. Wilson, "The Structure of the Psalter," 239.

mostly hopeful encouragement for those who remain loyal to Yahweh under the pressures of exile."[5]

J. Clinton McCann

J. Clinton McCann's study, "Books I–III and the Editorial Purpose of the Hebrew Psalter," is the first notable investigation into the final arrangement of Book III (MT) that sought to build upon Wilson's seminal work.[6] His aim was to develop Wilson's thesis that the Psalter addresses the apparent failure of the traditional Davidic/Zion covenant theology. Wilson argued that the answer to the problem documented in Books I–III comes in Books IV and V. McCann's burden is to show that "Books I–III already begin to answer the problem posed by the exile, dispersion and oppression of Israel by the nations in the postexilic era."[7] He argues this claim by considering the psalms opening Books I–III (Pss 1–2; 42–44; 73–74) and the shape of Book III itself. According to McCann, these considerations reveal a pattern "that serves to instruct the postexilic community not only to face the disorienting reality of exile but also to reach toward a reorientation beyond the traditional grounds for hope, that is, beyond the Davidic/Zion covenant theology."[8]

McCann begins with Book III because he believes that it most clearly reflects the failure of the Davidic covenant. He argues that the book has been significantly shaped by the experience of exile: it is communally oriented; it contains most of the communal laments in the Psalter; and Psalms 74, 79, 80, 83, 85, and 89 clearly reflect exilic influence.[9] Further, Psalm 73 pictures the psalmist maintaining hope in the midst of trouble, while Psalm 74 is a communal lament over the destruction of the Jerusalem Temple.

In fact, according to McCann, the arrangement of the entire book reflects exilic influence. Apart from Psalms 79–80, the book's communal laments do not occur side by side; they are punctuated with psalms that "grasp for threads of hope amid the experience of exile and dispersion by celebrating God as judge of all the earth

---

5. Ibid., 240. Wilson points to Ps 88 as an exception to this hopeful tone. It should be noted that Wilson's comments here are based on rather cursory observations. Unfortunately, his untimely death prevented him from carrying out an in-depth analysis of Pss 73–83 or Book III (MT) as a whole.

6. J. Clinton McCann, "Books I–III and the Editorial Purpose of the Hebrew Psalter," in *The Shape and Shaping of the Psalter*, ed. J. Clinton McCann, JSOTSup 159 (Sheffield: Sheffield Academic Press, 1993), 93–107. This essay is an expansion and refinement of ideas first set forth in chap. 5 of McCann's doctoral dissertation. See J. Clinton McCann, "Psalm 73: An Interpretation Emphasizing Rhetorical and Canonical Criticism" (PhD diss., Duke University, 1985), 123–79.

7. McCann, "Books I–III and the Editorial Purpose of the Hebrew Psalter," 95.

8. Ibid.

9. McCann, "Books I–III and the Editorial Purpose of the Hebrew Psalter," 96.

or by rehearsing God's past deeds on Israel's behalf despite Israel's unfaithfulness."[10] Thus, for McCann, the alternation between expressions of lament and hope in the book's final form is central to its message.[11] McCann claims that Psalm 73, with its movement from lament (vv. 1–16) to hope (vv. 18–27), anticipates this arrangement. In this way it "sets the tone" for the entire book.

McCann's central thesis, and most original claim, is that such an arrangement— the alternation between lament and hope—"serves to assist" the community both to face the horror of exile and to reach for fresh hope beyond the traditional Davidic/Zion theology. This is how Book III "already begins to answer" the problem posed by the exilic crisis. In McCann's view, this message is implied in the juxtaposition of the traditional Davidic/Zion theology and communal laments over its apparent failure throughout the book. He claims that these juxtapositions are intended to signal the rejection of the Davidic/Zion theology as a basis of hope. One example is the sequencing of Psalm 78:68–72, which recounts the Davidic/Zion theology, and Psalm 79:1–2, which laments the desecration of the temple and destruction of Jerusalem.[12]

In McCann's view, the message communicated by such juxtapositions is that hope for the future is not found in the theological traditions related to David and Zion. It is rather found in the psalms that stress God's role as judge (e.g., Pss 75–76) and that rehearse God's past deeds (e.g., Pss 77:12–21; 78). Further, Psalm 73 is "an example to the postexilic community of how to respond to the problem of exile and dispersion."[13] The remainder of McCann's essay focuses on how Books I and II bear out his central thesis.

Robert L. Cole

Robert L. Cole's *The Shape and Message of Book III (Psalms 73–89)* is the only full-length monograph devoted to an editorial-critical analysis of Psalms 73–89 (MT).[14] Cole seeks to build upon the work of Wilson and others by examining the purposeful arrangement of these psalms. He begins by briefly grounding his methodology in the field of poetics:

---

10. Ibid.

11. For example, the communal laments of Pss 74, 79, 80, 83, 85:1–8, 89:39–52 are offset with the hope expressed in Pss 75, 76, 81:12–17, 82, etc.

12. Other such juxtapositions are Ps 89:1–38/39–52 and Pss 73/74. It should be noted that McCann does think that the two "Zion psalms" (Pss 84 and 87) are "two-edged"; they remind the community of God's past deeds, but their juxtaposition with laments "makes the traditional hope ring hollow at best." Ibid., 98.

13. McCann, "Books I–III and the Editorial Purpose of the Hebrew Psalter," 100.

14. Robert L. Cole, *The Shape and Message of Book III (Psalms 73–89)*, JSOTSup 307 (Sheffield: Sheffield Academic Press, 2000).

It has become clear in recent years that the phenomenon of parallelism and repetition in the Psalter must be extended beyond that of the individual poems to surrounding psalms and finally the entire collection. The ordering and shaping of the collection casts the individual psalms in a new light. ... Such a focus moves from what the individual poem expresses to a meaning implied by the final compilation, the latter becoming a single "text." Consequently, the study of the final shape of the Psalter is simply a recognition that parallelism is not restricted to the individual poem.[15]

Cole proceeds to embark upon a 230-page analysis of Psalms 73–89. He works systematically through all seventeen psalms and constructs the book's "shape and message" on the basis of copious amounts of parallel features mined from these psalms. The links that Cole cites are lexical, phonological, thematic, and structural in nature. Cole's analysis is true to his method of treating these discrete psalms virtually as if they really were a single composition.

For Cole, "the dominant theme of Book III is the prolonged postponement of expectations that Ps 72 aroused."[16] He argues that the psalms of Book III communicate this theme by a "continuing dialogue," or even drama, centered around the fulfillment of promises contained in Psalm 72. In Cole's view, Psalm 72 serves as the basis for the lament, questioning, and promise of future restoration that run throughout Book III. The recurring themes that he detects correspond to different voices in a three-way "continuing dialogue"; a lamenting, sinful, and questioning nation (Pss 73:10; 74; 79; 80; 82; 83); a series of Divine responses to the nation (Pss 75; 76; 81:9–15; 82); and a righteous Davidide—distinguished from the nation by his obedience—who figures prominently in Cole's understanding of the book's message (Pss 73:15–17; 75:10–11; 77; 78:1; 80:18; 84; 85; 86; 88).

Book III begins in Psalm 73 with conditions that "are the opposite of those promised in Ps 72" (16). The "dialogue" begins in Psalm 74 with a communal lament to God. The "How long?" questions voiced first in this psalm (see vv. 9–10) will recur throughout the remainder of Book III (77:8–10; 79:5, 10; 80:5; 82:2; 85:6; 89:47) (34). But Psalm 74 does not simply complain; it requests the fulfillment of Psalm 72 (36).

This request is answered in Psalms 75 and 76. Psalm 75 answers both the "How long?" and "Why?" questions of Psalm 74 (38). In Psalm 75:3 God himself responds that he will judge with equity at a Divinely appointed time. On the other hand, the judgment of God mentioned in verses 3 and 8 provides an indirect response to the "Why?" of Psalm 74:1 and 11. It also responds to the problem of the wicked in Psalm 73 (38). Further, in promising the "long-awaited judgment" of the wicked, Psalm 75 "rekindles hope in the eventual fulfillment of ... Ps 72" (45). Psalm 76 is a "more detailed and vivid outworking" of the appointed time of God's judgment mentioned in 75:3. Many links with Psalm 74 indicate that "each point of Psalm

---

15. Ibid., 10.
16. Ibid., 61.

2. The Current State of Scholarship 43

74 is being answered by ... 76" (49). In addition, the promised salvation of "the afflicted ones" (v. 10) "reiterates the promise of a future kingdom of peace and justice seen in Psalm 72" (53).

According to Cole, the "dialogue" continues with the lament of Psalm 77. Cole observes, "Parallel vocabulary to Ps 77 in both 76 and 74 reveal continued discussion of the desired redemption" (55). Psalm 77 longs for the destruction of the enemies promised in the preceding Psalm 76. But Psalm 77 also reminds the people of their past failures; the community suffers under God's wrath (v. 10). An important aspect of Psalm 77 concerns the verb אזן in verse 2. In Cole's view, this verb "begins a string of the same through Psalms 77, 78 [v. 1], and 80 [v. 2], revealing a dialogue between God and the people at the canonical level ... the response of Ps 78 answers complaints voiced in 77, but due to the nature of that response Ps 80.2 ... again asks for a hearing" (60). Psalm 77 is to be understood as another appeal for the restoration promised in Psalm 72, while Psalm 78 provides a detailed response to the lament of Psalm 77. This response both explains the dismal situation of the people in terms of sin and disobedience, and provides "the pledge of an eventual restoration of Zion which now lies in ruins and of another shepherd like David. In the midst of complaints and laments, the promises of Psalms 72, 75, and 76 have been reaffirmed" (70).

The many links between the closing verses of Psalm 78 (vv. 67–72) and those opening Psalm 79 (vv. 1–3) indicate that the latter verses are a response to, and complete reversal of, the Davidic/Zion theology recounted at the conclusion of Psalm 78 (80). The "How long?" of the community continues in Psalm 79, a question that is "never fully answered in Book III" (81). Cole notes that the community continues to speak in Psalm 80. This lament is "another appeal to God by the faithful community" that responds "to issues raised in Psalm 78, but also repeats questions similar especially to those seen in Psalm 74. Furthermore, promises given in Psalm 72 are also recalled" (95).

Psalm 81 follows as a Divine response to the appeals of both Psalms 79 and 80. The answers that Psalm 81 provides for Psalm 80 "prove that God still answers, even if not in the desired manner" (98). In Psalm 81, God responds to the people's "Hear!" (Ps 80:2) in kind, exhorting them to "Hear!" (Ps 81:9, 12, 14). In Cole's view, the nature of this response is both sober and hopeful. God explains the people's sad state in terms of their disobedience (Ps 81:12–13). However, if his people would listen, God promises to turn his hand back upon their enemies and deliver them (Ps 81:14–17).

Psalm 82 continues the Divine response of Psalm 81. The prominent "How long?" of the community is now taken up on the "lips" of God himself (Ps 82:2): "In answer to the question of how long the desolation would last, the same is thrown back at the nation asking how long their corrupt judgment would continue."[17]

---

17. Cole, *The Shape and Message of Book III*, 103. Cole understands the plural אלהים of Ps 82 as a reference to corrupt "judges in Israel, and not a pantheon of foreign gods." Ibid. See the exegesis of Ps 82 in ch. 9 for the problems with this view.

In Cole's view, another reassertion of the promise of Psalm 72 is found here in the closing verse of Psalm 82. This verse promises that "all of the nations" will eventually be brought under "divine dominion."[18] At the same time, the request for God's action in Psalm 82:8 is "pleading for the promises of Psalm 72 to be fulfilled."[19] Regarding the concluding psalm of the Asaphite collection, Cole claims, "the oppressive situation described in Psalm 83 is a direct result of the disobedience described in 81. … Psalm 83 pleads for God's wrath upon the nations and ironically brings to the fore Israel's own guilt, as expressed in previous psalms of Book III."[20]

Christine Jones

In her 2009 dissertation, "The Psalms of Asaph: A Study of the Function of a Psalm Collection," Christine Jones aims to build upon the work of both McCann and Wilson.[21] Her study sought to fill two related gaps. The first was a scholarly lack of attention to questions of the collection's arrangement and placement within the MT Psalter. The second was the lack of attention given to smaller collections of psalms within "the canonical approach to the Psalter."[22]

Her central thesis is that the Asaph collection serves to "guide the reader through the turmoil experienced by the people as a result of the exile."[23] She notes that her approach will pay close attention to linguistic and thematic links between these psalms and to questions of arrangement. An important component of her method is attention to the "impact" of these considerations upon the reader.[24] After carrying out her analysis of the collection, Jones briefly considers its function in the MT Psalter as a whole.

In Chapter 5 Jones examines various linguistic and thematic links that communicate recurring messages to the reader. Her goal is to ask what these links reveal about the purpose of the collection as a whole. The main themes arising from her analysis are as follows: (1) God as the sole sovereign just judge of the world. Though presently judging the people, he can still be trusted to

---

18. Ibid., 104.

19. Ibid., 105.

20. Ibid., 111, 114. According to Cole, this irony results from the speaker of Ps 83 asking that the judgment of Ps 73 be brought to bear upon God's enemies. Cole explains that this request is ironic because, at the canonical level of Book III, such a judgment would include Israel. Ibid., 113.

21. Christine Dannette Brown Jones, "The Psalms of Asaph: A Study of the Function of a Psalm Collection" (PhD diss., Baylor University, 2009).

22. Ibid., 61.

23. Jones, "The Psalms of Asaph," 2.

24. By "reader" she means a careful exilic or postexilic reader strongly concerned about Judah's fate. Ibid., 5.

2. The Current State of Scholarship

save his people; (2) an antagonist who serves as a foil to demonstrate God's faithfulness; (3) a "faithful" group opposed to the antagonist, which highlights God's sovereignty; (4) the theme of "remembering," the key to remaining faithful; and (5) "the king."[25]

Chapter 6 contains her conclusions about the message that the arrangement communicates, as well as the collection's contribution to the Psalter as a whole. According to Jones, the message arises from a combination of the following: (1) the themes running throughout the psalms discussed in Chapter 5; and (2) the collection's arrangement. She discusses Psalm 50's placement first and suggests that it functions as a literary bridge between the Korahite collection (Pss 42–49), the Davidic collection (Pss 51–72), and the Asaphite collection (Pss 73–83).[26] Further, it "also establishes an idea that is challenged at the beginning of the Asaphite collection—the wicked will be punished and the righteous will be rewarded."[27]

Psalm 73 introduces the general problem of the main collection: the wicked prosper but hope still exists. Psalm 74 introduces the specific problem: the temple is destroyed because of God's anger. Psalms 75 and 76 function as responses to Psalm 74 by asserting God's role as judge of the wicked and assuring the reader that God will act. According to Jones, Psalms 77–79 are the heart of the collection. She explains that here the destruction of the temple as a consequence of God's anger is stressed again. But, she observes, so is the idea of remembering God's past deeds as a way forward. An appeal for God to turn from his anger follows in Psalm 80. A Divine speech in Psalm 81 (vv. 9–17) responds that such is contingent upon the people's repentance. Psalm 82 returns to the theme of God as judge and illustrates why the idolatry described in Psalm 81 is misplaced: other gods will perish. Finally, Psalm 83 pleads with God to commence this judgment with the surrounding nations. It concludes the Asaph collection by calling God to demonstrate his sovereignty in a definite manner.

Taken as a whole, Jones understands the collection as "an honest reflection of the confusion encountered after the destruction of the temple and the exile" (184). Its primary message is that the people should continue to obey and be faithful because God will one day judge the wicked and because God's past actions provide assurance of his faithfulness toward the people (185). According to Jones, the Asaph psalms pose something of a challenge to attempts to understand the MT Psalter as a whole (188). The reason is that many of the themes found elsewhere in the Psalter are tempered in these psalms, such as the role of David as king, God's kingship, and the faith of the righteous (188–90).

---

25. Ibid., 147–74.

26. Ibid., 141, 177. Her conclusion comes after reviewing various proposals for the compilation of the Elohistic Psalter (Pss 42–89) for clues regarding the placement of Ps 50. She admits that its position is a puzzle.

27. Ibid., 177.

Matthias Millard

In an important monograph, *Die Komposition des Psalters: Ein formgeschichtlicher Ansatz*, Matthias Millard brings the method of form-criticism (*Formgeschichte*) to bear upon the question of the shape and shaping of the MT Psalter.[28] Millard contends that form-criticism is able to shed light on the structure and function of psalm collections within the Psalter as it has individual psalms. In his view, the Psalter reached its present form in the Persian period and was intended for individual use rather than corporate worship.[29]

Millard begins with a form-critical analysis of individual psalms: untitled psalms, those grouped by common titles (e.g., the Asaph psalms; Korahite psalms; the Psalms of Ascents; etc.), the many "pairs of psalms" (*Zwillingspsalmen*) (e.g., Pss 9–10; 20–21), concentrically arranged groups (e.g., Pss 15–24), and so on. He focuses on what he calls clusters, the combination of motifs, genres, or formulas in a single psalm. The main portion of the study identifies similar kinds of clusters across the psalm groups he has identified.[30]

According to Millard, the fundamental feature around which these collections are organized is a "compositional arc" (*Kompositionsbogen*). This "arc" consists of the following elements: lament, oracle, and hymn (or thanksgiving). Like the form-critical analysis of individual psalms, not every element is or needs to be present in each collection. For example, the oracle is sometimes absent, as in the first collection of Korahite psalms.[31] An additional element may also be present, such as Psalm 82 in the first *Kompositionsbogen* of the Asaph psalms (see below).

Most relevant for present purposes is the way in which Psalms 73–83 bear out Millard's thesis. Millard contends first that the *Kompositionsbogen* mentioned above is twice repeated in the Asaph psalms. The first is composed of Psalm 74 (lament theme), Psalm 75 (oracle), and Psalm 76 (Zion psalm/hymn). Its conclusion is the lament of Psalm 77.

The second *Kompositionsbogen* consists of Psalms 79–80 (lament theme), Psalm 81 (oracle), and Psalm 82 (Zion psalm).[32] Like the first, this second *Kompositionsbogen* ends with the tone of lament (Ps 83). Further, as is true of other compositional arcs, Millard claims that wisdom psalms function to introduce both groups (i.e., Pss 73; 78), while, as just mentioned, laments function as conclusions (i.e., Pss 77; 83). Psalm 78 also functions as a "separator" (*Trenner*) between Psalms 77 and 79.[33] The hope of intervention that the psalm provides explains the presence

---

28. Matthias Millard, *Die Komposition des Psalters: Ein Formgeschichtlicher Ansatz*, FAT 9 (Tübingen: Mohr Siebeck, 1994).

29. Ibid., 240–8.

30. Ibid., 163–8.

31. Ibid., 162.

32. Ibid.

33. Millard, *Die Komposition des Psalters*, 90.

of Psalm 77 at the conclusion of the first sub-composition (vv. 12–21).[34] The same is true of the placement of Psalm 83 at the conclusion of the second.

Thus, for Millard, these psalms have a clear and deliberate structuration. They divide into two distinct groupings (Pss 73–77; 78–83) headed by "wisdom shaped psalms" (*weisheitlich geprägten Psalmen*) (Pss 73 and 78). Both compositional arcs mentioned above begin in a similar way, with complaints about the sanctuary's destruction (Pss 74 and 79) and progress in the analogous manner described.

Hossfeld and Zenger

Another important German contribution is the commentary on Psalms 51–100 by Frank-Lothar Hossfeld and Erich Zenger.[35] The authors first treat the individual psalm with more traditional methods. They then turn to consider its *Sitz im Buch* as a valid and important interpretative horizon. Like other German scholars (e.g., Beat Weber), diachrony plays a significant role in the analysis of Hossfeld and Zenger.[36] And like many North American studies, these scholars also give much attention to lexical and thematic links between psalms. In addition to psalm sequence and placement, these links form a significant basis for the conclusions they reach on the structure and message(s) of Psalms 73–83.[37] The major contours of their views are as follows.

Hossfeld and Zenger contend that Psalms 73–83 are structurally parallel to Psalms 84–88. In their view, both groupings were apparently influenced by the same "compositional arc,"[38] an interpretation reflecting the influence of Millard's study. This "arc" is repeated twice in the Asaph collection: teaching (Ps 73); community lament (Ps 74); oracle/Divine response (Pss 75–76); lament (Ps 77);

---

34. Ibid., 102.

35. Frank-Lothar Hossfeld and Erich Zenger, *Psalms 2: A Commentary on Psalms 51–100*, trans. Linda M. Maloney, Hermeneia (Minneapolis, MN: Fortress Press, 2005). The commentary was originally part of Herder's *Theologischer Kommentar zum Alten Testament*.

36. Meaning that they consider knowledge of the MT Psalter's historical growth as essential for understanding the message and purpose of its final form. Like Beat Weber (see below) and others, Hossfeld and Zenger deduce this process from synchronic observations on the MT Psalter.

37. In another place, Zenger outlined his approach as consisting primarily of attention to four main paratextual features: (1) connections between neighboring psalms; (2) the position of a psalm within its particular (redactional) unit or grouping; (3) psalm titles; (4) connections and repetitions of psalms within a collection. See Erich Zenger, "Was wird anders bei kanonischer Psalmenauslegung," in *Ein Gott, Eine Offenbarung: Beiträge zur biblischen Exegese, Theologie und Spiritualität: Festschrift für Notker Füglister*, ed. Friedrich V. Reiterer, OSB 60 (Würzburg: Echter, 1991): 397–413.

38. The authors also mention a "contextual link" between Pss 87 and 83 based upon common themes. Hossfeld and Zenger, *Psalms 2*, 387.

teaching (Ps 78); community lament (Pss 79–80); oracle/Divine response (Pss 81–82); lament (Ps 83).[39] Notably, Hossfeld and Zenger ground these arcs much more firmly in the links between psalms than does Millard. At the same time, their approach is much more conservative than Cole's, as it focuses on the *major* links that proximate psalms share.[40]

In addition to these "arcs," the authors identify Psalms 77–79 as a "triad" of psalms (294). These are so tightly bound by links, claims Hossfeld, that there is no "possibility of placing a caesura between the three psalms" (250). There is, however, evidence of a caesura between Psalms 76 and 77. This break is indicated by strong links between Psalms 77 and 78 but relatively weak ones between Psalms 77 and 76 (280).

The collection also has as an intentionally positioned introduction, Psalm 73, though the psalm was not created for its present context (237). Psalm 73 anticipates a number of ideas found in the following collection but also "acquires additional dimensions of meaning from the collection" (237). At the other end of the collection, Psalm 83 functions as a "programmatic conclusion" (345). It has been placed in its current, final, position "because it shares essential theological perspectives with the psalms here collected, and because … it is an effective conclusion to the collection."[41]

Importantly, Hossfeld and Zenger ascribe a central literary and theological (not merely numerical) position to Psalm 78, both within its "microcontext" (Pss 77–79) and the collection as a whole.[42] We will see below that others (e.g., Beat Weber; Judith Gärtner; Anja Klein) have taken a similar position on Psalm 78's importance. In support of this conclusion, Hossfeld and Zenger cite the many links that Psalm 78 shares with the surrounding psalms.[43] Following other scholars (i.e., Beat Weber), they conclude that these links suggest that Psalm 78 has significance as the "central Asaph psalm."[44]

O. Palmer Robertson

O. Palmer Robertson argues that the MT Psalter as a whole exhibits an intentional "flow" or development of thought progression.[45] In its broadest possible themes,

---

39. Ibid., 250, 271, and 336.

40. They observe that Pss 74–76 are cohesively bound by "the idea common to them all, of God as the (saving) judge (74:22; 75:3, 5; 76:9–10), the theologoumenon of divine wrath (74:1; 75:9; 76:8), and the theology of the Divine name (74:7, 10, 18, 21; 75:2; 76:2)" (Hossfeld and Zenger, *Psalms 2*, 250).

41. Hossfeld and Zenger, *Psalms 2*, 345–6.

42. Ibid., 294.

43. Ibid., 293–4.

44. Ibid., 293.

45. O. Palmer Robertson, *The Flow of the Psalms: Discovering Their Structure and Theology* (Phillipsburg, NJ: P&R, 2015).

Robertson conceives of the Psalter's "flow" along the following lines: confrontation (Book I); communication (Book II); devastation (Book III); maturation (Book IV); consummation (Book V).[46] Robertson's method focuses on the "substance" of the psalms themselves as the most important indicator of intentional structure in the Psalter.[47] He also takes into consideration genre, psalm titles, and thematic and key-word links.

Robertson's summary of Book III as "devastation" reflects his opinion that the book's "predominant message" is the devastation of the corporate community of God's people by foreign nations.[48] He contends that the book provides a completely different view on the continuing significance of the two major elements of Yahweh's covenant with David (i.e., "dynasty" and "dwelling place") than Books I and II of the MT Psalter.[49] The dynasty of David and the Lord's dwelling place have been devastated. In a significant departure from Wilson, Robertson argues that the Davidic covenant has not, therefore, failed. The repeated mention of the everlasting covenant with David in Psalm 89 anticipates a coming David-like descendent.[50]

Robertson holds that Book III of the MT Psalter has a deliberate structure. The discussion here is limited to his understanding of Psalms 73–83. On his view, Psalms 73–74 are thematic introductions (one individual [Ps 73], one communal [Ps 74]) introducing the book's focus on the devastation of God's people. Robertson cites parallels between Psalms 73–74 and the opening psalms of Book II (Pss 42–43 and 44) to justify the introductory function of both psalms. Next are two psalms asserting God's kingship over earthly kings (Pss 75–76). Psalm 75 is an intentional response to the cry for deliverance in the preceding psalm.[51] Psalm 76 "almost certainly describes the humiliation of Sennacherib king of Assyria."[52]

Seven psalms follow (Pss 77–83) that, according to Robertson, an editor/collector "appears to have deliberately grouped … at the midpoint of Book III … with the specific intent of relating the devastation of both kingdoms as well as their deliverance by their respective messianic figures."[53] These figures are Joseph and Jacob, who are referenced throughout these seven psalms. For Robertson, these figures function as a major disjunctive feature (he does not use that specific term) that segments these seven psalms as an intentional psalm grouping.[54] Robertson

46. Ibid., 52.
47. Ibid., 52n. 6, 92n. 8.
48. Robertson, *The Flow of the Psalms*, 122.
49. Robertson observes that these two themes appear first in Ps 2 and anticipate much of the MT Psalter's "flow." Ibid., 47–9.
50. Ibid., 146.
51. Ibid., 127.
52. Ibid. The basis of this claim is the psalm's title in the LXX (πρὸς τὸν Ἀσσύριον).
53. Ibid., 138. See his discussion on ibid., 128–38.
54. Another element of cohesion he observes is the shepherd imagery binding Pss 77–79 together (see Pss 77:20; 78:52, 72; 79:13; 80:1), noting that "this extension of a common phrasing across several psalms represents a typical technique of organizational arrangement." Robertson, *The Flow of the Psalms*, 129.

contends that the center of this collection is Psalm 80, a psalm focusing on a "son of man" that God has raised up as a deliverer (vv. 15, 17). After "rehearsing" the devastations of Psalms 74, 77, 79, and 80, Psalm 81 (vv. 6–13) "boldly declares that his [God's] people can be saved from all these oppressive armies [vv. 14–17]."[55]

For Robertson, an important message arising from Psalms 73–83 and Book III as a whole is the "failure of faith" and its negative consequences. The failure of the covenant people's faith explains how they could suffer the devastation described in the book: "Trust in Yahweh that might have functioned as the instrument of their deliverance appears at its weakest."[56] Robertson appeals to the scarcity of words for trust in Book III to support his interpretation, pointing to five words or phrases for trust that occur frequently elsewhere in the Psalter but seldom, or only in a negative sense, in Book III. These statistics suggest to Robertson that Book III is distinctive for its "paucity of references to the nation's response in faith."[57]

According to Robertson, in Psalm 82 God promises to judge the (human) judges of the nations. The Most-High God will arise and judge the earth, since he possesses all nations (v. 8). The final psalm of the collection (Ps 83) envisions "the ultimate end" of Israel's enemies. But surprisingly, this "end" consists of their seeking God's name (v. 16).

David Mitchell

David Mitchell's book, *The Message of the Psalter: An Eschatological Programme in the Book of Psalms*, seeks to demonstrate that the Psalter "may have been redacted as a literary unit with an intentionally eschatological reference" and that "this redaction takes the form of a programme of eschatological events."[58] The Asaph psalms (Pss 50, 73–83, 105–106[59]) are the first group of psalms on which he tests this thesis. Mitchell's burden is to show that the Asaph psalms "contain a sequence of events that can be read as depicting an eschatological programme."[60]

Mitchell appeals first to the heading לְאָסָף to support this thesis, which we have seen heads Psalms 50 and 73–83. Mitchell argues in detail that this heading evokes a "wide-image complex" that "involves the Asaphite guild of singers as cultic prophet-musicians, the cultic rite of 'remembrancing,' performed by the 'mazkir'

---

55. Ibid., 135.
56. Ibid., 143.
57. Ibid., 145. The lexica Robertson discusses are בטח ("to trust"); קוה ("to wait"); יראת יהוה ("the fear of the Lord"); חסה ("to seek shelter/refuge"); אמן ("to believe"). See his discussion on ibid., 144–5.
58. David C. Mitchell, *The Message of the Psalter: An Eschatological Programme in the Book of Psalms*, JSOTSup 252 (Sheffield: Sheffield Academic Press, 1997), 90.
59. In light of the observation that 1 Chr 16 (where David appoints Asaph to gives thanks) combines the text of these psalms, Mitchell refers to them as "deutero-Asaph Psalms."
60. Ibid., 90.

('remembrancer') at times of invasion and siege by foreign armies, the sounding of trumpets and the gathering of the people."[61] These traditions associated with the Asaphites are reflected in multiple ways in the Asaph psalms. The tradition of the Asaphites as prophet musicians is reflected in the presence of divine oracles, which is three times greater than in the rest of Psalter, and in the observation that Psalms 82:8 and 83:18 look forward to the future rule of Yahweh over all the earth.[62]

Asaph's function as a "remembrancer" (המזכיר) (Isa 36:22), closely tied to the zikhron (זכרון) or "remembrancing" ritual (1 Chr 16:4), is reflected in the following features of these psalms:[63] (1) the several references in the Asaph psalms to foreign invasion, such as the LXX superscriptions to Psalm 76 (πρὸς τὸν Ἀσσύριον) and Psalm 80 (ψαλμὸς ὑπὲρ τοῦ Ἀσσυρίου); (2) the reference to a foreign invasion in Psalm 79:1–3; (3) the oracle concerning the ten-nation confederacy in Psalm 83; (4) the predominance of the root זכר ("to remember") in the Asaph psalms, which occurs sixteen times (thirteen times in the main group and three more times in the "deutero-Asaph Psalms" 105 and 106). This is an impressive one-third of the total occurrences of this verb in the MT Psalter; (5) the "feature of historical review" in the Asaph psalms (i.e., Pss 74:12–23; 77:8–13), aimed at putting God in remembrance of his former acts on Israel's behalf; (6) the multiple places that mention calling out to God in the time of hostility (Pss 50:15; 77:2–3; 81:8); and (7) Psalm 81, which mentions the sounding of the trumpet and sets out terms of deliverance from enemies (vv. 4, 14–17).

Finally, Mitchell observes that the collection reflects the theme of ingathering. This theme is associated with the Asaphite tradition in the following ways: (1) the name "Asaph" (אסף) means "to gather" and so the heading לאסף "might be taken as meaning something like For the Ingathering";[64] (2) "the first word of the first divine oracle of the first Asaph psalm is a command to ingather" (i.e., Ps 50:5), and the last psalm "describes a ten nation alliance gathered against God and Israel" (100); (3) the Asaph psalms show an especial interest in Joseph, a name cognate to Asaph. He observes a similar interest in Jacob in the Asaph psalms, where seven of the Psalter's twenty-six references to Jacob occur. This observation is significant because it could be connected with his reputation as an ingatherer (Gen 49:1–2).

The next line of evidence Mitchell offers to support his thesis is the "eschatological orientation" of the Asaph psalms. He notes that several passages in these psalms "seem to refer intentionally to latter day events" (101). Mitchell's argument focuses

---

61. Ibid., 101.
62. Ibid., 93.
63. Mitchell deduces from texts in Chronicles, Numbers, and other places that the "remembrancer" (see 1 Chr 16:4) was a functionary in the cultic right of "remembrancing" Yahweh. This was apparently a rite that was central to Israel's Holy War traditions (ibid., 96). He argues that this role was tied closely to a rite that consisted of blowing hazozerot ("trumpets") before Yahweh in times of foreign invasion. This would bring Yahweh to remembrance of Israel's plight and obtain his deliverance.
64. Mitchell, *The Message of the Psalter*, 99.

mainly on reasons why Psalm 83, which describes an unattested ten-nation allegiance against Israel, "should be regarded as an intentionally eschatological prediction" (102). He also points to other psalms that "have a feeling of ultimacy about them," such as Psalms 50 and 82. Additional support for reading these psalms eschatologically, Mitchell argues, is that some later interpreters believed they referred to eschatological events.[65]

Mitchell's final consideration is the sequence of the collection. He tentatively argues that Psalms 73–83 contain "a sequence of events that can be read as depicting eschatological ingathering" that climaxes in battle.[66] The evidence supporting this claim is a narrative progression in thought that he detects from Yahweh's ingathering of Israel from exile for judgment (Ps 50) to the ingathering of nations against Israel in order to destroy them (Ps 83):[67]

1. Psalm 50. God commands the ingathering of Israel and pronounces sentence; the righteous are delivered while the wicked are torn to pieces.
2. Psalm 73. The wicked prosper now but God will destroy them when God rises up.
3. Psalm 74. The nations destroyed the temple and continue to mock God. God is reminded of such deeds and exhorted to repay them.
4. Psalm 75. Praise because God's judgment is near.
5. Psalm 76. Remembering that God has delivered in the past.
6. Psalm 77. God is called to remembrance and urged to act on Israel's behalf on the basis of God's former love for Israel.
7. Psalm 78. Recalling that Israel has failed but God is merciful.
8. Psalm 79. The nations have invaded and destroyed Jerusalem.
9. Psalm 80. A plea for God to restore the nation; in return the people promise.
10. Psalm 81. In an oracle God announces that the condition of deliverance is obedience.
11. Psalm 82. God responds by judging the deities of the nations.
12. Psalm 83. A ten-nation confederacy gathers against Israel signaling that the day of hostility spoken in Psalm 50 has arrived.

Beat Weber

Beat Weber has written extensively on the Asaph psalms.[68] This survey focuses specifically on his editorial-critical-oriented views. Pride of place here goes to

---

65. See the discussion on Mitchell, *The Message of the Psalter*, 103–4.
66. Ibid., 90.
67. This list is an adaptation of Mitchell's bulleted list on ibid., 106–7.
68. See, for example, the following studies: Beat Weber, *Psalm 77 und sein Umfeld: Eine poetologische Studie*, BBB 103 (Weinheim, Germany: Beltz Athenäum, 1995); Beat Weber, "'In Salem wurde sein Versteck …': Psalm 76 im Lichte literischer und historischer Kontexte neu gelesen," *BN* (1999): 85–103; Beat Weber, "Zur Datierung der Asaph-Psalmen 74 und

Weber's article "Der Asaph Psalter—eine Skizze." As the title indicates, this article sketches Weber's understanding of the Asaph collection. He first draws attention to the major literary similarities between these psalms: their largely collective nature; the focus on God's judgment; prophetic and wisdom accents; "name theology"; and knowledge of (early) historical (Moses) traditions.[69] He then turns to discuss what he argues is the "preexilic Asaph Psalter."[70] This discussion makes clear that, for Weber, diachronic concerns (i.e., the collection's historical growth) are crucial for understanding the shape and message of this collection.

In Weber's view, the crisis reflected in Psalms 74, 76–78, 80, and 83 is not the fall of the southern empire but (initially) the fall of the northern empire and the Assyrian crisis (129). Thus, each of these psalms is preexilic and was part of the preexilic Asaph Psalter. Psalm 78, which occupies a significant theological position in the collection (reflected in its numerical centrality), gives this group of psalms a theological interpretation of history (131).[71] And it responds to the open ending of Psalm 77, offering a theological explanation that makes God's judgment of Judah in Psalm 77 understandable (i.e., it is explained by disobedience) (134).[72] Though more tentative in his conclusions here, Weber proposes that Psalms 50, 81, 75, and 82 should also be given a preexilic dating (131–2). Thus, for Weber, Psalm 79—the only Asaph psalm that speaks explicitly of Jerusalem and its destruction—is the only exilic psalm in the collection (133, 135, 137).

Weber notes that the preexilic Asaph Psalter is open-ended; Psalm 83 does not resolve the tension between oppression and the hope for redemption in

---

79," *Bib* 81 (2000): 521–32; Beat Weber, "Psalm 78: Geschichte mit Geschichte deuten," *TZ* 56 (2000): 193–214; Beat Weber, "Psalm 83 als Einzelpsalm und als Abschluss der Asaph-Psalmen," *BN* (2000): 64–84; Beat Weber, "Der Asaph Psalter—eine Skizze," in *Prophetie und Psalmen. Festschrift für Klaus Seybold zum 65. Geburtstag*, AOAT 280, ed. B. Huwyler, H. P. Mathys, and B. Weber (Münster: Ugarit-Verlag, 2001), 117–41; Beat Weber, "Akrostichische Muster in den Asaph-Psalmen," *BN* (2002): 79–94; Beat Weber, "Psalm 78 als 'Mitte' des Psalters?—ein Versuch," *Bib* 88 (2007): 305–25; Beat Weber, "Von der Psaltergenese zur Psaltertheologie: Der nächste Schritt der Psalter-exegese?! Einige grundsätzliche Überlegungen zum Psalter als Buch und Kanonteil," in *The Composition of the Book of Psalms*, ed. Erich Zenger, BETL 238 (Leuven: Peeters, 2010), 733–44; Beat Weber, "Verbindungslinien von den Psalmen Asaphs (Ps 50; 73–83) zu den Psalmen des Psalterteilbuchs IV (90–106). Erwägungen zu einem asaphitischen Trägerkreis," in *Trägerkreise in den Psalmen*, ed. Frank-Lothar Hossfeld, Johannes Bremer, and Till Magnus Steiner, BBB 178 (Göttingen: V&R unipress/Bon University Press, 2017), 97–131.

69. See the discussion in Weber, "Der Asaph Psalter—eine Skizze," 118–27.

70. See ibid., 127–36.

71. In terms of Ps 78's importance, Weber asserts that its size alone suggests it was something of a "theological testament" in the collection and gives it its stamp. In his view, the psalm's importance is also indicated by its "central [numerical] position" within the group of Asaph psalms. See ibid., 34.

72. On this point, see also Weber, *Psalm 77 und sein Umfeld*, 290.

these psalms.[73] Further, he notes that a threefold movement can be discerned in this "Psalter." The first "arc" (134) consists of Psalms 74–76, which begins with complaint about the destroyed sanctuary (Ps 74) but ends in hymnic praise of God's theophanic intervention at Salem (Ps 76). The third movement is from Psalms 80–82. This "arc" begins with a request for restoration and leads to God as judge over the gods and all nations of the earth. Finally, the second "movement" is emphasized at the center of the collection: Psalms 77–78. This extends from a complaint of the people (77) to a message to the people (78), which culminates in the election of Judah and Zion.[74] In Weber's view, this preexilic Asaph Psalter likely can be traced to the time of Josiah (135).

According to Weber, Psalm 79 was added during the exilic period. This redaction "updated" not only Psalm 78 (with which Ps 79 is consciously linked [see 137]) but the collection as a whole (137), including the other complaints. Having first processed the fall of the northern kingdom, these complaints could easily be adapted to the analogous situation in the south (137). Thus, the addition of Psalm 79 did not substantially alter the *message* of the preexilic Asaph Psalter; it essentially only adapted that message for a new situation.

Furthermore, with the addition of Psalm 79 the second "arc" mentioned above was now expanded to include Psalms 77–79 (138). This core group, therefore, now contained the whole tension from the fall of the northern kingdom (Ps 77), to the theological interpretation of that event (Ps 78), to the lament over Jerusalem's fall (79) (138).[75] Importantly, Psalm 78 retained its significant "middle" position in the collection with this redaction (138), since, despite the exile, a theological problematization of the Davidic throne was not yet in sight.[76] According to Weber, Psalm 89 later assumed this function (141).

Martin Leuenberger

As the title of his book suggests, Martin Leuenberger's 2004 study *Konzeptionen des Königtums Gottes im Psalter: Untersuchungen zu Komposition und Redaktion*

---

73. Elsewhere Weber points out what appears to be a new and deliberate "horizon of meaning" created by Ps 83's concluding position: the judgment of God "inwardly" (i.e., Ps 50) on God's people and the judgment of God "outwardly" (i.e., Ps 83), on those outside of Israel who oppose God and his people. Here Weber also sketches his views on how Ps 83 marks the conclusion of the Elohistic Psalter. See Weber, "Psalm 83 als Einzelpsalm und als Abschluss der Asaph-Psalmen," 80–2.

74. For Weber, Ps 78 deals specifically with the rejection of the Northern tribes, not "all Israel." See the discussion of Ps 78 in Chapter 5 of the present study for an alternative view.

75. See the diagram in Weber, "Der Asaph Psalter—eine Skizze," 138.

76. In another place, Weber argues (with caution) that Ps 78 is the center of not only the Asaph psalms but the MT Psalter as a whole. See Weber, "Psalm 78 als 'Mitte' des Psalters?—ein Versuch."

der theokratischen Bücher IV–V im Psalter adopts a method that focuses on both compositional structures of the Psalter's final shape and its editorial history.[77] Leuenberger deals with Psalms 73–83 in Chapter 2.[78] After pointing out a lack of consensus on the structure of these psalms, Leuenberger focuses on what he considers to be clear correspondences to lay the groundwork for his views: Psalms 73 and 78 are wisdom-shaped didactic poems; Psalms 74 and 79–80 (and 83) are communal laments; Psalms 75–76 and 81–82 correspond in terms of both form (i.e., answer or reaction to God) and content (112).

Regarding Psalm 77, Leuenberger is aware of the disagreement over its relationship to Psalm 78. In his view, the strongest evidence suggests that it is something of a "hinge" (*Scharnier*) between two subcollections: 73–77 and 78–83. Suggesting this role are first of all the formal considerations sketched above: 73/78 (wisdom-didactic poems); 74/79–80 (communal laments); 75–76/81–82 (answer/reaction); and 77/83 (see below). According to Leuenberger, such formal correspondence points to a parallel relationship between Psalms 73–77 and 78–83.[79] Reinforcing and confirming this relationship is the content of these psalms, which he then traces out.

Psalm 73 opens with the programmatic statement of God's goodness, which will become "problematized" several times in both subgroups (73–77 and 78–83). The individual framework of Psalm 73 is then "collectivized and historically deepened" (*kollektiviert und geschichtlich vertieft*) in Psalms 74–76. The "How long?" of 74:1 is answered first in the assurance that "God is my King of old" (v. 12), and then again in Psalms 75 (the God of just judgment; see v. 3) and 76 (the terrible God of Zion; see v. 8).

Psalm 77 takes up again the questioning of Psalm 74 (v. 8). According to Leuenberger, the psalm itself provides an answer in God's works of old, centered on the Exodus deliverance (vv. 15–21). Yet this is an answer with reservations (in light of 11b), with the result that its implications for Israel's present are left open. Psalm 77 concludes the first subgroup, the first "arc of suspense/tension" (*Spannungsbogen*) (i.e., Pss 73–77) (113).

Thus, despite strong ties with Psalm 77, Psalm 78 "starts again" with a call for the people to "listen!" (v. 1). The psalmist recounts not only the people's sins but also God's great acts, for the purpose of evoking fresh trust in God (v. 7). In Leuenberger's view, Psalm 78 recounts God's rejection of the northern tribes in particular (vv. 56–59). But God' grace continues in the choice of David (Judah). Psalm 79 begins historically (v. 1) where Psalm 78 ends (vv. 65–72): the nations have desecrated the temple and made Jerusalem a heap of rubble. Importantly, a parallel relationship with Psalm 74 is established both by the clear topical

---

77. Martin Leunberger, *Konzeptionen des Königtums Gottes im Psalter: Untersuchungen zu Komposition und Redaktion der theokratischen Bücher IV–V im Psalter*, ATANT 83 (Zürich: Theologischer Verlag, 2004).

78. Ibid., 112–15.

79. See the chart on ibid., 115.

correspondence and by other significant parallels (e.g., the "How long?" [79:5; 74:10]; Yahweh's anger [79:5; 74:1]). Psalm 80 opens by "continuing" the request of Psalm 79 (v. 2) and pleads for return from exile (vv. 8, 20). Psalm 81 begins on a positive note (v. 2) but is then dominated by a Divine speech emphasizing God's (unheeded) call to "Listen!" Psalm 82 bears clear resemblances with Psalm 75, both of which have significant Divine speeches centering on judgment. Also, the concern for the lowly in 82:4 recalls 76:10.

Psalm 83 takes up the exilic theme of Psalms 79 and 80 and expresses it in terms of a plan to eradicate the people of God (v. 4). This is a highpoint in the threat to the peoples in Psalms 73–83. The threat is answered in the request for the enemy's annihilation in Psalm 83 (see vv. 10, 14). Yet verse 19 indicates that total annihilation is not in view, as its goal is that "they shall know" that Yahweh alone is "the Most High over all the earth." Psalm 83, contends Leuenberger, clearly parallels Psalm 77: the individual Psalm 77 advances from the repudiation of the people to their redemption; the collective Psalm 83 progresses from a threatened annihilation of the people to the future establishment of Yahweh's sovereign position as the Most High for Israel.

Thus, with Psalm 83 the two historical–theological explanations of the threat to the people (73–77; 78–83) come to a conclusion. The first (73–77) focuses on the distant past and concludes with exile, which appears to remain open from the perspective of the presumed author. The second (78–83), on the other hand, continues this perspective into the postexilic period, with definitive resolution to the people's problems only in the future. This implies a degree of hope for the present in light of the anticipated demonstration of Yahweh's royal power (74:12; 80:2) (114).

Looking at the larger unit of Books II and III, Leuenberger suggests that, in the horizon of the Asaph Psalter (Pss 50, 73–83), the opening confession of 50:1 will be fulfilled when the expectation of 83:19 occurs.[80] However, he suggests that the "outer frame" of the Korah psalms (see Pss 42–49; 84–88) puts this outlook into perspective, and it does not come about within the horizon of the "messianic Psalter" (2–89). This expectation, argues Leuenberger, will receive a major emphasis in Book IV of the MT Psalter (115).

Judith Gärtner

Judith Gärtner has argued that the "historical psalms" (i.e., Pss 78, 105, 106, 135, and 136) are key hermeneutical texts in the MT Psalter.[81] What is relevant

---

80. Leuenberger takes the view, reflected in other studies, that Books II and III of the MT Psalter are chiastically arranged. Leunberger, *Konzeptionen des Königtums Gottes im Psalter*, 112. By "Asaph Psalter" he means either the Asaph psalms on their own or as a frame around the composition of Pss 50–72.

81. See Judith Gärtner, *Die Geschichtspsalmen: Eine Studie zu den Psalmen 78, 105, 135 und 136 als hermeneutische Schlüsseltexte im Psalter*, FAT 84 (Tübingen: Mohr Siebeck,

here is the key interpretive role she ascribes to Psalm 78 in the collection under investigation. Gärtner considers Psalm 78 to be the theological center of Psalms 74-79.[82] She summarizes her argument as follows: "In the context of the Asaph collection, the position and the macro-structural features of Psalm 78 with respect to the composition and redaction of the Psalter shows that Psalm 78 was designed as a reflective text, both in terms of its neighboring Psalms 77 and 79 and of the Masoretic sequence from Psalm 74 to Psalm 79."[83]

Gärtner begins with Psalms 77-79, noting that they are bound together by Yahweh's anger limiting mercy (formulated in 78:38-39). Psalm 78 is a "reflective text" to these neighboring psalms by first "taking up and continuing" crucial aspects of Psalm 77 (308). In Psalm 77 the question in verse 10 reminds God of his anger-limiting mercy, but in Psalm 78 the relation between "anger and mercy is part of the historical and creation-theological foundation of the psalm" (380). As a "reflection text," Psalm 78 consequently "raises the individual remembrance of the days of old from Ps 77:6, 12 to a higher level of reflection" (380). Further, the "issue of guilt is shifted to the days of old and reflected with relation to creation theology" (308).

Psalm 78 is also a "reflective text" for Psalm 79. First, in Psalm 79 the topic of guilt is expressed in relation to petitions and forgiveness (vv. 8-9). The "covering" of guilt in 79:8-9 is then "taken up again in 78:38f. at the level of creation theology. This means that petitioners who pray Psalm 79 in light of Psalm 78 are aware not only of their guilt as anthropologically anchored, but also the mercy of the creator" (380-81). In this way, 78:38f serves as a "hermeneutical key" that gives Psalm 79's petition for forgiveness "a theological dimension beyond what would have been possible had Psalm 79 been on its own" (381).

2012). See pp. 36-132 for the discussion of Ps 78. A condensed version of her argument can be found in Judith Gärtner, "The Historical Psalms. A Study of Psalms 78; 105; 106; 135, and 136 as Key Hermeneutical Texts in the Psalter," *Hebrew Bible and Ancient Israel* 4 (2015): 373-99. In consultation with her monograph, Gärtner's discussion of Pss 73-83 in the latter article is the primary basis of my summary here.

82. Anja Klein has similarly argued that Pss 73-83 are structured around Ps 78. See Anja Klein *Geschichte und Gebet. Die Rezeption der biblischen Geschichte in den Psalmen des Alten Testaments*, FAT 94 (Tübingen: Mohr Siebeck, 2014), 80-185. Klein understands Ps 78 as occupying a key editorial position in its literary context of the Asaph collection. It takes up and brings together various aspects of the biblical story. The focus, however, is no longer on the foundational saving acts of God but on the peoples' guilt. In this way, Ps 78 can be understood as a "relecture" of the historical outline of Ps 81. With its historical review from the Exodus to David, Klein argues, Ps 78 "closes the gap" between the early Mosaic period in the first part of the collection (Pss 74-77) and the situation of the threat to the community in the second (Pss 79-83), and offers a perspective of hope that overcomes it. Further, with its references to Ps 44, Ps 78 has implications far beyond the Asaph collection and gives the Elohistic Psalter a "historical stamp." See the concise summary on pp. 185-6 of Klein's book.

83. Gärtner, "The Historical Psalms," 380.

Gärtner follows Weber in postulating multiple "compositional arcs" at work in these psalms. She holds that two such arcs can be detected in the sequential reading of Psalms 74–79. First, in Psalms 74–76, both Psalms 75 and 76 "answer" the collective lament of Psalm 74. The second "arc" involves Psalms 74, 77, and 79. Psalm 77 "continues" the lament of Psalm 74 from the perspective of a "paradigmatic individual" (381). In this connection, Gärtner claims that "the salvation history perspective of 74:1–3 is taken up and maintained in 77:17–21 with the hope of a renewed coming of YHWH," an issue that Psalm 79 also addresses (381).

On the basis of this interpretation, Gärtner postulates that Psalms 75 and 76 have been redactionally inserted in the "arch of composition" consisting of Psalms 74, 77, and 79 (381).[84] More specifically, her reasoning is as follows: "This observation is mainly supported by the fact that already executed judgment on the poor in Ps 76:9–10 assumes the hope in Ps 75:3–4, 8 that YHWH will intervene as judge, simultaneously connecting this hope with the addition of the petition for the poor in Ps 74:19, 21" (382). Gärtner holds that Psalm 78 was the final psalm deliberately inserted into the context of Psalms 74–79 (382). As was the case with Psalms 77–79, Psalm 78 is also a "reflection text" for the arc under discussion: "This psalm [Psalm 78] takes up the collective, salvation-historical and creation-theological perspective begun in Psalm 74, embedding them in a comprehensive context of historical and creation theology" (382). Consequently, Psalm 78 is a focal point for Psalms 74–79 that "collects and theologically refines the formative themes" (382).

Peter Ho

Peter Ho has recently undertaken the formidable task of seeking to "understand the logic and design of the MT Psalter and whether any overarching architectural schema can be assigned to it."[85] He explains that his general approach "can be situated under the titles 'Rhetorical Criticism,' 'New Criticism,' and 'Close Reading'" (40). In addition, Ho's approach is canonical literary or editorial critical (40). He elaborates, "My interests are primarily in the literary shape of the hundred-and-fifty Hebrew poems and how they are designed as a single composition, if at all, in shaping a coherent theological program for its readers" (41).

Ho contends that the MT Psalter can (and should) be read in a linear fashion, concentrically, and intertextually. These three approaches are not in competition but are complementary. Further, Ho detects thirty-two organizational principles (thirteen formal and nineteen tacit), though noting this is not an exhaustive list.[86] These principles are applied primarily on a macrostructural level in the study. That

---

84. She points out that the name theology common to Pss 74–76 is an important aspect of their "Psalter-compositional connection." Gärtner, "The Historical Psalms," 381n. 22.

85. Peter C. W. Ho, *The Design of the Psalter: A Macrostructural Analysis* (Eugene, OR: Pickwick, 2019), 2.

86. See the charts on ibid., 35–7. Ho culls these techniques from previous studies.

is, Ho does not focus on inter-psalm relationships between smaller sequences or collections of psalms. He is instead concerned with how "certain lexemes or motifs, superscriptions, Davidic collections, and other poetical features function within the entire Psalter" (41). According to Ho, such an approach "avoids the difficulties associated with analyses of a limited number of psalms, yet at the same time, takes advantage of their gains by consolidating them under a macroanalysis" (41).

The "difficulties" Ho seeks to avoid refer especially to those associated with lexical/thematic approaches (e.g., David Howard's, *The Structure of Psalms 93–100*). In Ho's view, such a methodology "seems to be increasingly counterproductive" (11). He expounds, "The plethora of lexical links generated made it increasingly hard [in past studies] to find the dominant idea across the unit of concern, let alone the entire Psalter" (11). He also implies that the method is deficient given the difficulty of identifying "truly significant" connections between psalms (i.e., those reflective of editorial intent). Further, in Ho's view, it is "difficult for such studies to expand beyond the single literary unit" (11).

In the end, Ho's analysis leads him to detect three major divisions in the MT Psalter. Book I is its own unit, Books II and III form a (chiastically arranged) second unit, and Books IV and V constitute the third. Each of these groups has a number of subgroups, which Ho explores at length in his study. Central to the message arising from the whole is the Davidic covenant:

> The design of the Psalter is an intertwining structure of at least three narratives expressed via garbs of Hebrew poetry. The first is a larger metanarrative of God's purpose expressed through the prophetic (mantological exegesis) understanding and unfurling of the Davidic covenant. Within this metanarrative, two smaller narratives representing the life-journeys of the Davidic king and the chasidim of God to the paradisical garden city of bliss, are skillfully interwoven (legal and aggadic exegesis). The reader's own journey becomes the unspoken fourth narrative that is fused with the above three as the Psalter is read.[87]

The primary concern here is with Ho's understanding of Psalms 73–83. As noted above, Ho (like Weber and Mitchell before him) argues that Books II and III of the MT Psalter are arranged chiastically. In this structuration, Psalms 42–49 and 84–89 parallel each other as the outer frame, and Psalms 50–72 and 73–83 constitute the inner frame.[88] Ho explains that the primary reason these four psalm sequences can be seen as a chiasmus is their central motifs.[89] Regarding the inner frame, the parallel structural relationship is established by the following parallel

---

87. Ho, *The Design of the Psalter*, 5.

88. See the diagram on ibid., 95.

89. There are other indicators, but this is the primary one. For instance, Ho believes Ps 50 originally belonged to Pss 73–83 but was separated in the final form of the MT Psalter to establish this chiastic relationship. The reader should recall in this connection that, on Ho's schema, Pss 50–72 and 73–83 are parallel psalm sequences.

in central motifs: Yahweh rejects the Davidic kingship because of sin (50–72); Yahweh rejects the Temple because of sin (73–83) (95).[90]

In terms of Psalms 73–83 themselves, on one level Ho proposes a structuration similar to both Millard and Hossfeld and Zenger. He argues that the group as a whole divides into two parallel halves at Psalm 78: Psalms 73–77; 78–83. Consistent with his macro-level method, Ho bases this interpretation upon genre considerations rather than an in-depth analysis of the lexical and thematic links between these psalms. Psalms 73 and 78 are considered parallel because they are "Didactic/Sapiential," Psalms 74 and 79–80 because they are "Communal laments," Psalms 75–76 and 81–82 because they are "Divine responses," and 77 and 83 because they are "Laments."[91]

Further, according to Ho, each subgroup (Pss 73–77; 78–83) is concentrically structured with multiple psalms at the prominent central location. In one place, Ho identifies the structural centers as 75–76 and 80–81 respectively, thus revealing a focus on YHWH's kingship and deliverance (96). However, in another place Ho expands these centers, listing them as Psalms 74–76 and 79–82 respectively (143). This expansion brings the fall of the Zion temple (74; 79–80) into the picture at the center of each subgroup, which is followed by a "Divine response" in each case.

Ho suggests that the superscriptions of these psalms help identify Psalms 74–76 and 79–82 as the center of these groupings. Psalms 74–76 are distinguished by having משכיל (Ps 74) and מזמור (Pss 75 and 76) in their superscriptions, while the framing Psalms 73 and 77 have מזמור לאסף. On the other hand, "in a striking reversal," Psalms 79 and 82 are linked by מזמור לאסף, while Psalms 78 and 83 have משכיל and מזמור respectively. Ho concludes, "The organization of the superscription and genre of these psalms is unlikely to be fortuitous. And by their arrangement, the central position of Pss 74–76 and 79–82 can be discerned" (144).

Finally, also consistent with his method, Ho reads these psalms not only concentrically but also in a linear narrative–like fashion.[92] For example, consider the following interpretive comments: "The hope reawakened at the temple (73:17–28) is quickly quashed by descriptions of the destruction of the temple a few verses later (74:3–4). The destruction of the temple (79) and YHWH's people (80) effectively negate any sustained prospects of Ps 73" (98). Ho sees other organizing principles at work in these psalms,[93] but the above summary captures the major contours of his approach to Psalms 73–83.

---

90. See Ho, *The Design of the Psalter*, 142–3, for further elaboration upon the central motif of Pss 73–83. Here he points out in particular how the parallel structure of this collection "emphasizes the fall of Zion."

91. See the diagram on ibid., 92.

92. "While concentric reading identifies structural core focuses of compositional units in the Psalter, a linear reading tracks a trajectory. In the Psalms, they complement each other to reveal a skillful design to the Psalter" (Ho, *The Design of the Psalter*, 165).

93. See, for example, his discussion of "nexus words." Ibid., 298–9.

Commentaries

In addition to that of Hossfeld and Zenger, several other Psalms commentaries have appeared that seek to integrate an editorial-critical approach with more traditional methods. J. C. McCann's contribution to the *New Interpreters Bible Commentary* is one such example. McCann's understanding of Book III has already been discussed above. The more recent commentary by Walter Brueggemann and Bill Bellinger occasionally explores a psalm's position within the MT Psalter, or its relationships with neighboring psalms.[94] This method is only applied a handful of times in Book III. For example, commenting on Psalm 74, they note that "the centrality of the temple in the resolution of the crisis of faith in Psalm 73 makes the destruction of the temple even more disturbing."[95] Brueggemann and Bellinger observe that Psalm 75 reads like a response to Psalm 74 when Psalms 73–75 are read in sequence. Psalm 83 is a fitting conclusion to the Asaph collection given its thematic ties with Psalms 82 and 73.[96]

Published in the same year, the commentary by DeClaissé-Walford, Jacobson, and Tanner also incorporates editorial criticism.[97] Beth Tanner's introduction to Book III notes her agreement with McCann that Psalms 73–89 appear to have been decisively shaped by the exile. Her comments on the individual psalms bear this point out.[98] However, being a "poetic rendering of theodicy," Book III "represents every time when the world and its violence makes no sense, times when we do not understand why God does not simply fix it."[99] There is a consistent effort to read Book III as a literary unit in the above commentaries. The main contribution of these commentaries is not so much their conclusions but the fact that they reflect the growing interest in editorial criticism among Psalms scholars.

Miscellaneous Studies

A number of studies explore the function of a single psalm within the final shape of Book III (MT). Only three notable studies will be mentioned here.[100] Thomas Hieke argues for the purposeful placement of Psalm 80 in the final form of Book

---

94. Walter Brueggemann and William H. Bellinger Jr., *Psalms*, NCBC (New York: Cambridge University Press, 2014).

95. Ibid., 325.

96. Ibid., 321, 325, 360.

97. Nancy L. DeClaissé-Walford, Rolf A. Jacobson, and Beth L. Tanner, *The Book of Psalms*, NICOT (Grand Rapids, MI: Eerdmans, 2014).

98. Ibid., 583. On this point, see especially the discussions of Pss 73, 74, 77, 79, 80, and 89.

99. Ibid., 583.

100. Others could be mentioned, such as numerically based approaches to the structure of these psalms. See Ho, *The Design of the Psalter*, 31–3, 265–309.

III.[101] He argues that lexical and thematic parallels with Psalm 79 indicate that Psalm 80 (originally composed for a different setting) should be read with Psalm 79 as a response to the fall of Jerusalem. Links with Psalm 81 suggest that Psalm 80 answers "Why?" (למה) the community is experiencing God's anger in a "deuteronomistic" way (v. 13). This answer is provided by the God-speech stressing Israel's disobedience (Ps 81:12–15). Psalm 81 thus answers the problem of theodicy left open in Psalm 80.[102] Consequently, in Hieke's view the meaning of Psalm 80 in the final form of the book "contradicts the original intention and expression of the text."[103]

Joseph Jensen explores the relationship of Psalm 75 to its neighbors in the book's final shape.[104] Jensen argues that the sequence of Psalms 74–76 develops a progression first occurring in Psalm 73. The lament of Psalm 74 corresponds to the wicked's prosperity in Psalm 73:1–16. Psalm 75, with its assurance of divine justice, corresponds to the revelatory experience in the temple in Psalm 73:17. The celebration of God as warrior and ruler of Zion in Psalm 76 "develops the meditation on the fate of the wicked in Psalm 73:18–28."[105] Jensen suggests that Psalm 75 may have functioned as an important link between these neighboring psalms in a liturgical setting where these four psalms were employed together.[106]

The third study under this heading is Lawrence Boadt's analysis of Psalms 73–78.[107] Boadt begins by citing the research of Leslie Allen and John Kselman, both of whom have argued that "panels" or large blocs (e.g., sizeable sections of lament or praise) were used in the diachronic construction of various psalms, such as Psalms 69, 101, and 132. Boadt's study asks whether such "paneling" was used in the construction of psalm sequences, particularly Psalms 73–78 (534). He begins by noting a number of factors important to analyzing panels: parallelism, repetition, chiasmus, and acrostics (535-7). Boadt proceeds to analyze Psalms 73–78 individually and then considers whether "these same psalms are interrelated structurally so that the panels actually help give unity to the group of psalms" (537). His analysis leads to the conclusion that panels unify these psalms, but the panels "are not strictly identical to regular strophes or stanzas; the panels we found work in pairs, usually functioning contrastively" (549).

---

101. Thomas Hieke, "Psalm 80 and Its Neighbors in the Psalter: The Context of the Psalter as a Background for Interpreting Psalms," *BN* 86 (1997): 36–43.

102. Ibid., 40-1.

103. Hieke, "Psalm 80 and Its Neighbors in the Psalter," 41. The intentional placement of Ps 80, according to Hieke, also reveals the (Deuteronomistic) theological perspective of the collection's editors.

104. Joseph E. Jensen, "Psalm 75: Its Poetic Context and Structure," *CBQ* 63 (2001): 416–29.

105. Ibid., 419.

106. Ibid., 427–8.

107. Lawrence Boadt, "The Use of 'Panels' in the Structure of Psalms 73–78," *CBQ* 66 (2004): 533–50.

For purposes of this study, two particular elements of the unity Boadt detects between Psalms 73–78 should be noted. First, Boadt sees a single idea explaining the progression of Psalm 73 to 78: "The movement from liturgical praise to God's maintenance of the divine order in the universe to the hope of a new exodus to rescue the nation from exile" (546). Second, the wisdom/didactic correspondence between Psalms 73 and 78 suggests that they are deliberate "bookends" to this unit (548). Thus, for Boadt, Psalms 73–78 are a unified subgroup within this collection.

The Present Study

While other studies could be added, the above survey sufficiently maps the scholarly landscape of editorial-critical views on Psalms 73–83. And it reveals that much, good, work has been done on these psalms since Wilson's seminal study. At the same time, it highlights a number of problem areas that collectively point to the need for the fresh analysis offered in the present study. I outline three major areas here.

First, while there is some agreement on the collection's structure, there is currently no consensus on this issue. This applies to both aspects of structure discussed in Chapter 1: the number and boundaries of the collection's psalm groups and the organizing principle(s) that govern psalm sequencing. For instance, is Psalm 73 the collection's sole introduction (Hossfeld and Zenger)? Or should Psalm 74 be included as well (Robertson)? Are Psalms 73–77 a literary unit? (Leunberger; Millard; Weber)? Or is the real unity between Psalms 73–78? (Boadt)? Is the structural and theological center Psalm 78 (Gärtner, Klein, Weber, Hossfeld and Zenger), Psalm 80 (Robertson), or neither (e.g., McCann; Ho)? In terms of organizing principles, does a linear narrative-like principle govern the sequencing of some or all of these psalms (Mitchell; Cole; Jones)? Or should these psalms be read in a parallel, inverted parallel (i.e., concentric/chiastic), *and* narratival way (Ho)? Or perhaps the major structuring principle is yet to be discovered (the present study)?

Additionally, there are unresolved tensions within the structural analyses of more than one scholar. I gave one such example in the last chapter.[108] Here I provide one additional example. Above we noted Ho's contention that there are two subgroups in the collection (Pss 73–77; 78–83), and that these are chiastically arranged. This interpretation hinges on Psalms 74 and 77, and Psalms 79 and 83, being in an inverse parallel relationship (i.e., 73 [A1], 74 [B1], 75–76 [X], 77 [B2]; 78 [A1], 79–80 [B1], 81–82 [X], 83 [B2]). However, I noted how later in the study Ho proceeds to expand the centers of each chiasm from Psalms 75–76 and 80–81 ("X") to Psalms 74–76 and 79–82 respectively. But by incorporating Psalm 74 and 79 ("B1") into the center units ("X"), these laments are no longer parallel to Psalm

---

108. See p. 33.

77 and 83 ("B2") respectively—the very relationship required to form the chiasm Ho proposed earlier in the study.

Issues such as those outlined here indicate the need for further work on the collection's structure. The lack of consensus over this issue is not a peripheral matter. As pointed out in Chapter 1, there is a close relationship between structure and *meaning*. Thus, if we want to understand the meaning associated with this collection's present shape (e.g., its message[s] and purpose[s]), it is essential to nail down its literary structure.

This first problem area naturally leads into the second: methodology. This issue manifests itself in some studies by the lack of a robust and/or explicitly articulated methodology. Some move directly to interpretation either without any, or with very minimal, methodological discussion (e.g., McCann; Cole; Jones; Robertson). The most in-depth investigation into these psalms (i.e., Cole's work), for example, adopts a potentially promising method (i.e., the extension of Berlin's approach to parallelism) but applies it in an extremely undisciplined way. As Snearly has pointed out, Cole "tends to see any similarity whatsoever as evidence of editorial significance."[109] What is missing is criteria for weeding out incidental links.[110]

This omission has at least two unfortunate results in Cole's study. First, the truly significant connections between psalms often get lost in the mix. Second, the distinct issues of design "indicators" and design "significance" get collapsed into one interpretive move.[111] But, as discussed in Chapter 1, it is crucial that these related issues be kept distinct and that the former precede the latter in one's

---

109. Michael K. Snearly, *The Return of the King: Messianic Expectation in Book V of the Psalter*, The Library of Hebrew Bible/Old Testament Studies 624 (New York: Bloomsbury, 2016), 19.

110. One is often left questioning whether the connections cited truly reflect deliberate design, or simply Cole's creativity.

111. Jones's study reflects the same shortcoming. See Jones, "The Psalms of Asaph," 176–90. Here she explores the "impact" or "affect" of the collection's arrangement upon the reader (i.e., the informed exilic/postexilic reader). Her conclusion is that "the psalms of the collection move in an ebb and flow of waves of despair over the reality that the wicked are still present and threatening [e.g., Pss 74, 77] and waves of remembrance that God delivered before and can/will deliver again [e.g., 75–76, 78]." Jones, "The Psalms of Asaph," 48. The reader who simply works through the collection in a sequential manner encounters a rather obvious alternation between psalms of lament and psalms of hope (e.g., the linear progression from Ps 74 to Pss 75–76). This is a self-evident characteristic of the collection. But characterizing this alternation as an "ebb and flow" between "waves of despair" and "waves of remembrance" represents an *interpretation* of the collection's literary structure that has important implications for the collection's message. This interpretation only holds *if* a linear organizing principle has been used to structure the collection, the very thing Jones has assumed rather than argued. Thus, the distinct issues of design "indicators" and design "significance" are collapsed into a single interpretive move. On this point, see the earlier discussion on pp. 20–1.

analysis. Otherwise, as Cole's study shows, editorially unintended "design" gets read into the collection.

The mention of Cole's work raises what is, in my view, another important methodological weakness of previous research: conceiving of the literary unity between these psalms in a narratival way. This is seen especially in the works of Cole and Jones, though it appears in others (e.g., Mitchell and Ho). We saw, for example, that Cole discerns a dramatic three-way "continuing dialogue" between God, the community, and the righteous Davidide in these psalms. The following types of statements (found throughout the work) illustrate this hermeneutic: "In Psalm 77 *we return apparently to the present pre-judgment time*, since the complaints of Psalm 74 are *raised again*"; "Parallel vocabulary to Ps 77 in both 76 and 74 reveal *continued discussion* of the desired redemption" (emphasis added).[112]

Similar statements can be found throughout Jones's dissertation: "the struggles of Psalm 73 and 74 *seem to fade* at the beginning of Psalm 75"; "it does not seem that *the people's situation has changed* significantly from that of Psalm 73 and 74"; "the praises of Psalm 76 *are dimmed by the anguished cries* of Psalm 77"; and "the apparent celebration of the last verses in Psalm 78 *does not last for long*" (italics mine).[113] Such statements clearly assume a kind of linear "plot development" in the progression from one psalm to the next. To give only one more example, consider Ho's comments on the relationship between Psalms 73 and 74: "The hope reawakened at the temple (73:17–28) is *quickly quashed* by descriptions of *the destruction of the temple a few verses later* (74:3–4)" (emphasis added).[114]

The problem with such approaches, however, can be seen by recalling Waltke's insight mentioned in Chapter 1: the inherent nature of the object being studied dictates the best methods for elucidating its properties. When considered in light of the Psalter's inherent nature, it becomes apparent that a narratival approach is not the best method for "elucidating its properties."[115] Adam Hensley explains,

> Unlike biblical narrative, the Psalter explicitly represents itself as a collection of existing compositions, i.e., individual psalms. This difference suggests that one should not expect the Psalter to conform to the standards of linear plot

---

112. Cole, *The Shape and Message of Book III*, 55, 61. Many similar statements could be cited.

113. Jones, "The Psalms of Asaph," 73, 78, 90.

114. Ho, *The Design of the Psalter*, 98.

115. It should be noted that there is a sense in which narrative (or at least narrativity) is part of the Psalter's inherent nature. Robert Alter has shown that a type of narrativity is observable between the lines of individual psalms. See Robert Alter, *The Art of Biblical Poetry* (New York: Basic Books, 1985), 27–61. The point being made above, however, concerns the fundamental nature of a "text" like the collection under investigation, or the MT Psalter as a whole, not certain aspects of their constituent parts. Neither presents itself as a narrative text. Consequently, a narrative-like hermeneutic is not the best method of elucidating its properties.

development expected in narrative. ... Narrative approaches ... risk reading into sequences of psalms an editorially unintended narrative-like plot development.[116]

Thus, reflection upon the type of "text" editorial critics are dealing with reveals that narratival interpretations are particularly susceptible to being grounded less in the "text" than in the creativity of the modern interpreter. Just because sequences of discrete psalms (e.g., Pss 73–83) *can* be read in a narratival way does not mean that is how they *should* be read (i.e., the actual editorial agenda at work).[117]

At the very least, a linear narrative-like organizing principle should be argued, not simply be assumed. In the studies of Cole and Jones, for example, there is never any discussion (or very little) that such interpretive moves are even being made.[118] A linear narrative-like *literary structure* is simply imposed upon the *linear sequence* of the collection.[119] One is left with the impression that a "storyline" or "dramatic" approach is the natural consequence of applying Berlin's observations on parallelism at the inter-psalm level. In Chapters 4–8 of this study I aim to show that such is not the case.

Another (related) weakness relates to the issue of literary discontinuity or editorial separation discussed in Chapter 1. We saw there that structure is a function of literary continuity *and* discontinuity. But a number of important studies surveyed focus almost solely on the former. For example, Cole's extreme concern to demonstrate the concatenation of psalms leaves virtually no room for discontinuity on his conception of the shape and message of these psalms (and Book III of the MT Psalter as a whole). A similar critique applies to Jones's study, though she shows considerably more restraint in arguing for literary continuity. Further, even

---

116. Adam D. Hensley, *Covenant Relationships and the Editing of the Hebrew Psalter*, LHBOTS 666 (London: Bloomsbury T&T Clark, 2018), 13. Hensley does think that the Psalter's editors used a narrative organizing principle at times (e.g., Pss 71–72). His comments here are a caution against simply assuming that such a principle is at work, rather than another (e.g., a concentric pattern). A major proponent of the narratival approach in editorial criticism is Robert Wallace. See Robert E. Wallace, *The Narrative Effect of Book IV of the Hebrew Psalter*, Studies in Biblical Literature 112 (New York: Peter Lang, 2007); Robert E. Wallace, "The Narrative Effect of Psalms 84–89," *Journal of Hebrew Scriptures* 11 (2011): 2–15, accessed June 8, 2020, https://jhsonline.org/index.php/jhs/article/view/11525/8843. Though his approach differs considerably from Wallace's, Snearly has recently argued that the Psalter should be read as a "multiple-focus narrative." See Snearly, *The Return of the King*, 80–5. For one of the most recent attempts to trace a linear trajectory throughout the entire MT Psalter, see chap. 3 of Ho's *The Design of the Psalter* (especially pp. 165–92).

117. In this regard, the reader should recall especially Wilson's "working hypothesis pitfall" mentioned in Chapter 1: "Especially in such a thematically diverse literature as the Psalms, a hypothesis set out beforehand can allow the researcher to see what supports the thesis and ignore what does not."

118. Ho's study is more methodologically sound at this point. He discusses linear reading at length in chap. 3 of his work.

119. See n. 111 above for an example.

when claims implying discontinuity are made, they are often not given sufficient justification from the texts themselves.[120] Other studies do give attention to literary discontinuity or editorial separation (e.g., Ho; Weber; Hossfeld and Zenger). But, as we have seen, there is disagreement over its location(s), nature, and extent.

A third important methodological issue relates to the relationship between "psalms exegesis" and *Psalterexegese* discussed in Chapter 1. There is a tendency to propose editorial-critical interpretations that read "against the grain" of one or more psalms to arrive at the proposed interpretation. This issue has arisen particularly (though not solely) in connection with the collection's lament psalms. In this regard, the reader should recall McCann's central thesis that the arrangement of Psalms 73–83 (and Book III of the MT Psalter as a whole) "serves to assist" the community both to face the horror of exile and to reach for fresh hope beyond the traditional Davidic/Zion theology. Psalms like 74 and 79 are the central pillar of this thesis since they lament the destruction of Jerusalem/the Temple, and their juxtaposition with other psalms supposedly signals "the rejection of the Davidic/Zion theology as a basis of hope."[121] Also based upon laments like Psalms 74 and 79 are (1) Robertson's one-word summary of Book III ("devastation") and his view that "the failure of faith" is a major message arising from these psalms; and (2) Ho's claim that the central motif of Psalms 73–83 is "YHWH rejects the Temple because of sin."

Such interpretations, however, are predicated upon either a misreading of the purpose of the laments in this collection (i.e., that their function is primarily to "recount," "document," or bemoan the devastation)[122] or a misplaced focus in their

---

120. For example, we noted earlier Jones's claim that Pss 77–79 "are at the heart of the collection." Jones, "The Psalms of Asaph," 179. This statement implies not only continuity but also discontinuity; the psalms flanking these are presumably *not* at "the heart of the collection." But there is no discussion of the evidence indicating that Ps 77 begins a group that Ps 79 concludes, and consequently why the preceding Ps 76 and the following Ps 80 are excluded from this group.

121. The reader should recall here the example given earlier. We noted McCann's claim that the sequencing of Ps 78:68–72, which recounts the Davidic/Zion theology, and Ps 79:1–2, which laments the desecration of the Temple and destruction of Jerusalem, signals the rejection of the Davidic/Zion theology as a basis for hope.

122. This is a common view of so-called "lament" psalms reflected in editorial-critical studies. It has arisen particularly in relation to the function of Ps 89 in the MT Psalter. A frequent claim since Wilson's seminal work has been that Ps 89 "documents" (or similar language) the failure of the Davidic covenant in the Psalter's macro-structure. But as Whybray rightly points out,

> It is hardly correct to see it [Ps 89] in its present position in the Psalter as having been used editorially to document the failure of the Davidic monarchy and the unlikelihood of its restoration, as some scholars have done (notably McCann and Howard). It is important to bear in mind that laments in the Psalter … are not expressions of despair. However much the psalmists may accuse God of breaking

interpretation (i.e., on the devastating events *behind* the text [i.e., the Temple's destruction] rather than on the text itself). A close reading of texts like Psalms 74 and 79 (and the collection's other laments) reveals that they are carefully crafted *appeals* or *arguments* that seek change and arise from a robust *trust* in God.[123] As a consequence, these so-called "laments": (1) are not interested in any sort of "reorientation" predicated upon the *failure* of the "traditional Zion theology" (contra McCann); its failure is precisely what these psalmists refuse to accept; (2) do not represent faith's failure but its high point (contra Robertson);[124] and (3) are not *communicating the message* that "YHWH has rejected the Temple because of sin," the impression (whether intended or not) that Ho's summary statement gives. Ho's statement is more appropriate for the narrative text of 2 Kings 25, not appeals such as Psalms 74 and 79.[125]

> his word and becoming an enemy, hope always remains that intercession will be effective.
>
> R. N. Whybray, *Reading the Psalms as a Book*, JSOTSup 222 (Sheffield: Sheffield Academic Press, 1996), 93. In recent years, editorial-critical studies have increasingly assigned a more hopeful function to Ps 89 in the Psalter's macro-structure. See, for example, the discussion in Snearly, *The Return of the King*, 94–8.
>
> 123. "The aim of these psalms ... is never simply to complain, for this protest is always directed towards the purpose of summoning God to conform to his promises." Craig C. Broyles, *The Conflict of Faith and Experience in the Psalms: A Form-Critical and Theological Study*, JSOTSup 52 (Sheffield: Sheffield Academic Press, 1989), 221. See Broyles's study for a detailed analysis of the lament psalms in Pss 73–83 (minus Ps 83). Ingvar Fløysvik's dissertation on the complaint psalms concluded that the major theological contribution of complaints like Pss 74 and 79 can be summarized as follows: "faith sticks to God's self-revelation in the midst of conflicting evidence." Ingvar Fløysvik, *When God Becomes My Enemy: The Theology of the Complaint Psalms* (St. Louis, MO: Concordia Academic, 1997), 176.
>
> 124. Discussing the type of faith exhibited in laments such as Pss 74, 77, 79, and 80, Andrew Davies rightly observes that it is a "'faith despite,' *the height of religious commitment* rather than its waning" (emphasis added). Andrew Davies, "My God ... 'Why?' Questioning the Action And Inaction of YHWH In The Psalms," in *Why? ... How Long? Studies on Voices of Lamentation Rooted in Biblical Hebrew Poetry*, ed. LeAnn Snow Flesher, Carol J. Dempsey, and Mark J. Boda, LHBOTS 552 (London: Bloomsbury T&T Clark, 2014), 52. Robertson's argument regarding the paucity of words for "trust" in Book III does little to prove his point. As noted in Chapter 1, themes (here "trust") are not always apparent on the surface of the text but must sometimes be "abstracted" by interpretation.
>
> 125. Additionally, claiming that such is the "central motif" of Pss 73–83 is disproportionate to the number of psalms that actually contain this motif (i.e., Pss 74 and 79). Relatedly, a close reading of Ps 74 reveals that the people's sin ("YHWH rejects the Temple *because of sin*") is not even mentioned in that psalm. The focus of the appeal is that, although sin may have been the *initial* cause, such is no longer the major problem; *God* is. See the analysis of Ps 74 in Chapter 4 of the present study. While the community's sin is mentioned explicitly

Thus, (reasonably) assuming that the collection's editor(s) were reading "with the grain" of these "laments," it is unlikely that they would have used them to communicate the ideas or messages that the above scholars propose. Consequently, such proposals are problematic since they require doing "violence" (albeit unintentionally) to one or more psalms in the sequence to arrive at the "canonical" meaning. As alluded to above, we will encounter similar approaches with respect to other psalms in the collection as the study progresses.[126]

A related tendency is to essentially collapse "psalms exegesis" into *Psalterexegese*. What I have in mind here is the tendency to read two or more discrete texts as if they are virtually a single continuous psalm. The earlier quote from Ho's study illustrates this tendency: "The hope reawakened at the temple (73:17–28) is quickly quashed by descriptions of *the destruction of the temple a few verses later*" (74:3–4) (emphasis added). The claim that the temple's destruction comes a "few verses" after "the hope reawakened at the temple"—the latter taking place in a discrete, albeit adjacent, text—virtually treats Psalms 73 and 74 as a single psalm. But they are not a single psalm; they are two discrete units, each having their own structure, purpose, and message. Conflating them in this way unintentionally distorts the purpose and message of them both, and, as a consequence (I will argue), the collection's structure and message.

Cole's study, which is most characteristic of this tendency, provides additional examples. For instance, consider his explanation of the "sanctuaries of God" (מקדשי אל) in Psalm 73:17. He begins by noting that "this plural (i.e., מקדשי אל) has provoked a variety of opinions among scholars. ... Here the important point is its relation canonically to the following psalm."[127] This statement leaves the reader wondering whether the meaning of verse 17 within Psalm 73 is somehow different from its "canonical meaning." Cole reasons as follows to determine the "canonical meaning" of this verse: (1) there are lexical parallels between the destroyed Temple sanctuary in Psalm 74:2–8 and the psalmist's arrival at the sanctuary in 73:17–18; therefore (2) the psalmist arrived at a destroyed sanctuary *in 73:17*. Thus, Cole explains, the juxtaposition of these psalms implies that "arrival at the sanctuaries brought enlightenment because, as Psalm 74 *later explains*, they were in ruins" (emphasis added).[128]

---

in Ps 79 (see v. 8), the same applies to that psalm. See the analysis of Ps 79 in Broyles, *The Conflict of Faith and Experience in the Psalms*, 157–60. There Broyles points out that, in terms of the actual appeal, "Although God's anger has some justification relative to the people's sin alone, *the psalmist for the sake of his argument focuses upon other factors* that would indicate God is actually acting against his own interests" (emphasis added). Broyles, *The Conflict of Faith and Experience in the Psalms*, 158.

126. I refer the reader particularly to the discussion of Pss 78, 80, and 81 in Chapters 5 and 7.

127. Cole, *The Shape and Message of Book III*, 22.

128. Ibid., 23.

I am not questioning whether the parallels Cole recognizes reflect deliberate design. Neither am I questioning the validity of arguing from Psalm 73 itself that the psalmist arrived at a sanctuary that was in ruins.[129] I am objecting to the validity of an editorial-critical hermeneutic that collapses the boundary between Psalms 73 and 74 and treats them essentially as a single psalm. Later I attempt to show that the "canonical meaning" comes into focus by leaving this boundary firmly intact.

Another example is Cole's claim that parallels between Psalms 82 and 83 suggest that Psalm 83 "ironically brings to the fore Israel's own guilt, as expressed in previous psalms of Book III."[130] But not a seed of such irony is present in Psalm 83 itself. Here too the underlying hermeneutic seems to be that the interpretive horizon provided by a neighboring psalm can (legitimately) modify a psalm's *fundamental meaning*. This hermeneutic is not limited to Cole's study. For example, it also appears in Hieke's claim that Psalm 80's placement next to Psalm 81 "*contradicts the original intention* and expression of the text [i.e., Ps 80]" (emphasis added).[131] Parting ways with such approaches, I argue throughout this study that one psalm can provide a new interpretive horizon for another without making "a fruit purée" of either.

Other problem areas could be discussed, but these are sufficient to reveal the need for a fresh editorial-critical appraisal of Psalms 73–83. In the pages that follow, I argue that previous analyses have largely overlooked the two most important "paratextual" features related to the collection's design.[132] As a consequence, I suggest, scholarship on this collection has not yet fully grasped the nature of its structure, message, and purpose. As will become clear, I believe that recognition of these features resolves many of the problems that have arisen in the editorial-critical study of these psalms. It is also my hope that the analysis makes a contribution to editorial-critical methodology more broadly.

It goes without saying that the views articulated in the following chapters are, in one way or another, deeply indebted to the studies reviewed above (as well as others not mentioned). If I have seen further than others in any way, an evaluation I leave solely to the reader, it is by standing on their shoulders.[133]

---

129. For such an argument, see Harris Birkeland, "Chief Problems of Ps 73:17ff," *ZAW* 67 (1955): 100.

130. Cole, *The Shape and Message of Book III*, 114.

131. See the discussion of Hieke's article earlier in this chapter. See Chapter 7 of the present study for an alternative view.

132. See the summary on pp. 35–7.

133. Here I am of course borrowing from Sir Isaac Newton's famous words: "If I have seen further than others, it is by standing upon the shoulders of giants."

Chapter 3

PSALM 73: "GOD IS GOOD TO ISRAEL"—DESPITE CONFLICTING EVIDENCE

Chapters 3 through 8 are the heart of this study: an editorial-critical investigation into Psalms 73–83. This chapter focuses on the collection's initial psalm, Psalm 73. As I noted in the previous chapter, the major argument running through Chapters 3–8 is that four psalm sequences/pairings following Psalm 73 stand in a deliberate parallel relationship with that psalm. The following analysis of Psalm 73 is thus foundational for the rest of this study.

Analysis of Psalm 73

There is a long-standing debate over the *Gattung* of Psalm 73.[1] I will not, therefore, attempt to locate this psalm among any one of the traditional genre classifications. In fact, I agree with John Vassar that Psalm 73 resists such classification.[2] It is sufficient to observe that the psalm contains elements of a number of different *Gattüngen* and also reflects a wisdom influence.[3]

There has also been considerable debate over the psalm's structure.[4] My own analysis yields the following arrangement:

---

1. For detailed discussions of the various proposals, see Leslie C. Allen, "Psalm 73: An Analysis," *TynBul* 33 (1982): 107–18; J. Clinton McCann, "Psalm 73: An Interpretation Emphasizing Rhetorical and Canonical Criticism" (PhD diss., Duke University, 1985), 88–101; Marvin E. Tate, *Psalms 51–100*, Word Biblical Commentary (Nashville, TN: Thomas Nelson, 1990), 231–3.

2. John S. Vassar, *Recalling a Story Once Told: An Intertextual Reading of the Psalter and the Pentateuch* (Macon, GA: Mercer University Press, 2007), 67.

3. I have intentionally avoided the language "wisdom psalm." I agree with Murphy's suggestion that it is better to "speak of wisdom influence on certain psalms ... rather than argue for a wisdom classification." Roland E. Murphy, *The Gift of the Psalms* (Peabody, MA: Hendrickson, 2000), 15–16.

4. For a thorough discussion of the numerous proposals, see Allen, "Psalm 73," 92–106; McCann, "Psalm 73," 49–75. McCann discusses thirty-four different structural proposals in his study.

    A1. The problem: the prosperity of the wicked (vv. 1–3)
       B1. Elaboration on the problem: the stability of the wicked (vv. 4–12)
          C1. Initial response: the instability of the psalmist (vv. 13–16)
             D. Resolution: restored confidence in God's justice/goodness (v. 17)
          C2. Final response: the instability of wicked (vv. 18–20)
       B2. Elaboration on the resolution: the stability of the psalmist (vv. 21–26)
    A2. Summary of the resolution (vv. 27–28)

The psalm clearly divides into two major halves (vv. 1–16; 18–28) arranged in an inverted parallel fashion. The particle אך in verses 1 and 18 marks the beginning of these two parts.[5] This particle also heads verse 13, but there it marks the opening of a sub-unit within the first major unit (i.e., vv. 13–16). The psalm's two parts pivot upon verse 17, the psalm's turning point.

The Problem: Verses 1–16

The psalm's first half (vv. 1–16) details the problem facing the psalmist, the perception of a severe incongruity between the doctrine "God is good to Israel, to the pure of heart" (v. 1) and the perpetual prosperity of the wicked (vv. 3–12). Craig C. Broyles has labeled such a perceived tension between core Israelite beliefs about God and Israel's current experience of God a "conflict of faith and experience," terminology I adopt in this study.[6] This half of the psalm divides into three sub-units: verses 1–3 summarize the problem; verses 4–12 elaborate upon the problem; and verses 13–16 describe the psalmist's initial response to the problem.

Verses 1–3 summarize the problem that faced not merely an individual psalmist but "Israel" as a whole (v. 1).[7] The seemingly perpetual prosperity of the wicked

---

5. In addition to the factors mentioned below, further evidence supporting unit boundaries at vv. 18 and 27 (as well as v. 13) are the "unusual parallelisms/colon arrangements" of these verses. See the discussion in Nicholas P. Lunn, *Word-Order Variation in Biblical Hebrew Poetry: Differentiating Pragmatics and Poetics*, Paternoster Biblical Monographs (Milton Keynes: Paternoster Press, 2006), 160–76, 184–7, 194. Lunn shows that such parallelisms have a structuring function.

6. Craig C. Broyles, *The Conflict of Faith and Experience in the Psalms: A Form-Critical and Theological Study*, JSOTSup 52 (Sheffield: Sheffield Academic Press, 1989). Broyles does not use this terminology specifically of Ps 73. His study focuses on lament psalms he labels "God-laments." However, as we will see, while not a "God-lament" proper, Ps 73:1–16 centers on the same fundamental theological dilemma as they do.

7. As is well-known, interpreters (especially of the twentieth century) have often emended לישראל ("to Israel") to לישר אל ("to the upright") because it seemingly creates "better" parallelism. But an emendation is unnecessary and there is no textual support for it. The LXX τῷ Ισραηλ ("to Israel") supports the MT. An emendation would obscure the fact that the psalm addresses Israel as a whole.

(see עוֹלָם ["forever"] in v. 12) appeared to contradict a core Israelite belief: "God is good to Israel, to the pure of heart (טוֹב לישׂראל אלהים לברי לבב)" (v. 1). In the Hebrew Bible this belief is foundational to Israel's conception of God's character, as God himself had revealed it. Its close connection to the core Israelite credo of Exodus 34:6–7 illustrates this point. When Moses asked God, "Please, show me your glory" in Exodus 33:18, the author places the words "I will cause all of my *goodness* (טוּבִי) to pass before you" on God's own "lips." The foundational Israelite credo of Exodus 34:6–7 is a fulfillment of *this* promise. This credo, therefore, consists of God's own self-description of various "good" expressions of God's character that his people benefit from (e.g., mercy, grace, and steadfast love). The many echoes of Exodus 34:6–7 in the Hebrew Bible, together with the many affirmations that "God/the Lord is good,"[8] confirm the foundational nature of the belief expressed in Psalm 73:1.

The other side of this belief is that God is *not* good to the wicked. They instead (should) experience God's judgment. This belief was so entrenched in Israel that citations are virtually unnecessary.[9] The biblical writers place this belief on God's lips as well, revealing the central role that it played in their conception of God's character. In Psalm 75:2, for instance, God himself promises, "At an appointed time, I will judge uprightly." And the following verses describe how "all the wicked of the earth (כל רשעי ארץ)" will be made to drink of the cup of God's judgment (v. 9). Instances where God's failure to judge the wicked evokes complaint also evince the centrality of justice to God's basic character (e.g., Hab 1:2–4, 12–17). Thus, the theology expressed in the affirmation of verse 1 was deep-seated in Israel and rooted in God's own self-revelation.

The psalmist explains in verse 3 that lived experience seemed to severely undermine the theology of verse 1: those who were *not* pure of heart (i.e., the wicked/boasters) seemed to perpetually experience שָׁלוֹם ("well-being/prosperity").[10] Conversely, verse 14 indicates that the psalmist's experience was one of suffering. But the psalmist's conception of retribution does not appear to have been simplistic or naive. He did not expect the wicked to never experience prosperity, nor the righteous to never suffer, an assumption reflected in verses 12–14. Here the psalmist explains that both the wicked's prosperity and his own suffering were of an exceedingly long duration (see especially עוֹלָם ["forever"] in v. 12; "continually"; "every morning" [v. 14]). It was thus the persistent, ongoing nature of these realities (and so of God's continued absence) that, over time, had

---

8. See Nah 1:7; Pss 25:8; 34:9; 86:6; 100:5; 106:1; 107:1; 118:1, 29; 136:1; Jer 33:11; Lam 3:25.

9. Nevertheless, see the following sampling of texts: Pss 50; 76:8–10; 82; Gen 18:22–33; Mal 3:13–18; Pss 96:13; 98:7–9.

10. The expected recipients of שָׁלוֹם were those obedient to God (Isa 48:17–18; 54:14; Jer 6:14; 14:13; Ezek 13:16), not the wicked (Isa 57:18–20). Also reflecting this point are texts in which שָׁלוֹם ("peace") and טוֹב ("good") are parallel ideas or otherwise clearly associated (Gen 26:29; Deut 23:7; Jer 8:15; 14:19; 33:9; Ps 34:15; Esth 10:3; 9:12).

eroded the truthfulness of the doctrine in verse 1—it was not the wicked's prosperity or the psalmist's suffering *as such*.[11] The psalmist candidly confesses his envy (קנא) of the wicked (v. 3) amid these circumstances, and how it nearly turned him away from a life characterized by purity of heart (v. 2).

The next sub-unit (vv. 4–12) shifts the spotlight onto the wicked. This extended description of the wicked firmly establishes the incongruity of lived experience with the doctrine of verse 1. After expounding upon the wicked's condition of שלום mentioned in verse 3 (vv. 4–5), the psalmist underscores the apparent failure of Divine justice by turning to an extended moral assessment of the wicked in verses 6–12. Importantly, in these verses the reader discovers that so far the psalm has had non-Israelite wicked in view.[12] The first clause of verse 10 explains that some of "his [i.e., God] people (עמו)" apostatized (שוב) and joined the wicked ("here" [הלם]), the implication being that the wicked in view are not God's people (i.e., non-Israelites). The apostasy of God's people was a consequence of the powerful and secure position of these non-Israelite wicked (vv. 6–9), and God's apparent indifference toward it (v. 11).

Verses 11 and 12 close out this sub-unit. The "enemy quotation" in verse 11 summarizes the stance that the non-Israelite wicked (vv. 4–9) and apostate Israelites (v. 10) adopted toward God in light of their impunity: "How can God know? Is there knowledge in the Most High?" This sentiment is an affirmation of God's apparent indifference, apathy, and possibly approval of the wicked. The quotation is especially significant for what it reveals about the psalmist's attitude toward God at the time. It gives explicit voice to the psalmist's own questioning of whether God was perhaps indifferent, uninterested, or, worse, approving of the wicked. The "God of experience" described in verse 11 bore little resemblance to the "God of faith" in verse 1. The final verse of this sub-unit (v. 12) summarizes the wicked's prosperity: "Look! These are the wicked; forever at ease, they increase wealth."

Verses 13–16 constitute the final sub-unit of the psalm's first half.[13] Verse 13 allows listeners/readers to eavesdrop on the verbal expression of the psalmist's near apostasy mentioned in verse 2:

---

11. Psalm 73 thus assumes what Kenneth Kuntz has called a "realistic" stance on retribution (contra Kuntz's own classification of Ps 73): "notwithstanding his fidelity to Yahweh, the צדיק is forced to cope in an imperfect world and to suffer moments of hardship, hostility, and anguish. Nevertheless ... sooner or later the destruction of the רשע and the deliverance of the צדיק will be effectively secured." J. Kenneth Kuntz, "The Retribution Motif in Psalmic Wisdom," *ZAW* 89 (1977): 232.

12. McCann, "Psalm 73," 188–91; Tate, *Psalms 51–100*, 229.

13. Two factors indicate that v. 13 marks the beginning of a new textual unit: (1) there is a clear shift in focus from the wicked in vv. 4–12 to the psalmist in vv. 13–17; (2) the summary statement about the wicked in v. 12 clearly marks a closing boundary, indicating that v. 13 begins a new unit.

> Surely (אַךְ), in vain I have cleansed my heart (לבב)
> and washed my hands in innocence
> For I was stricken continually
> and rebuked every morning (Ps 73:13–14)

These verses constitute the psalmist's preliminary conclusion amid the circumstances recounted in the preceding verses: striving to maintain a pure heart had been futile. The retributive principle of verse 1 appeared to have been turned on its head. God's absence in the wicked's prosperity/the psalmist's suffering challenged whether the psalmist really was the recipient of God's "good" benefits.

This point is signaled by an allusion to the opening credo of verse 1 in verse 13.[14] Both verses 1 and 13 make equally strong affirmations about the benefit of striving to maintain purity of heart (see אַךְ ["surely"] in vv. 1 and 13)—but they represent contradictory assessments of it (see "good" [v. 1]; "vain" [v. 13]). The intention is to lay before the reader the jarring crisis of faith that the psalmist faced: lived experience implied "a contradiction that reflects on God himself," raising the question, "is God, in fact, 'good' ... to those who are pure of heart?" (v. 1).[15]

Verse 15 explains that concern for the faithfulness of other Israelites (see "the generation of your sons [דור בניך]") led the psalmist to refrain from uttering this conclusion publicly. This decision is significant: even though experience appeared to contradict the doctrine in verse 1, the psalmist remained a part of Israel.[16] Verse 16 closes out the psalm's first half by describing the inner turmoil and intellectual burden (עמל) that lived experience had brought upon the psalmist.

Turning Point: Resolution at the Sanctuary: Verse 17

Verse 17 explains that the intellectual burden was lifted when the psalmist entered the Temple sanctuary (v. 17).[17] The entire mood and direction of the psalm

---

14. Some interpreters think that these similar verses form an inclusion bracketing what they believe to be the first major unit of the psalm (i.e., vv. 1–13) (e.g., Craig C. Broyles, *Psalms*, NIBC [Peabody, MA: Hendrickson, 1999, 300]). But the concluding summary statement of v. 12 indicates that v. 13 begins a new unit.

15. Broyles, *Psalms*, 300.

16. In light of its significance in the psalm, McCann argued in his dissertation on Ps 73 that v. 15 is "the theological turning point of Ps 73." McCann, "Psalm 73," 68–9, 209. But as will be seen below, there are better reasons for identifying v. 17 as the psalm's turning point.

17. The Hebrew has מקדשי אל ("the sanctuaries of God"). The plural מקדשי has been variously interpreted. For a summary of views, see McCann, "Psalm 73," 37–39, 212–13. Using the plural מקדשי to refer to the sanctuary is rare in the Psalter, but not unprecedented (see קדשיך ["your sanctuaries"] in Ps 68:36. See the singular in vv. 16–18, 25, and 30). See also the plural "dwelling places (משכנות)" as a reference to the temple in Ps 84:2. The plural in 73:17 may be a "plural of intensification," in which case it would highlight the "holiness

changes after verse 17, clearly indicating that it forms the psalm's turning point.[18] Consequently, verse 17 divides Psalm 73 into two clearly distinct halves: verses 1–16 and 18–28. Verses 18–28 demonstrate that these two halves reflect markedly different postures toward God and perspectives on his involvement in the affairs of his people/the world.

The second half of verse 17 reveals what removed the psalmist's intellectual burden: "I understood their (i.e., the wicked) end (אחרית) (i.e., outcome/future)." Verses 18–20 make clear that by "end" the psalmist means God's future, material, destruction of the wicked.[19] This statement shows that it was not a new belief that changed the psalmist's perspective; it was reassurance of an "old" one. At the temple the psalmist gained fresh assurance of the "other side" of the credo in verse 1, which experience had formerly led him to doubt: God's certain judgment of the wicked. Whatever the catalyst at the temple,[20] the resultant reassurance of the wicked's disastrous "end" brought about resolution to the conflict between faith and experience recounted in the psalm's first half. The clear implication is that the psalmist's confidence in God's goodness had been restored.[21]

The statement in verse 17 also shows that the resolution to the psalm's crisis of faith did not consist of changed circumstances; the psalmist became confident of God's involvement in the affairs of his people/the world but had not yet experienced it. Rather, resolution consisted in a changed perspective on the wicked, and especially God, amid unchanged circumstances (i.e., the wicked still prosper [vv. 3–12]; the psalmist still suffers [v. 26]). The second half of the psalm is largely an elaboration upon this resolution that the psalmist found at the sanctuary.

---

of the place." If it is a "plural of local extension," it would refer to the "temple and all its precincts (Jer 51:51; Ezek 21:7; Lev 21:23; and others)." Tate, *Psalms 51–100*, 229 n17a.

18. "The center [of a concentric pattern] serves as a turning point that shifts the focus from one level of meaning to another." John Breck, *The Shape of Biblical Language: Chiasmus in the Scriptures and Beyond* (Crestwood, NY: St. Vladimir's Seminary Press, 1994), 336.

19. McCann's claim that vv. 18–20 have "nothing to do with the outward, material condition of the wicked" (McCann, "Psalm 73," 214–15) is unconvincing. It is difficult to see how these verses could be read any other way. A perusal of how the language of these verses is used elsewhere makes this point clear: חלקות ("slippery places") (v. 18; Ps 35:6; Jer 23:12); נפל ("fall") (v. 18; Ps 35:8; Jer 23:12); משואה ("ruins") (v. 18; Zeph 1:15; Ps 35:8, Isa 47:11) שמה ("destruction") (v. 19; Isa 13:9); רגע ("in a moment") (v. 19; Isa 47:9 [God as logical subject, v. 3]); סוף ("utter end") (v. 19; Isa 66:17); בלהה ("terrors") (v. 19; Ezek 26:21; Job 27:20); כחלום ("like a dream") (v. 20; Isa 29:7; Job 20:8 [vv. 4–7 for context]); קיץ ("awake") (v. 20; Ps 78:65). McCann is aware of such usage but surprisingly does not draw the natural conclusion for Ps 73:18–20: the psalmist has in view the outward, material, destruction of the wicked.

20. This point has been the cause of much (unnecessary) speculation among scholars. The text focuses on the result of having entered the temple (i.e., renewed assurance of the wicked's "end"), not on what brought about that result.

21. See the discussion of v. 28 below for further evidence of this interpretation.

Resolution: Verses 18–28

The particle אך ("Surely") in verse 18 marks the opening of the second part of the psalm (vv. 18–28) just as it did the first (see v. 1). As just mentioned, these verses reflect and elaborate upon the resolution brought about at the sanctuary (v. 17). McCann has demonstrated that their language and imagery deliberately signal a complete reversal in the psalmist's perspective from that of the psalm's first half. An example that will factor prominently in this study is McCann's observation of seven words in vv. 18–28 that are deliberately repeated from vv. 4–12. These words function as a unified network of repetitions aimed at highlighting the psalmist's dramatic perspectival shift.[22] I argue in Chapters 4–8 that this network of repetitions plays a prominent role in the collection's design.

This second half of the psalm consists of three sub-units that stand in an inverted parallel relationship with the first three. The first sub-unit (vv. 18–20) elaborates on the "end/future" (אחרית) of the wicked mentioned in verse 17. It consists of the psalmist's confident affirmations about God's future, though certain, destruction of the wicked. As such, verses 18–20 stand in a sharp contrastive parallel relationship with the psalmist's former response to the wicked's prosperity (vv. 13–17).[23] And they represent a complete reversal in the psalmist's perspective on the wicked amid the circumstances recounted in verses 2–14. But most significantly, they represent a markedly different perspective on God's involvement in the affairs of the world/his people. God's certain future activity means that God's current inactivity, though enigmatic, does not imply injustice or indifference—despite apparent evidence to the contrary (vv. 3–12).

Verses 21–26 form the next sub-unit.[24] These verses stand in a contrastive parallel relationship to verses 4–12.[25] Verses 4–12 had described the stability and security of the wicked. Verses 21–26, on the other hand, describe the stability and security of the psalmist. Thus, this section also reflects a radical reversal in perspective from the psalm's first half. The psalmist admits that his former envy of the wicked was behavior characteristic of a brute beast (vv. 21–22). Verses 23–26 reflect a confident assurance of the experience of God's presence. This provides the

---

22. See McCann, "Psalm 73," 79–82. In this discussion, McCann also draws attention to parallels in imagery that function in the same way (e.g., "slippery places" [v. 18]; "my feet nearly had nearly slipped" [lit. "were poured out [שפכו]"] [v. 2]).

23. The contrastive statements beginning with אך in vv. 13 and 18 highlight this parallel relationship. The particle introduces a statement reflecting the instability of the psalmist in v. 13, and a strong affirmation of the future instability of the wicked in v. 18 ("you will set them in slippery places").

24. Verses 21–26 are framed by references to the psalmist's "heart (לבב)" in vv. 21 and 26. Giving them inner cohesion is the repetition of the prepositional phrase "with you (עמך)" (vv. 22, 23, 25), a key phrase in this section.

25. Both sections begin with the particle כי (vv. 4, 21) and conclude with contrastive statements about the security of the wicked and psalmist respectively. Each statement contains the noun עולם ("always") (vv. 12, 26).

psalmist with newfound stability and security ("God is the rock [צוּר] of my heart and portion [חֶלְקִי] forever").[26] It thus appears that assurance of God's certain (albeit future) destruction of the wicked awoke in the psalmist the corresponding realization that God had *not* abandoned the righteous, despite conflicting evidence (vv. 13–14, 26). The psalmist had, in fact, been "with (עִם)" God (v. 23) all along, receiving God's guidance (v. 24).[27]

The final two verses of this section form a succinct conclusion to the psalm as a whole: the instability of the wicked (v. 27); the stability of the psalmist (v. 28). As the psalm's conclusion, verse 27 fittingly returns to the realization that brought about resolution to the crisis of faith: God's certain judgment of the wicked (see vv. 18–20). Except here in verse 27 the scope of God's judgment is narrower than in verses 18–20. The reason is that one burden of the psalm is clearly to warn against the perils of apostatizing based upon God's apparent absence. The psalmist himself had nearly apostatized for this very reason (vv. 2–3; 13–14). But, receiving reassurance of God's active involvement at the temple, the psalmist concludes with a strong affirmation about the perils of straying "far (רחק)" from God (v. 27; see v. 2). All Israelites who "commit harlotry from you (זונה ממך)"[28]—like those mentioned in verse 10—will "perish" and be destroyed by God. Thus, reassurance of the wicked's future (though certain) instability (v. 27) had put their current stability (v. 12) into perspective for the psalmist.[29]

The instability of the wicked in verse 27 is contrasted with the stability of the "pure of heart" in verse 28. Doubt over whether God was, in fact, "good (טוֹב) to the

---

26. Both "rock of my heart" and "portion" are metaphors for security. A parallel passage is Ps 142:5, where "portion (חלק)" parallels "refuge (מחסה)": "You are my refuge (מחסה), my portion (חלק) in the land of the living." William Brown rightly notes that being parallel to "refuge" (which conveys an analogous image as "rock [צוּר]" in 73:26), "portion" is here a metaphor for protection. William P. Brown, *Seeing the Psalms: A Theology of Metaphor* (Louisville, KY: Westminster John Knox, 2002), 205.

27. The meaning of the much-discussed אחר כבוד תקחני in the second clause of v. 24 need not detain us here. Whatever its precise meaning, it is clearly an affirmation reflecting the reversal in perspective that is characteristic of the psalm's second half.

28. The verb זנה is used almost exclusively to refer to Israelite apostasy, and idolatry in particular, in the Hebrew Bible (e.g., Lev 17:7; 20:5; Deut 31:16; Judg 2:17; 8:27; Jer 2:10; 3:1, 6, 8; Ezek 6:9; 16:15, 35, 41; 23:3, 19, 30, 43; Hos 1:2; 2:7; 4:12, 15; 9:1; Ps 106:39. Particularly relevant are the two other occasions where, like Ps 73:27, the verb זנה is followed by the preposition מִן ("from") (Hos 4:12; 9:1). With the preposition, זנה more clearly conveys the idea of leaving God, and therefore indicates Israelites are in view. McCann observes that the only place where the verb זנה is applied to non-Israelites is Nah 3:4 (i.e., Nineveh). McCann, "Psalm 73," 228.

29. The psalmist highlights this point by evoking his former conclusion about the wicked (see v. 12) in v. 27: "Look! (הנה) These are the wicked; forever at ease, they increase wealth" (v. 12); "Look! (הנה) Those far from you shall perish; you will destroy all who commit harlotry from you" (v. 27).

pure of heart" had placed the psalmist on unstable ground at the beginning of the psalm (vv. 1–2). It had led to questioning the benefit gained by striving for purity of heart. Verse 28 makes explicit that the psalmist regained confidence in both the value and necessity (v. 27) of striving for "purity of heart" through the experience recounted in the psalm: "But as for me, nearness to God is good (טוב)."[30]

This statement, which many have (rightly) noted forms an inclusion with verse 1, is not defining or equating "nearness to God" with the adjective "good" (i.e., "good" = "nearness to God"). That is, the psalmist is not claiming that "purity of heart is its own reward."[31] The statement is instead predicating something about "nearness to God" (i.e., "purity of heart"), namely, that it is beneficial (i.e., "good"); it "pays off." It therefore becomes evident that the affirmation "nearness to God is good (i.e., beneficial)" in verse 28 and "God is good ... to the pure of heart" in verse 1 is two different ways of saying the same thing. Verse 28 brings the psalm full circle.

However, unlike verse 1, verse 28 fleshes out what is meant by "beneficial": the pure of heart experience God as their "refuge (מחסה)." God provides them with stability and security, as the psalmist could readily testify (vv. 21–26), even amid continual suffering (v. 26; see v. 14). But the psalmist most likely has in view primarily refuge/security from God's own judgment given the parallel verse 27 ("Those far from you shall perish ...").[32] Thus, as the psalmist looks to God for refuge from the coming judgment, he "recounts (ספר)" all of God's works,[33] eagerly expecting a future demonstration of them. This statement reflects a complete

---

30. The construct chain קרבת אלהים translates "nearness to God" above. It is best taken in the sense of a Greek "objective genitive" (the psalmist's nearness to God), not a "subjective genitive" (God's nearness to the psalmist). This is indicated first by the parallel expression "those far from you (רחקיך)." The antonymic nature of "near" and "far" indicates that the psalmist intends to make a contrastive parallel between the conduct and respective "end" of the wicked and the righteous: the wicked are unfaithful ("far") and perish (v. 27); the psalmist remains faithful ("near") and experiences God as a refuge (v. 28). Second, the only other occurrence of the expression קרבת אלהים in the Hebrew Bible (Isa 58:2) refers to faithfulness/obedience to God. McCann, "Psalm 73," 48, 229–30. The expression is equivalent to "pure of heart" in the psalm.

31. Contra ibid., 231.

32. Nahum 1:7–8 is another text that fleshes out God's goodness in terms of his being a "refuge" from judgment: "The Lord is good (טוב יהוה), a place of protection in the day of distress (למעוז ביום צרה); He knows all who take refuge in him (וידע חסי בו). But with an overflowing flood he will make a complete end of his adversaries [i.e., Nineveh]."

33. The infinitival clause "recounting all your works (לספר כל מלאכותיך)" in v. 28 most likely has the "works" of God's judgment in view. The verb ספר is only used with מלאכה in Ps 73:28. In fact, apart from Ps 73:38, only five of the remaining 166 occurrences of the noun מלאכה in the Hebrew Bible refer to "works" performed by God of any kind (Gen 2:2 [2×], 3; Jer 48:10; 50:25). Three are irrelevant for Ps 73 since they refer to God's works of creation (Gen 2:2 [2×], and 2:3). The remaining two refer to God's works of judgment, not salvation

reversal from the psalmist's former temptation to publicly "recount (ספר)" that purity of heart is futile (v. 15).

Main Theological Message

The major theological message that emerges from the above analysis may be summarized as follows: "faith sticks to God's self-revelation [i.e., 73:1] amid conflicting evidence [i.e., vv. 3–12]."[34] The psalmist confidently affirms the truthfulness of the core Israelite belief that "God is good to Israel, to the pure of heart" (v. 1) in the face of apparent evidence to the contrary, the wicked's perpetual prosperity (vv. 3–12), and continual personal suffering (vv. 14; 26). This message hangs like a banner over the entire psalm in verse 1 "as a summary of the whole psalm: In spite of everything, I nevertheless maintain that God is good."[35]

(Jer 48:10; 50:25). Given that judgment is prominent in the immediate context, it is preferable to interpret מלאכה in Ps 73:28 as a reference to God's judgments.

34. As noted already in Chapter 2, this is the conclusion that Ingvar Fløysvik reached regarding the major theological contribution of the complaint psalms. See Ingvar Fløysvik, *When God Becomes My Enemy: The Theology of the Complaint Psalms* (St. Louis, MO: Concordia Academic Press, 1997), 176. Though not a complaint psalm, Ps 73 has many similarities, as will become clear as the study progresses.

35. N. H. Snaith, "The Meaning of the Hebrew אך," *VT* 14 (1964): 223. Many others recognize v. 1 as a proleptic summary of the psalm's conclusion. See, for example, John Calvin, *Commentary on the Book of Psalms: Psalms 36–92* (Grand Rapids, MI: Baker, 2005), 124; Tate, *Psalms 51–100*, 233–5; John Goldingay, *Psalms 42–89*, Baker Commentary on the Old Testament (Grand Rapids, MI: Baker, 2007), 400; Frank-Lothar Hossfeld and Erich Zenger, *Psalms 2: A Commentary on Psalms 51–100*, trans. Linda M. Maloney, Hermeneia (Minneapolis, MN: Fortress Press, 2005), 226.

Chapter 4

PSALMS 74–76: YAHWEH IS ZION'S GREAT KING—DESPITE CONFLICTING EVIDENCE

In this chapter I make the case that Psalms 74–76 is the first of four psalm sequences/pairings that stand in a deliberate parallel relationship with the initial Psalm 73 just considered. After laying out the evidence for such design, I consider its significance for the collection's structure and message.

Analysis of Psalms 74, 75, and 76

To ensure (as much as possible) that *Psalterexegese* is rooted firmly in "psalms exegesis," I begin with a concise analysis of the three psalms under consideration.

Psalm 74

Psalm 74 is a communal lament likely composed in response to the destruction of the Jerusalem temple in 586 BCE (vv. 3–8).[1] It is one of the psalms that Craig C. Broyles identifies as a "God-lament" in his form-critical and theological study

---

1. Contra scholars holding that Ps 74 likely dates to the preexilic period. For example, Beat Weber, "Der Asaph Psalter—eine Skizze," in *Prophetie und Psalmen. Festschrift für Klaus Seybold zum 65. Geburtstag*, AOAT 280, ed. B. Huwyler, H. P. Mathys, and B. Weber (Münster: Ugarit-Verlag, 2001), 128; W. C. Bouzard Jr., *We Have Heard with Our Ears, O God*, SBLDS 159 (Atlanta, GA: Scholars Press, 1997). Bouzard bases a preexilic date upon (1) evidence within the psalm of a Mesopotamian literary milieu, and (2) various linguistic features betraying a preexilic date. See Bouzard, *We Have Heard with Our Ears*, 174–85. However, in my view (along with the majority of scholars), Ps 74 clearly has the sixth-century crisis in view. But even if scholars like Weber and Bouzard are correct, a close examination of the collection indicates that Ps 74, whatever its origin, is used to respond to the sixth-century crisis *in the collection's final form*, as Weber himself points out. See Weber, "Der Asaph Psalter—eine Skizze," 135–7. It is the latter point that is most significant for the present study.

of the lament category.² For our purposes, this designation is significant because it highlights the fact that Psalm 74 (like other "God-laments") forms its appeal by "drawing God's attention" to the faith crisis that we saw characterizes Psalm 73, a severe conflict between "faith" and "experience."³ As we shall see, the purpose is not merely to bemoan the situation but to motivate God to resolve it. In terms of date, the psalm's emphasis on the prolonged duration of God's inactivity (vv. 1, 3, 9–10, 23) suggests a date later in the exilic period for its composition.⁴

Graeme E. Sharrock has convincingly shown that the psalm has a five-part concentric arrangement, signaled by inversely parallel verbal patterns:⁵

A1. Imperatives (apart from introductory complaint [v. 1]) (vv. 1–3)
    B1. Perfects (with supplementary imperfect in v. 9) (vv. 4–9)
        C. Imperfects (vv. 10–11)
    B2. Perfects (with supplementary imperfect in v. 14) (vv. 12–17)⁶
A2. Imperatives (and supporting jussives, etc.) (vv. 18–23)

Sharrock demonstrates that correspondences in the content of the parallel sections confirm the psalm's concentric structure.⁷ The following discussion adopts Sharrock's structuration but is not organized in terms of it.

The community interprets the catastrophe (i.e., an enemy's destruction of God's dwelling place [vv. 4–12]) as God's wrathful (אַף) rejection (זנח) of his people

---

2. See the discussion in Craig C. Broyles, *The Conflict of Faith and Experience in the Psalms: A Form-Critical and Theological Study*, JSOTSup 52 (Sheffield: Sheffield Academic Press, 1989), 150–4. See also Ingvar Fløysvik, *When God Becomes My Enemy: The Theology of the Complaint Psalms* (St. Louis, MO: Concordia Academic Press, 1997), 68–92. Fløysvik's book develops Broyles's insights by providing an even more in-depth look at the theology of the "God-lament" psalms.

3. In his study, Broyles makes the case (convincingly in my view) that only a subset of "laments" distinctively form their appeals by drawing God's attention to such a severe crisis (6; 9–10; 13; 22; 35; 39; 42–43; 44; 60; 74; 77; 79; 80; 85; 88; 89; 90; 94; 102; and 108). Broyles contends on form-critical grounds that this subset should be considered a distinct subgenre of lament (i.e., the "God-lament"). See Broyles, *The Conflict of Faith and Experience in the Psalms*, 35–51. For present purposes, it is unimportant whether Broyles is correct about the latter point. What is important is his insight that the appeal of these "laments" in particular has been carefully crafted to "draw God's attention" to a severe conflict of faith and experience in hopes that he will resolve it.

4. Broyles, *The Conflict of Faith and Experience in the Psalms*, 151.

5. Graeme E. Sharrock, "Psalm 74: A Literary-Structural Analysis," *Andrews University Seminary Studies* 21 (1983): 211–23.

6. Further support that v. 17 concludes a section begun in v. 13 is the subtle variation in style from the preceding verses. See the discussion in Gary A. Rendsburg, *How the Bible Is Written* (Peabody, MA: Hendrickson, 2019), 276–7.

7. Sharrock, "Psalm 74," 214–19.

(v. 1).⁸ However, the enemy is not characterized as the instrument of God's anger. They are instead God's enemy (see "your adversaries" [v. 4]) acting on their own accord (vv. 4–9). Thus, as Broyles notes, God's "disposition is considered one of wrathful rejection but his conduct one of restraint."⁹

The central problem facing the community is not the temple's destruction per se. It is the theological implications of God's inactivity in the wake of this calamity. God's absence implies either indifference or, worse, that the Great King has been defeated by the enemy's god.¹⁰ The former is implied by the prolonged nature of God's inactivity,¹¹ and the latter by an enemy who has set up military standards carrying the emblem of their god into God's own dwelling place.¹² All of this, the psalmist stresses, is threatening God's great "name (שם)"; it threatens God himself and particularly God's reputation as King.¹³

The psalmist highlights this conflict between faith and experience by placing multiple God-laments at the prominent central location of the psalm's concentric arrangement:

How long will the adversary reproach?
> Will they despise your name forever?
Why do you withdraw your hand, even your right hand?
> (Take it) out from your bosom! Destroy! (Ps 74:10–11)

Zenger rightly observes that the "withdrawal" of God's hand and hiding of his "right hand" in his garment (v. 11) is an "accusation of actual and deliberate inactivity" that "stand[s] in contradiction to his 'exodus action.' … With this, the accusation of God reaches its climax: the situation lamented in the psalm is a

---

8. "Why do you reject forever? Why does your anger smoke against the flock of your pasture?" (v. 1).

9. Broyles, *The Conflict of Faith and Experience in the Psalms*, 151.

10. Rolf A. Jacobson, *Many Are Saying: The Function of Direct Discourse in the Hebrew Psalter*, Library of Hebrew Bible/Old Testament Studies 397 (New York: T&T Clark, 2004), 46. Jacobson considers this to be the central theological dilemma of the psalm, which is named by the enemy quotation in v. 8: "Let us destroy [the Lord's sanctuaries] altogether." See also similar comments in Fløysvik, *When God Becomes My Enemy*, 87–91.

11. Prolonged Divine inactivity is a prominent theme in the psalm: "Why … do you reject *forever* (לנצח)?" (v. 1); "*perpetual* (נצח) ruins" (v. 3); "How long?" (vv. 9–10); "Will the enemy despise your name *forever* (לנצח)?"; "the uproar of those who rise against you goes up *continually* (תמיד)" (v. 23).

12. Fløysvik, *When God Becomes My Enemy*, 87.

13. God's "name (שם)" is a major theme in Ps 74 (vv. 7, 10, 18, and 21). It is a "metonym for the total character, presence, reputation, and authority of God." Sharrock, "Psalm 74," 222. While true, God's "name" is tied particularly to his reputation as king in Ps 74. On the importance of this theme Sharrock notes, "If indeed C [vv. 10–11] is the axis of the petition, then the primary theme of the psalm is the status of God's name and reputation." Ibid., 223.

contradiction within God himself!"[14] The juxtaposition of a "reference to God's earlier saving deeds" as the mighty "king of old (מלכי מקדם)" (vv. 12–17) with these complaints reveals that the calamity undermines God's past self-revelation as King. As the Great King, God had defeated all chaotic forces in the past (vv. 12–14) and ordered the created world (vv. 14–17). This Divine portrait stands in stark contrast with the "God of experience" who appears to be indifferent to the chaos currently ensuing in Zion (vv. 1–11).

This contrast is deliberate (see "B1" and "B2" in the psalm's structure) in the psalm and is central to the way Psalm 74 forms its appeal. The juxtaposition of the hymnic verses 12–17 with a lament over the chaos ensuing in Zion (vv. 1–11) indicates that these verses are not "straight praise." They are instead "praise" in the service of lament.[15] Their function in the appeal is to highlight the massive discrepancy between God's past praiseworthy behavior as the subduer of chaos/orderer of creation and the chaos/disorder prevailing in Zion *in order to motivate God to resolve it*. These verses "remind" God of "what his conduct should be" so that he will intervene and show himself to be king once more.[16] Consequently, the appeal is predicated upon an extremely robust commitment to the "God of Israel's faith" reflected in verses 12–17.

Psalm 75

Psalm 75 does not fit any one of the traditional Gattüngen.[17] The psalm progresses as follows. It opens with a praise introduction (v. 1), in which the community

---

14. Frank-Lothar Hossfeld and Erich Zenger, *Psalms 2: A Commentary on Psalms 51–100*, trans. Linda M. Maloney, Hermeneia (Minneapolis, MN: Fortress Press, 2005), 247–8.

15. Broyles, *The Conflict of Faith and Experience in the Psalms*, 43. Others have observed this point as well. Fløysvik, *When God Becomes My Enemy*, 89; John Goldingay, *Psalms 42–89*, Baker Commentary on the Old Testament (Grand Rapids, MI: Baker, 2007), 430; Marvin E. Tate, *Psalms 51–100*, Word Biblical Commentary (Nashville, TN: Thomas Nelson, 1990), 253–4. Jones claims that vv. 12–17 "assure the people that God does indeed have the power to right the situation." Christine Danette Brown Jones, "The Psalms of Asaph: A Study of the Function of a Psalm Collection" (PhD diss., Baylor University, 2009), 70. But these verses do not so much "assure" the people of God's power to "right the situation" as they do reflect their deep-seated belief that God is able to bring this situation about. As Tate notes, "The hymnic section in vv. 12–17 is more description than declarative and is not really praise but rather prayer intended to emphasize God's painful inactivity. The language of praise is put to use in the service of lament." Tate, *Psalms 51–100*, 253–4.

16. Broyles, *The Conflict of Faith and Experience in the Psalms*, 43.

17. Rejecting Gunkel's designation "prophetic liturgy," Matthias Millard proposes the designation "Orakelpsalm" for Ps 75 and other similar psalms (see Pss 81, 82, 95). Matthias Millard, *Die Komposition des Psalters: Ein Formgeschichtlicher Ansatz*, FAT 9 (Tübingen: Mohr Siebeck, 1994), 95–6. But such a designation is unhelpful since the term "oracle" can only be applied to the Divine speech in Ps 75 in a very loose sense. See below.

praises God because his "name (שם)" is "near" (v. 2).[18] This is followed by a God quotation, the length of which is not entirely clear. I have adopted a conservative approach by limiting it to verses 3–4 in light of the "Selah" at the end of verse 4, but it possibly extends further. The voice addressing the wicked in verses 5–10 is then that of the psalmist. The confident admonition for the wicked not to "boast" or "lift up" their horn in pride arises from, and is firmly rooted in, the divine self-disclosure of verses 3–4:[19]

> When I take an appointed time,
>   I will judge with equity.
> When the earth and its inhabitants melt/totter,
>   it is I who keeps its pillars steady. (Ps 75:3–4)

This Divine speech most directly depicts God as the universal Judge (מישרים אשפט ["I will judge uprightly"]). But similar language elsewhere (e.g., Pss 9:9; 96:10; 98:9; 99:4) reveals that the fundamental image reflected is that of Israel's God as the Great and Sovereign King;[20] judgment is a central function of God's role as King.

---

18. The verb הודינו in v. 2 (which occurs twice) is best understood as a performative *qatal*, not a past tense statement (contra Hossfeld and Zenger, *Psalms 2*, 252–3, 255): "we give you thanks/praise you!" That is, the *qatal* "does not describe anterior (perfect), past, present, or even future events or situations" but "is employed in order to perform determined acts, such as blessing, thanking, and challenging … by uttering the sentence, the speaker does not state how reality was, is or will be, but imposes an immediate modification of the adjacent world." Alexander Andrason, "Making It Sound—The Performative Qatal and Its Explanations," *Journal of Hebrew Scriptures* 12 (2011): 37, accessed July 5, 2018, https://jhsonline.org/index.php/jhs/article/view/18390/14375.

19. Similar language elsewhere supports the psalmist as the speaker. Compare, for example, these verses with Ps 66:7: "Let the rebellious not exalt themselves [אל ירומו]" [reading the Qere ירומו], and sections of the "Song of Hannah" in 1 Sam 2. In terms of the latter text, compare especially תדברו גבהה גבהה ("Do not speak proudly") in 1 Sam 2:3 and תדברו בצואר עתק ("Do not speak with a haughty neck") in Ps 75:6.

20. Compare the following texts, both lexically and thematically, with Ps 75:3–4 ("I will judge uprightly [מישרים אשפט]. When the earth totters, it is I who steadies its pillars"). Notice especially how God's sovereign control and "upright" judgment mentioned in Ps 75:3–4 is understood as a function of God's kingship: "Say among the nations, The Lord reigns (מלך)! Surely the world is established; it shall not be moved; he will judge (ידין) the people with uprightness (ידין עמים במישרים)" (Ps 96:10); "Shout in joy before the king (המלך), the Lord … he comes to judge the earth (לשפט הארץ). He will judge (ישפט) the world with righteousness, and the peoples with uprightness (במישרים)"; "The King is mighty; he loves justice (משפט). You have established equity (מישרים)." Others have observed this point as well. See Hossfeld and Zenger, *Psalms 2*, 255.

Jacobson cautions that the (common) designation "oracle" should only be used of this Divine speech "with the greatest of care."[21] He points out that an oracle implies present communication from God. But the Divine speech in this and other similar psalms (Pss 50, 81, 95) is best understood as "either a quotation of words of God that had been communicated in the past ... or as artistic liturgical compositions that drew upon the theological traditions of Israel's past."[22] The focus should therefore be on the rhetorical function of the Divine speech in the text's present form.

The content of the oracle is best interpreted as the "wonders" of God judgment recounted by the congregation praising God (see ספרו נפלאותיך [v. 2]). Thus, God's promise of future judgment to bring order to the chaos (vv. 3–4) is "a 'wonder' to which the faithful of God look forward and for which they give praise."[23]

The psalmist's admonition of the wicked to not arrogantly "lift up" (רום) their horn is rooted in the oracle of verses 3–4 and is the central motif in the psalm (see vv. 5, 6, 7,[24] 8, and 11). This motif functions to highlight God's sole sovereign authority as Judge and the certainty of his judgment of the wicked. The Great King is the one who "lifts up" and "brings low," who will make "all of the wicked of the earth" drain the cup of his wrath to its dregs (vv. 8–9).

This confident admonition is followed by a vow to "sing" praise to God (v. 10), clearly prompted by the reality of God's sovereign justice. And the psalm ends with a closing oracle (v. 11) reinforcing the certainty of the Divine King's judgment. The Divine King will "cut off" all the horns of the wicked but "lift up" all the "horns" of the righteous. This closing oracle, like that of verses 3–4, is also introduced by and subordinate to praise: "I will declare [your judgment][25] forever; I will sing praises to the God of Jacob" (v. 10).

This summary suggests that Psalm 75 reflects a delay in God's judgment as the wicked flourish.[26] Such delay is suggested by the psalm's preoccupation with the

---

21. Jacobson, *Many Are Saying*, 92.

22. Ibid., 109. See Jacobson's discussion on ibid., 92–3, 111–12. As Jacobson points out, Ps 75 is a liturgical composition (cf. v. 1) and the God-quotation would be repeated every time the psalm was performed. In short, the "oracle" recorded in vv. 3–4 is "more a liturgical than a prophetic phenomenon." James L. Mays, *Psalms*, Interpretation (Louisville, KY: Westminster/John Knox Press, 1994), 266 (quoted in Jacobson, *Many Are Saying*, 112).

23. Jacobson, *Many Are Saying*, 110.

24. In v. 7 the form is הרים. Some interpret this form as a plural of the noun הר ("mountain"). This reading is supported by the LXX's ὀρέων. While possible, I have read it instead as a hiphil infinitive construct from the verb רום ("to lift up/exalt"), given that this verb is a keyword in the psalm (vv. 6, 7, 8, 11). Thus, לא ממדבר הרים in v. 7 is translated as, "not from the wilderness is lifting up/exaltation."

25. The words "your judgment" are not in the text, which simply reads, "I will declare (אני אגיד)." I have supplied "your judgment" since God's judgment is clearly the implied object of the verb "to declare" in context.

26. Others have observed this point as well. Jacobson, *Many Are Saying*, 111. Hossfeld and Zenger, *Psalms 2*, 255–8.

arrogant wicked (vv. 5–9) and the focus on God's *future* judgment. The oracles of verses 3–4 and 11 provide a Divine, authoritative, answer to these circumstances. The purpose is to elicit and bolster the faith of God's people. But it is also to warn the wicked among them.[27] The righteous maintain, on the basis of God's self-revelation (vv. 3–4, 11), that God will "cut off" the horns of the wicked in due time (v. 11).

Psalm 76

Psalm 76 has traditionally been labeled one of the "Songs of Zion."[28] It is a hymn that celebrates God as the leonine[29] warrior who is "renowned (נודע)" in Judah and whose "name (שם)" is great in Israel (v. 2). But he is also sovereign over the "kings of the earth (מלכי ארץ)" (v. 13). The main section of the psalm (vv. 5–10) puts on vivid display the basis for the praise in the opening verses:[30] God's self-revelation as the incontestable defender of Zion, who comes in judgment (משפט) to protect/save its poor inhabitants (v. 10).

Though implied all along, the final verses (vv. 12–13) make explicit that the majestic image of God in the psalm is a picture of his mighty kingship.[31] Tate notes that "Yahweh is presented as a great king who overcomes the raging of humankind

---

27. Jacobson notes in his conclusion on such God quotations in the Psalter: "These psalms give a divine answer to the problem of sin and the seeming absence of God." Jacobson, *Many Are Saying*, 111.

28. Other psalms so labeled are Pss 46, 48, 84, 87, and 122. Some reject this designation because the focus is Zion's lion/warrior and not the city as such. Erhard S. Gerstenberger, *Psalms (Part 2) and Lamentations*, FOTL (Grand Rapids, MI: Eerdmans, 2001), 87. However you classify it, Zion is clearly a prominent feature in the psalm.

29. The psalmist applies lion imagery to God in v. 3 with the terms סך and מענה. The terms סך and מענה occur in parallel in Job 38:40 to describe the dwelling of a lion. The term מענה is used elsewhere in this way in Amos 3:4, Nah 2:13 Ps 104:22, Cant 4:8. For סך, see Jer 4:7, 25:38, Ps 10:9. Zenger thus rightly notes that in 76:3 these terms reflect "the imagery of YHWH as a lion who has chosen Salem/Zion as his 'covert' (סך) and his (hidden) 'camp' … in order, from there, to fall upon the armies and destroy their weapons." Hossfeld and Zenger, *Psalms 2*, 265.

30. It is common to take the *nipʿal* participles in vv. 2 (נודע ["known"]), 5 (נאור ["majestic"]), and 8 (נורא ["feared"]) as structural indicators, marking the beginning of the first three sections of the psalm. The final section then consists of vv. 11–13. Others (e.g., Tate, *Psalms 51–100*, 264) consider the term סלה ("selah") at the end of vv. 4 and 10 to be the major structural indicator, yielding a three-part structure for the psalm: vv. 2–4, 5–10, 11–13. The latter is preferable because it does not break up vv. 5–10, which form one section delineating God's incontestable defense of Zion and salvation of its people.

31. "Make vows to the Lord your God and repay them! Let all around him bring tribute to the one who is to be feared! He cuts off the spirit of princes. He is one to be feared by the kings of the earth" (Ps 76:12–13).

(v. 11) and waits for the fulfillment of vows to him by homage-paying vassals. The neighboring people, along with the Israelites, are exhorted to bring tribute to God who awes kings and mortifies the rebellious wills of princes."[32]

This hymn is undoubtedly rooted in (and its content informed by) historical occasions where Yahweh was believed to have acted mightily. But the position that Psalm 76 has a specific battle in view should be rejected. The psalm employs generalized imagery of God as the great leonine king that is rooted in specific occasions.[33] The hymn is clearly forward looking (vv. 11-13) but is not strictly eschatological. Tate's judgment seems to accurately capture the "direction" that the psalm is pointing the reader: "Psalm 76 invites the reader to look backward and forward, but especially to the latter, to the time when the resplendent majesty of Yahweh will be demonstrated in great acts of rebuke and judgment. The shape of the future lies in the past."[34] Thus, the psalm looks backward to provide a solid foundation for future hope and confidence in God.

Formal Correspondence with Psalm 73: Evidence

Here we consider three lines of evidence that collectively suggest a deliberate parallel relationship between this sequence of three psalms and the opening Psalm 73.[35]

Analogous Literary Progression

Close analysis reveals that the sequence of Psalms 74-76 mirrors the major literary progression of Psalm 73 on an inter-psalm level.[36] Psalm 74 corresponds to the first part of this progression (73:1-16), while Psalms 75-76 relate to the second (73:18-28) (Table 4.1).

Column 2 shows that Psalm 74 centers on the same fundamental theological crisis as 73:1-16: God's prolonged inactivity results in the perception of a vexing conflict between faith and experience. This is a significant thematic correspondence. In the lament-like 73:1-16, God's prolonged inactivity amid the wicked's prosperity

---

32. Tate, *Psalms 51-100*, 266. See also the comments of Hossfeld and Zenger, *Psalms 2*, 271.

33. Tate, *Psalms 51-100*, 266. The LXX interprets the psalm historically, where the title diverges from the MT by including πρὸς τὸν Ἀσσύριον ("concerning the Assyrian").

34. Ibid., 264.

35. The reader should recall here from Chapter 1 (pp. 20-1) the importance of keeping the distinct (though closely related) issues of "indicators of design" and "significance" separate in one's analysis.

36. As noted in Chapter 1, a couple of scholars have made a similar observation (see p. 35n. 131). I will contend, however, that neither fully grasps the nature of the correspondence between Ps 73 and the Pss 74-76 or its interpretive implications. Both considerations are explored in detail below.

Table 4.1 Analogous Literary Progression of Psalm 73 and Psalms 74–76

Core aspect of Israelite "faith" challenged	Confrontation with a severe conflict of faith and experience	Radical shift in perspective on God's posture/ involvement
God's goodness	Psalm 73:1–16	Psalm 73:18–28
God's status as Zion's Great King	Psalm 74	Psalms 75–76

and the psalmist's (and all Israel's) suffering (experience) appears to contradict the thesis "God is good to Israel" (v. 1) (faith). The faith crisis confronting the psalmist challenges that core Israelite belief in the extreme (column 1).

The appeal of Psalm 74, on the other hand, centers on the communal perception that God's prolonged inactivity in the face of an enemy wreaking havoc in Zion (experience) severely threatened Yahweh's reputation as Zion's Great King (faith) (column 1), even suggesting his potential defeat.

Column 3 indicates that the transition from Psalm 74 to Psalms 75–76 marks a radical shift in perspective that mirrors the progression to verses 18–28 in Psalm 73. We saw that Psalm 73's second half is clearly distinguished by a radical shift in perspective on God's posture toward his people/the wicked and involvement in the world relative to the crisis recounted in the first. We noted how verse 17 explained that this shift originated at the temple, after which the psalm's entire tone dramatically changes. In spite of God's inactivity, the psalmist becomes resolute in the belief that God is *not* indifferent to either the wicked's prosperity or Israel's suffering; in due time, God will utterly destroy the wicked (vv. 18–20, 27) and prove to be the refuge of the righteous (vv. 26, 28). Thus, in the psalm's second half, the core Israel belief challenged in the first is upheld and confidently (re)affirmed (i.e., God's goodness).

The progression to Psalms 75–76 witnesses an analogous shift in perspective. In marked contrast to Psalm 74, God's kingship is not perceived to be severely challenged in Psalms 75–76 but is confidently affirmed and extolled. Here the dominating Divine profile is not a King who is seemingly indifferent to the wicked or Zion's plight, or even potentially defeated. Rather, it is of the Great King who currently reigns supreme and who will administer justice with certainty in due time (Ps 75) and who is portrayed as Zion's incontestable Savior and Defender (Ps 76). These adjacent psalms, therefore, enthusiastically promote the core Israelite belief perceived to be severely threatened in the previous lament (God's reputation and status as the Great King).

Thus, the sequential movement from Psalm 74 to Psalms 75–76 mirrors the major literary progression of Psalm 73 in terms of the distinctive semantic/conceptual relationship between the psalm's two main halves.

Analogous Network of Parallels

A second line of evidence builds on the first. We noted in Chapter 3 McCann's observation of a network of parallels that highlights the radical shift in perspective

Table 4.2 Lexical Parallels between Psalms 73:4–15 and 18–28

Lexical item	Verses 4–15	Verses 18–28
עם ("with")	"... *with* man, they (i.e., the wicked) are not afflicted." (v. 5)	"When my heart was embittered, I was a beast *with* you."; "I am continually *with* you." (vv. 22, 23) See also v. 25.
עולם ("forever")	"Behold, these are the wicked ... *forever* they increase riches." (v. 12)	"God is the rock of my heart and my portion *forever*." (v. 26)
שית ("set/make")	"They (the wicked) *set* their mouth in heaven." (v. 9)	"Surely, you *set* them (i.e., the wicked) in slippery places." (v. 18); "I have *made* the Lord God my refuge." (v. 28)
בארץ + בשמים ("in heaven/"on earth")	"They (the wicked) set their mouth in *heaven*, and their tongue walks through the *earth*." (v. 9)	"Who is there for me in *heaven*, but with you I am pleased on the *earth*." (v. 25)
איך ("how")	"*How* does God know?" (v. 11)	"*How* they become destroyed in a moment." (v. 19)
ידע ("to know")	"How does God *know*?" "Is there *knowledge* in the Most High?" (v. 11)	"When my soul was embittered ... I was without *knowledge*." (v. 22)
הנה ("look/behold")	"*Behold*; these are the wicked; always at ease, the increase in riches." (v. 12)	"*Behold*, those far from you shall perish; you destroy all who are unfaithful to you." (v. 27)
כל ("all")	"*All* day long I have been stricken." (v. 14)	"You destroy *all* who are unfaithful to you." (v. 27); "I have made the Lord God my refuge, declaring *all* your works." (v. 28)
ספר ("to declare/speak")	"If I said, 'I will *speak* thus I would betray a generation of your sons.'" (v. 15)	"I have made the Lord God my refuge, *declaring* all your works." (v. 28)

observable in Psalm 73's second half. These parallels are displayed in tabular form in Table 4.2.

Table 4.2 shows that a group of words or roots that occur in verses 4–15 is repeated in verses 18–28. A quick glance at the table reveals that in verses 18–28 the word or root does not occur in the same type of context, or even the same sense, as in verses 4–12. But, as McCann points out, the repetitions nevertheless appear to be intentional: "In each case, the repetition serves to mark the reversal that has taken place in the psalmist's perspective."[37] A few examples will suffice to illustrate McCann's point.

In verse 11, for instance, the wicked use the word איכה (interrogative) to assert their superiority: "*How* does God know?" (i.e., God does *not* know). But in verse 19 איך occurs in an exclamation that emphasizes the certain downfall of the wicked,

---

37. J. Clinton McCann, "Psalm 73: An Interpretation Emphasizing Rhetorical and Canonical Criticism" (PhD diss., Duke University, 1985), 79.

reflecting a reversal in perspective: "*How* they become destroyed in a moment!" Or consider עולם ("forever"). In verse 12 the word comes in a description of the wicked's prosperity: "Behold, these are the wicked ... *forever* they increase riches." But when עולם is repeated in verse 26, it is "not associated with the prosperity of the wicked but with the destiny of the psalmist, whose 'portion is God forever.' A reversal has occurred. The psalmist, not the wicked, is secure forever."[38] To look at only one more example, in verse 9 the psalmist describes the wicked as asserting their authority "in the heavens" (בשמים) and "on the earth" (בארץ). But verse 25 reflects a reversal in the psalmist's perspective: "The psalmist recognizes no one in the heavens [בשמים] besides God, and because he is with God, he has no desire on earth [בארץ]."[39]

A close consideration of the remaining repetitions reveals that all follow this same pattern. McCann, therefore, concludes, "It is possible that some of the instances cited above [i.e., the repetitions presented in Table 4.2] are coincidental. However, the number of cases involved and their pattern suggest that repetition is used intentionally as a rhetorical device to highlight the reversal that has taken place in the psalmist's perspective."[40] Thus, McCann discovered a unified network of links (not a disparate group) between the psalm's two halves. Though the word or root does not occur in the same type of context when repeated, and some not even in the same sense, its repetition is nevertheless intentional.[41] In fact, the rhetorical effect McCann describes comes about *precisely because* the repetition appears in a radically different context.

In light of the semantic/conceptual parallel with Psalm 73 already uncovered, it is striking to find the network of links between Psalm 74 and Psalm 75 and/or 76 presented in Table 4.3. Table 4.3 shows that an entire group of linguistic features in Psalm 74, mostly words but also images and motifs, is repeated in the following two consecutive psalms, Psalms 75 and 76. Like the rhetorical device used in Psalm 73, each repetition marks the radical shift in perspective that characterizes the inter-psalm progression to Psalm 75 and/or 76. A few examples will illustrate this point.

38. Ibid., 80.
39. Ibid.
40. Ibid., 82.
41. It should be noted here that some editorial critics dismiss certain words or roots as reflecting intentionality because they do not occur in the same type of context when repeated. For example, Snearly claims in his study that parallels between Pss 118 and 119 pointed out by Yair Zakovich should not be considered significant since "in every case the words are not used in the same type of contexts." Michael K. Snearly, *The Return of the King: Messianic Expectation in Book V of the Psalter*, LHBOTS 624 (New York: Bloomsbury, 2016), 114. But regardless of whether or not these parallels reflect intentionality, McCann's observations on Ps 73 show that the grounds upon which Snearly dismisses them are invalid. In addition to Ps 73, there are many instances in Hebrew poetry where words or roots "not occurring in the same types of context" or even the same sense are meaningfully repeated.

Table 4.3 Parallels between Psalm 74 and Psalms 75–76

Parallel	Psalm 74	Psalm 75	Psalm 76
God's status as the "Great King"	Undermined by lived experience (i.e., the chaos ensuing in Zion)	Confidently affirmed and extolled	Confidently affirmed and extolled
שם ("name")	"They defile the dwelling place of your *name*." (v. 7); "Will the enemy despise your *name* forever." (v. 10); See also vv. 18, 21.	"We praise you, for your *name* is near." (v. 2)	"God has made himself known in Judah; in Israel his *name* is great." (v. 2)
God as the "Guarantor of cosmic stability"	Conception of God undermined by Divine inactivity (vv. 16–17)	Conception of God forming basis for praise and confidence (v. 4)	
מועד ("appointed time/place")	"Your adversaries roar in the midst of your *appointed place*" (i.e., the sanctuary) (v. 4) (see also v. 8).	"At the *appointed time*, I [God] will judge uprightly." (v. 3)	
רום ("to lift up/exalt")	"*Lift up* your steps to the eternal ruins!" (v. 3)	"I say to the wicked, do not *lift up* your horn!" (vv. 5, 6); "Not from the wilderness is *lifting up*, but God is judge." (v. 8); See also vv. 7, 11.	
יד ([God's] "hand")	"Why do you draw back your *hand* …?" (v. 11)	"A cup is in the *hand* of the Lord … all of the wicked of the earth will drain it to its dregs." (v. 9)	
Theology of the poor/afflicted (עני;ענו)	"Do not forget the life of your *poor* forever." (v. 19; see also v. 21)		"When God arose for judgment, to save all the *poor* of the earth" (v. 10)
ישע/שבר ("to save"/"to shatter")	Used to describe conception of God undermined by experience (vv. 12–13)		Used to describe the Great King's mighty defense of Zion/judgment (vv. 4, 10)
מלך ("king")	"O God, my *king* from of old." (v. 12) (conception of God undermined in Ps 74)		"… God … who is to be feared by the *kings* of the earth." (v. 12)
Lion imagery	"Your [i.e., God's] adversaries have *roared* amid your meeting place." (v. 4)		"In Salem was his [i.e., God's] *covert* (סך), his *dwelling place* (מענה) in Zion." (v. 3)
ציון ("Zion")	"Why do you reject forever? …. Remember Mt. *Zion* … where you dwelt." (v. 2)		"His dwelling place is in *Zion*. There he broke the flashing arrows." (v. 2)
קום ("to rise")	"*Arise*, O God, defend your cause!" (v. 22); "Do not forget … the uproar of *those who rise* against you." (v. 23)		"When God *arose* for judgment, to save all the poor of the earth." (v. 10)

In Psalm 74 the noun מועד is closely associated with the image of God as a potentially indifferent and defeated King. Here it refers to the "appointed places of God (מועדי אל)" burned by the enemy (v. 9), and the appointed place (מועד) of God's dwelling (i.e., the Temple) that they occupy (v. 3). But in Psalm 75 מועד occurs in a description of the Great King who currently rules and reigns: "At the *appointed time* (מועד) I set, I will judge uprightly" (v. 3). Or consider the verb רום ("to lift up/exalt"). In Psalm 74 the verb is part of a desperate plea for the potentially defeated King to defend his dwelling place: "*Lift up* your steps to the eternal ruins!" (v. 3). But in Psalm 75 it is *the* key word repeated to describe God's current status as the Great King/Judge (see vv. 5, 6, 7, 8, and 11).

The word יד ([God's] "hand") is a final example from Psalms 74 and 75. In Psalm 74 it comes in a rhetorical question expressing the inexplicability of God's prolonged inactivity: "Why do you draw back your *hand*?" (v. 11). However, when יד is used in Psalm 75, it appears in an affirmation of God's current status as the Great King: "A cup is in the *hand* of the Lord ... all of the wicked of the earth will drain it to its dregs" (v. 9). The remaining links between Psalms 74 and 75 follow the same pattern.

The links between Psalms 74 and 76 are of the same nature. Consider first the verb קום ("to rise"). In Psalm 74 it is used in desperate pleas for the inexplicably inactive King to "Rise up! (קומה)" and not forget the uproar of "those who rise up against you (קמיך)" (vv. 22, 23). But in Psalm 76 the verb occurs in a description of God as the incontestable regal Defender and Savior of Zion: "From heaven you uttered judgment; the earth was afraid and silent; when God *arose* (קום) for judgment, to save all the oppressed of the earth" (v. 10). Or we can consider the noun ציון ("Zion"). In Psalm 74 it is associated with the Great King's seemingly undue neglect of Zion: "Why do you reject forever?. ... Remember Mt. *Zion* ... where you dwell." (v. 2). In Psalm 76, however, it is associated with the Great King's mighty, leonine, defense of Zion: "His dwelling place is in *Zion*. There he broke the flashing arrows" (v. 2). Finally, in Psalm 74 the verbs ישע/שבר ("to save"/"to shatter") are used to "remind" a seemingly negligent God of what his conduct "should" be as the Great King (see vv. 4 and 8).[42] But when the verbs appear in Psalm 76, they extol the Great King's past defense of Zion, set forth as a basis for praise and confidence in God among future generations (vv. 4, 10). The remaining two links follow the same pattern.

These observations show that Psalm 74 shares a network of links with Psalm 75 and/or 76 that strikingly resembles the intentional rhetorical strategy McCann detected between the two halves of Psalm 73. At the inter-psalm level as well, we find an entire group of words (and other linguistic features) whose repetition—though not occurring in the same type of context or even the same sense (e.g., מועד)—follows a consistent pattern of marking the radical shift in perspective observable in the following literary unit(s) (Pss 75 and 76). In fact, as noted in the case of Psalm 73, this effect comes about *precisely because* the repetition occurs in

---

42. The reader should recall here that the section in which these verbs occur (vv. 12–17) is not "straight praise" but praise in service of lament. See the analysis of Ps 74 earlier in the chapter.

a completely different context. The number and consistent pattern of these links suggest that their repetition is *intentional*. And, in light of the semantic/conceptual parallel with Psalm 73 already uncovered, these repetitions further point to a deliberate relationship with the proximate Psalm 73.

Evaluating these links in light of the principles/criteria outlined in Chapter 1 corroborates their intentionality.[43] Consider first the links between Psalms 74 and 75:

1. God's profile as the Great King/Judge occupies a central literary "location": it is *the* central image of God and a major theme in both psalms (e.g., 74:12, 22; 75:3–4).
2. "Name" (שֵׁם) theology (and so the word שֵׁם) reflects the above thematic parallel in both psalms (74:7, 10, 18, 21; 75:2) and is a keyword in Psalm 74. This theology plays a particularly prominent role in Psalm 74, being a major motif (Ps 74:7, 10, 18, 21). Its presence at the pivot of Psalm 74, a structurally prominent location, strengthens the case for its intentionality ("Will the enemy despise your name [שֵׁם] forever?" [v. 10]).[44] After Psalm 76, which belongs to the same grouping as Psalms 74 and 75 (see below), "name" theology does not appear again until Psalm 79.[45]
3. The motif of God as the "Guarantor of cosmic stability" (74:16–17; 75:4)[46] does not appear again until Psalm 82.
4. The occurrences of the noun מוֹעֵד ("appointed time/place") in these *adjacent* psalms (74:4, 8; 75:3) account for three of the five total in MT-150. The remaining two come in Psalms 102:14 and 104:19.
5. The occurrences of the root רוּם ("to lift up/exalt") in these adjacent psalms account for seven of the nine total in Psalms 73–83 (Ps 74:3; 75:5, 6 [2×], 7, 8, 11). In addition to such clustering, the central role of this root in Psalm 75 further supports its intentionality: רוּם is *the* key root/word repeated to underscore God's sovereign justice and universal kingship.
6. Apart from Psalms 74:11 and 75:9, there are three other specific references to God's "hand" (יָד) in Psalms 73–83 (78:42; 80:18; 81:15). Elsewhere there are related references to God's "right hand" (77:11; 78:54; 80:16, 18). That such references reflect a consistent pattern in the collection—always appearing in *adjacent* psalms (i.e., 74–75; 77–78; 80–81)—suggests their intentionality here. This link receives further corroboration as the case is made for the deliberate juxtaposition of these adjacencies. It is also not insignificant that the reference to God's "hand" in Psalm 74 appears at the prominent structural location of verse 11.

---

43. In this connection, see the methodological discussion on pp. 27–32.

44. See the earlier discussion of Ps 74 for justification of the psalm's concentric arrangement.

45. Observations such as this reflect the "concentration" criterion discussed in Chapter 1 (see p. 29).

46. Hossfeld and Zenger, *Psalms 2*, 258.

7. The final link is the motif of praise (see הלל ["to praise"] in 74:21 and ידה ["to give thanks/praise"] in 75:2 [2×]. See also 75:10).⁴⁷ The verb ידה occurs elsewhere only at Psalm 79:13; הלל occurs one other time (78:63).⁴⁸

Consider next the links between Psalms 74 and 76:

1. As in both Psalms 74 and 75, the profile of God as the Great King/Judge dominates in Psalm 76. This thematic link is the major conjunctive feature binding Psalms 74–76 together. This claim receives additional support from the next link ("name," שם), a keyword reflecting this larger theme in all three psalms.
2. The occurrences of the noun שם in Psalms 74–76 represent six of the thirteen total in Psalms 73–83 (i.e., 74:7, 10, 18, 21; 75:2; 76:2).⁴⁹ This clustering of the noun שם, and the larger theme of God's kingship it reflects, is the most significant feature joining and distinguishing this psalm sequence amid its proximate context. As noted above, the noun שם does not occur again until Psalm 79.
3. A similar reference to "Zion (ציון)" as God's dwelling place (74:2; 76:3) is only found once elsewhere in Psalms 73–83 (78:68).
4. The link שבר/ישע ("to save"/"to shatter") is a particularly distinctive parallel. In both psalms, the verb שבר ("to shatter") appears in the *pi'el* (74:13; 76:4) with a word built from the root ישע ("to save") (ישועות [74:12]; עישוהל [76:10]) in descriptions of God's great deeds. The former verb (שבר), in any stem, appears nowhere else in Psalms 73–83. A word built from the root ישע does not occur again until Psalm 78:22. Outside of Psalms 74 and 76, there are only three other psalms in the collection that contain such words (78 [v. 22]; 79 [v. 9]; 80 [vv. 3, 4, 8, and 20]).
5. The occurrences of the verb קום ("to rise") in these psalms account for three of the six total in Psalms 73–83 (74:22, 23; 76:10; 78:5, 6; 82:8). Further, the verb is connected in both psalms to the image of God as Judge/King, something only true once elsewhere in the collection (Ps 82:8).
6. The occurrences of the noun מלך ("king") in these psalms (74:12; 76:12) are the only two in Psalms 73–83.
7. The theology of the poor/afflicted (עני; ענוו) (74:19, 21; 76:9–10) that these psalms share does not appear again until Psalm 79.

---

47. The semantic overlap of הלל and ידה is evidenced by cases where they occur in parallel or otherwise proximate contexts (e.g., Isa 38:18; Pss 35:18; 44:9; 106:1; 109:30; 111:1; Ezra 3:11; Neh 12:24; 1 Chr 16:4; 23:30; 25:3; 29:13; 2 Chr 5:13; 7:6; 31:2).
48. This link does not appear in Table 4.3 but follows the same pattern as those links.
49. As observed earlier, Sharrock argues that the status of God's name or reputation may be the major theme of the psalm. Sharrock, "Psalm 74," 223.

8. The lion imagery that these psalms employ does not occur anywhere else in the collection (see 74:4 ["Your adversaries roar [שאג] in the midst of your sanctuary"]⁵⁰; 76:3).
9. Regarding the motif of praise (see הלל ["to praise"] in 74:21 and ידה ["to give thanks/praise"] in 76:11), (1) the verb ידה occurs again only at Psalm 79:13; and (2) הלל occurs one other time (i.e., in addition to 74:21 [78:63]).⁵¹

The links that the parallel relationship with Psalm 73 singles out thus meet the criteria outlined in Chapter 1. This observation strengthens the case for the deliberate nature of this relationship.

Linguistic Parallels with Psalm 73

This third line of evidence builds upon the first two. The striking correspondence between the sequence of Psalms 74–76 and Psalm 73 observed so far invites (and warrants) the search for other parallels. A closer look reveals a number of significant linguistic ties:⁵²

1. The Divine profile of God as the Just Judge features prominently in both Psalm 73 (vv. 18–20, 28) and Psalms 75–76.
2. The wicked/enemy in the sequence of Psalms 74–76 is described with the same uncommon lexemes as in Psalm 73: מצה ("to drain," 73:10; 75:9) (*dis legomenon* in the MT Psalter);⁵³ חמס ("violence," 73:6 and 74:20) (*dis legomenon* in Pss 73–83);⁵⁴ הלל ("to boast") (73:3; 75:5 [2×]);⁵⁵ רשע ("wicked") (73:3, 12; 75:5, 9, 11);⁵⁶ and הלל ("to boast") (73:3; 75:5 [2×]).

---

50. This statement almost certainly evokes lion imagery. In all but two of its twenty occurrences in the Hebrew Bible (i.e., Ps 38:9; Job 37:4), the verb שאג either literally or figuratively has the "roaring" of a lion in view. See Judg 14:5; Isa 5:29; Jer 2:15; Jer 25:30 (3×); Jer 51:38; Ezek 22:25; Hos 11:10 (2×); Joel 3:16; Amos 1:2, 3:4, 8; Zeph 3:3; Ps 22:14; 104:21.

51. This link does not appear in Table 4.3 but follows the same pattern as those links.

52. Most of these parallels have been cited in one study or another. For example, Robert L. Cole, *The Shape and Message of Book III (Psalms 73–89)*, JSOTSup 307 (Sheffield: Sheffield Academic Press, 2000), 37–45. My contention, however, is that previous studies have failed to recognize their implications for the collection's design, discussed in the next section.

53. In this study I borrow the terminology "*dis legomenon*" (i.e., a word occurring only twice in the named corpus) from Cole. Cole, *The Shape and Message of Book III*, 236.

54. The noun only occurs in nine other psalms in the MT Psalter, for a total of twelve occurrences (7:17; 11:5; 18:49; 25:19; 27:12; 35:11; 55:10; 58:3; 72:14; 140:2, 5, 12).

55. This verb occurs nowhere else in the collection. It only appears two other times in the MT Psalter (Pss 5:6; 102:9).

56. This term is very common in the Hebrew Bible (over three hundred times) but only occurs in one other psalm in this collection (see 82:2, 4).

3. The clause "they recount your [God's] wonders" [ספרו נפלאותיך] in 75:2 closely resembles "recounting all your [i.e., God's] works [לספר כל מלאכותיך]" in Psalm 73:28.
4. The parallel למשאות/למשואות ("to ruins") in 74:3 and 73:18 is a *dis legomenon* in the Hebrew Bible.[57]
5. Both contain the motif of an enemy quotation by a foreign nation introduced by the quotative frame "they say (74:8; 73:11)" (אמרו). Such quotations appear only two other times in Psalms 73–83 (79:10; 83:5).[58]
6. Like Psalm 73, where the resolution comes about at *the Temple* (lit., "sanctuaries of God" [מקדשי אל] v. 17), Zion theology plays a significant role in Psalms 74–76. Psalm 74 centers on an enemy's attack upon God's sanctuary (קדש/מקדש) in Zion (vv. 3, 7); Psalm 76, often deemed a "song of Zion," focuses on God's mighty kingship in Zion.

These parallels are further suggestive of a deliberate literary correspondence between the sequence of Psalms 74–76 and the opening Psalm 73.

Formal Correspondence with Psalm 73: Interpretation

The last section made the case that the sequence of Psalms 74–76 (1) mirrors the major literary progression of Psalm 73; (2) is characterized by an analogous group of significant repetitions (i.e., ones appearing to reflect intentionality); and (3) shares additional significant parallels with the opening Psalm 73. The striking nature of this formal correspondence (particularly the first two considerations) suggests intentionality: the sequence of Psalms 74–76 stands in a *deliberate* parallel relationship with the opening Psalm 73.

The key to understanding the significance of this observation lies in the close relationship between structure and meaning, or form and function, discussed in Chapter 1. Edward Greenstein's observations on the tendency for grammatical and semantic parallelism to co-occur highlights the application of this relationship relevant here:

> Most significantly parallelism contributes to the meaning of Biblical verse by structuring the ways in which we perceive its content. *The presentation of lines in parallelism has the effect of reinforcing the semantic association between them*. It has long been observed that *when discrete materials appear to us in similar form, we are led to seek, and find, some meaningful correlation between them* (emphasis added). This, for example, is the underpinning principle of rhyme: rhyme creates

---

57. Cole, *The Shape and Message of Book III*, 236.
58. Israel's complaint in Ps 78:19–22 is also an "enemy quotation." See Jacobson, "*Many Are Saying*," 37–8. This instance is excluded from the count here since it does not appear on the lips of a foreign nation as in Pss 79:10 and 83:5.

or tightens an association between two or more words or phrases. Repetition of syntactic structure ... can perform the same function. The psychological nexus between semantic sense and syntactic structure has been demonstrated experimentally. When subjects were presented with a sentence of a particular grammatical form and were then asked to produce another sentence having the same form, subjects tended to formulate a sentence that not only mirrored the structure of the model but also echoed something of its semantics. For example, the test sentence *The lazy student failed the exam* elicited such responses as: *The smart girl passed the test. The industrious pupil passed the course. The brilliant boy studied the paper.* (Emphasis original)[59]

Greenstein's basic point about parallelism here is that similarity in *structure* leads to a perception of, and promotes, a correlation in *meaning*. Because of the "psychological nexus" between "semantic sense" and structure, most often structural or formal correspondence reveals and/or reinforces an underlying semantic relationship.[60]

Greenstein's observations on parallel lines apply equally to parallel relationships such as the one being considered here: that the "discrete materials" of Psalm 73 and the sequence of Psalms 74–76 "appear to us in similar form" leads us to "seek, and find, some meaningful correlation between them." On a basic level, this parallel relationship implies that, like Psalm 73 itself, Psalms 74–76 are a literary unit—a distinct and deliberately arranged psalm group. But even more significantly, this parallel relationship functions as a paratextual indicator that the sequence of Psalms 74–76 develops Psalm 73's topic on an inter-psalm level (Table 4.4).

That the core Israelite belief challenged/promoted is different in each case (column 4) seems to prima facie contradict this claim. A closer look, however, suggests otherwise. In Psalm 73, the perspective on God challenged/reaffirmed is broad in nature ("God is good to Israel"), the historical setting is unspecified, and the identity of the non-Israelite wicked is undefined.[61] On the other hand, in the grouping of Psalms 74–76, the core belief challenged is more defined (God's status as the Great King), the historical setting is specific (the aftermath of the Temple's destruction), and the identity of the non-Israelite wicked receives a concrete face in the enemy nation hacking the temple to pieces (74:1–11).

These observations suggest that the relationship between Psalm 73 and the parallel Psalms 74–76 resembles that of many parallel lines of Hebrew poetry.

---

59. Edward L. Greenstein, "How Does Parallelism Mean?" in *A Sense of Text: The Art of Language in the Study of Biblical Literature*, Stephen A. Geller, Edward L. Greenstein, and Adele Berlin, Jewish Quarterly Review Supplement (Winona Lake, IN: Eisenbrauns, 1982), 64. Quoted from Adele Berlin, *The Dynamics of Biblical Parallelism* (Grand Rapids, MI: Eerdmans, 1994), 23.

60. There are, of course, exceptions. See Berlin, *The Dynamics of Biblical Parallelism*, 22.

61. See the exegesis of Ps 73 in Chapter 3 for reasons to identify the wicked in this psalm as non-Israelites.

Table 4.4 The Semantic Relationship between Psalm 73 and Psalms 74–76

Psalm/psalm group	Confrontation with a severe conflict of faith and experience	Resolution to the conflict of faith and experience	Core Israelite belief challenged/promoted
Psalm 73	vv. 1–16	vv. 18–28	"God is good to Israel" (v. 1)
Psalms 74–76	Psalm 74	Psalms 75–76	God's status as the Great King

Robert Alter explains that, between many parallel lines, "the characteristic movement of meaning is one of heightening or intensification ... *of focusing, specification, concretization*" (emphasis added).[62] In this case, the sequence of Psalms 74–76 takes up the *same* topic as the parallel Psalm 73 but *develops it in a more specific and concrete direction*. Marvin Tate's observation on Psalm 73 supports this view, namely, that Psalm 73 is "a good example of what Miller has called 'openness to new contexts,'" the psalm not being "locked into any one particular setting in history."[63] This quality makes Psalm 73 particularly suitable for having its topic developed within a more specific context in the following psalm sequence.

Formal correspondence with Psalm 73, therefore, implies the view that the severe threat to Divine Kingship in Psalm 74 is to be interpreted as, more fundamentally, a challenge to God's *goodness* (73:1) (Table 4.4, column 4). Thus, an editorial-critical investigation confirms Tate's conclusion on Psalm 73:1 ("God is good to Israel"): "the reader knows right away that this thesis is going to be tested severely in this section of the Psalter, both in terms of individual faith and in terms of the nation Israel."[64] However, it also reveals that Tate's claim requires modification. In the sequence of Psalms 74–76, this thesis is not merely or even primarily *tested*. Rather, we have discovered an editorial concern to *resolve* tension over its enduring truthfulness and *reaffirm* it in the face of conflicting evidence (columns 3 and 4).

The repetitions identified between Psalm 74 and Psalm 75 and/or 76 (Table 4.3) corroborate this interpretation. We saw earlier that, in each case, the repetition marked the radical shift in perspective on God's kingship in Psalms 75–76. But we have yet to consider the significance of such editorial marking. Its significance is found in the analogous network of repetitions in Psalm 73. The reason is that, as argued above, the significant repetitions in Psalms 74–76 reflect deliberate literary correspondence with that rhetorical device. Psalm 73 is thus something of a hermeneutical key that unlocks the interpretive significance of these repetitions.

---

62. Robert Alter, *The Art of Biblical Poetry* (New York: Basic Books, 1985), 19.
63. Tate, *Psalms 51–100*, 233.
64. Ibid., xxv.

We saw that McCann observed how the repetitions in Psalm 73 were used intentionally as a rhetorical device for the purpose of highlighting the psalmist's reversal in perspective. In so doing, they highlighted the *resolution* the psalmist reached in relation to the crisis of verses 1–16. And we noted that the resolution reached consisted essentially in a renewed commitment to what the psalmist/Israel already believed about God (i.e., God's goodness and justice) but had nearly collapsed under the weight of lived experience.

By analogy, the repetitions in Psalms 75 and 76 are used to *highlight the resolution that these psalms are promoting* in relation to the community's confrontation with a conflict of faith and experience in Psalm 74. The same rhetorical device used in the parallel Psalm 73 appears to be at work, just at a higher literary level in the collection. Consequently, these repetitions corroborate the interpretation already tacitly indicated by the parallel sematic/conceptual relationship discovered between Psalms 75–76 and 73:18–28 (Table 4.4, column 3): Psalms 75–76 are sequenced after Psalm 74 to promote resolution to the conflict of faith and experience at the center of that appeal.

And the resolution promoted is of the same nature as the parallel Psalm 73. As we have seen, Psalms 75 and 76 feature the same Divine profile as Psalm 74 (i.e., Yahweh as the Great King). But they reflect a radical shift in perspective on the Great King's posture toward his people/the wicked and involvement in the affairs of the world. The deliberate sequencing of these psalms thus directs singers/readers to extol and affirm the sovereign saving kingship (Pss 75–76) of a God whose kingship in Zion was seen to be severely threatened (Ps 74). The implication is that the editorial purpose driving the arrangement is to undergird the deep faith commitment to the "God of belief" (i.e., Zion's Great King) reflected (but violently disrupted) in the appeal of Psalm 74 itself (see vv. 12–17):[65] Zion's Great King is *not* indifferent, has *not* been defeated, and in due time *will* order the chaos that has ensued in Zion (75:3–4; 76:4–10)—in spite of conflicting evidence (74:1–11).

Thus, resembling Psalm 73, resolution consists in promoting confidence in what was already believed about God but had nearly collapsed under the weight of lived experience. Significantly, this grouping grounds such confidence in God's own self-revelation in both word (75:3) and work (76:1–7).

The Theological Message of Psalms 74–76

A distinct theological message arises from the sequence of Psalms 74–76. It is essentially the same as that of Psalm 73, which is unsurprising given the parallel relationship with that psalm: "Faith sticks to God's self-revelation [i.e., God's status as the Great King, more fundamentally 'God is good to Israel'] amid

---

65. The proposed interpretation does not, therefore, make a "fruit purée" of these psalms (see pp. 18–20). Such an editorial concern to undergird confidence in *Zion's* Great King is notable in light of previous claims that the collection's arrangement points readers away from the "traditional David/Zion theology" (McCann). More on this point in later chapters.

conflicting evidence." This message is a consequence of the following observations on the sequence's design: (1) its shape shores up confidence in Yahweh's status as the Great King (Pss 75–76) in the face of conflicting evidence (Ps 74:1–11); and (2) the parallel relationship with Psalm 73 tacitly indicates that the core belief at issue is, more fundamentally, God's goodness (Table 4.4, column 4).

Importantly, this is not an abstract theological message communicated in a vacuum. As we have seen, it is contextualized within a specific historical circumstance, namely, the aftermath of the temple's destruction in 586 BCE (74:1–11). While the message certainly transcends that historical context, it cannot be severed from it. As we will see in later chapters, this observation has important implications for the collection's design.[66]

Implications for the Collection

At least three important implications emerge from the analysis carried out above. One is that the first four psalms are a literary unity consisting of two distinct but closely related units: Psalm 73 and a psalm group consisting of Psalms 74–76. The analysis has, therefore, identified both significant literary continuity and discontinuity between these first four psalms. In terms of the latter, it has revealed tacit indicators that the *psalm* boundary between Psalms 73 and 74 is also an *editorial* boundary (i.e., a boundary distinguishing Ps 73 from the grouping of Pss 74–76). If correct, proposals that conceive of Psalms 73 and 74 as a joint introduction (Robertson) or otherwise detect no significant literary discontinuity between these psalms (e.g., Jones; Cole) have overlooked an important aspect of editorial separation in the collection. Chapters 6 and 8 explore these matters in more detail.

Second, as already noted, Psalms 74–76 emerge as the collection's first distinct and deliberately arranged psalm group. An important implication is that, like the parallel Psalm 73, this literary unit is not "open-ended"; it is an internally coherent, self-contained, grouping that *resolves* the theological crisis it addresses (i.e., the conflict of faith and experience voiced in Ps 74). Chapter 6 fleshes out the implications of this point in the context of previous research.

A third implication relates to the organizing principle that structures these first four psalms. I have presented evidence that Psalms 74–76 deliberately *parallel* Psalm 73. And, as we have seen, this means that the sequence of Psalms 74–76 does not progress in a linear and/or narrative-like fashion from the topic of Psalm 73. This psalm sequence takes up Psalm 73's general topic (i.e., a conflict between God's goodness and the wicked's prosperity) and develops it in a more specific direction (i.e., in terms of a threat to God's status as the Great King) and within more specific historical circumstances (an enemy's attack upon the Temple in the sixth century). Thus, the relationship between Psalms 73 and 74–76 is not one of linear progression but topical recursion.

---

66. See in particular Chapters 6 and 8.

The analysis has thus identified a *recursive* organizing principle at work in the sequencing of Psalms 73–76, what I referred to (following Peter Gentry) as "progressive repetition" in Chapter 1: the common approach in Hebrew literature where a single topic is treated multiple times ("repetition") but developed differently when repeated ("progressive").[67]

This structural insight is significant in light of studies like those of Cole, Jones, Ho, and others. We saw in Chapter 2 that such approaches assume the operation of a linear narrative–like principle at work in the sequencing of these psalms. But if the above analysis is sound, such interpretations are misguided; they are predicated upon a misunderstanding of the organizing principle that structures these psalms.[68] As we shall see, progressive repetition surfaces time and again as the principle governing psalm sequencing in this collection.

---

67. See pp. 36–7.

68. One might conceivably object that a linear principle is not at odds with, but can complement, the parallel structuration suggested here (in this connection, see Peter C. W. Ho, *The Design of the Psalter: A Macrostructural Analysis* [Eugene, OR: Pickwick, 2019], 165). While such may be the case with certain types of parallelism, it is excluded here. Progressive repetition is *by definition* a nonlinear structuring principle.

Chapter 5

PSALMS 77–78: THE LORD IS GRACIOUS AND COMPASSIONATE—DESPITE CONFLICTING EVIDENCE

In this chapter we continue our investigation of the design of Psalms 73–83. The main argument here is that Psalms 77–78 is a second psalm sequence that stands in a deliberate parallel relationship with Psalm 73. As will become clear in the course of the analysis, the design of this second grouping bears a striking resemblance to the first.

Analysis of Psalms 77 and 78

We begin once again with a concise analysis of the psalms under consideration.

Psalm 77

The focus on national deliverance (i.e., the Exodus event) in this lament (vv. 12–21) suggests that "the 'I' of Psalm 77 speaks on behalf of the nation."[1] The particular occasion of the lament is unspecified, the psalmist mentioning only the "day of my distress" (v. 3). It becomes clear as the psalm progresses that the major problem is an apparent incongruity between "faith" and "experience." Thus, like Psalm 74, Psalm 77 is one of the "God-laments."[2]

Similar to Psalm 74, Psalm 77 appears to be concentrically arranged, with multiple God-laments at its center:[3]

---

1. Craig C. Broyles, *The Conflict of Faith and Experience in the Psalms: A Form-Critical and Theological Study*, JSOTSup 52 (Sheffield: Sheffield Academic Press, 1989), 155; Mitchell Dahood, *Psalms II: 51–100*, Anchor Bible Commentary (Garden City, NY: Doubleday, 1968), 224.

2. See Broyles's discussion of this psalm in ibid., 154–7.

3. What follows is an adaptation of the structural proposal in Beat Weber, *Psalm 77 und sein Umfeld: Eine poetologische Studie*, BBB 103 (Weinheim: Beltz Athenäum, 1995), 40–184. The key structural indicators are the verbs זכר ("to remember") and שיח ("to meditate/muse") in vv. 4, 7, 12–13 in conjunction with סלה ("Selah"), which marks the conclusion of a section in vv. 4, 10, and 16. The shift to questions in v. 8 marks the beginning of the psalm's central section. The

A1. Description of (unanswered) cry for intervention (vv. 2–4)
   B1. Reflection on God's past deeds (vv. 5–7)
      C. Interrogative God-laments (vv. 8–10)
   B2. Reflection on God's deeds (vv. 11–16)
A2. Exodus theophany aimed at intervention (vv. 17–21)

The psalmist recounts in verses 2–3 that God has been unresponsive in the face of continual appeals to "hear" (v. 3).[4] In this context, "remembering (זכר)" and "pondering (שׂיח)" of God and the "days of old, years of long ago" (v. 6) only exacerbate the psalmist's distress, producing not comfort but groaning (המה) and faintness (עטף) of soul (v. 4). The psalmist voices the central theological dilemma confronting him in a series of questions at the psalm's axis:

Will the Lord reject forever,
   and not again be favorable?
Has his lovingkindness ceased?
   Has his promise come to an end for all generations?
Has God forgotten to be gracious?
   Has he shut up his compassion in anger? (Ps 77:8–10)

---

major adaptations of Weber's proposal are as follows: (1) I have taken vv. 11–16 as a single strophe instead of Weber's two (11–13; 14–16 [Weber, *Psalm 77 und sein Umfeld*, 94–137]). This strophe is bracketed by references to God's "right hand" (v. 11) and "arm" (v. 16). And the references to God's "work/deeds" in vv. 12–13 and "wonders" in v. 15 argue for the unity of vv. 11–16; (2) I have also taken vv. 17–21 as a single strophe, instead of Weber's two (17–19, 20–21 [Weber, *Psalm 77 und sein Umfeld*, 138–73]). I see no good textual reason for a division in the middle of the theophanic vision that unifies vv. 17–21; and (3) based upon the previous two decisions, vv. 8–10 form the hinge of the psalm. This contrasts with Weber's view that vv. 11–13 form the hinge section (*Scharnierglied*). Weber, *Psalm 77 und sein Umfeld*, 179. The structural centrality of these questions in the psalm reflects their theological centrality. Others have made similar observations about the importance of questions in vv. 8–10. See, for example, J. S. Kselman, "Psalm 77 and the Book of Exodus," *JANESCU* 15 (1983): 51–8; Marvin E. Tate, *Psalms 51–100*, Word Biblical Commentary (Nashville, TN: Thomas Nelson, 1990), 273.

4. The Hebrew of v. 2 is קולי אל אלהים ואצעקה קולי אל אלהים והאזין אלי ("My voice to God and I will cry out, my voice to God that he will hear me"). The *yiqtol* אקרא ("I will call out") has most likely been elided in each line: "my voice to God (I will call out) and I will cry out! My voice to God (I will call out) in order that he will hear me!" See Ps 3:5 (קולי אל יהוה אקרא). The form והאזין (which I have taken as a *hipʿil weyiqtol*) indicates the purpose of the "calling out" after the gapped אקרא, namely, in order that God would hear the psalmist. This is not a direct address to God but a third person musing on the psalmist's continual address to God (to no avail). The predominance of the first singular and third-person references to God in vv. 1–11 (see vv. 2, 4, 9–11) suggests that these verses are best taken as the personal meditations/musings of the psalmist. The shift in appeal from personal meditations to addressing God comes in v. 12. From then on the second-person address to God dominates.

Unlike those in Psalm 74, the third-person nature of these questions suggests that they are *real* (i.e., not rhetorical) questions reflecting the inner pondering of the psalmist/community.⁵ Reflection on the past only exacerbated the psalmist's anguish because it impressed upon him the massive "discrepancy between divine activity in the past and the lack of intervention in the present."⁶ God's prolonged inactivity, a manifestation of Divine anger (אָף) (v. 10), raised the question of whether God had rejected (זנח) his people forever (v. 8). This in turn seemed to contradict God's past self-revelation as a God characterized by lovingkindness, promise keeping, graciousness, and compassion (vv. 9–10).

John Kselman has shown that the questions in verses 9–10 are framed in terms of the foundational Israelite credo of Exodus 34:6-7—but they strikingly refute it point by point.⁷ The clear implication of this intertextual reference is that God's behavior amid the present circumstances appeared to undermine Israel's most basic beliefs about God, as God himself had revealed it. Verse 11 is really the shocking climax of the questions in verses 8–10: God's mighty "right hand," and so God himself, had apparently changed.

Many have detected a change in mood/perspective/understanding in verses 12–21; from questioning, doubt, and confusion, to confident trust and resolution of the dilemma in verses 8–11.⁸ Along these lines, some (e.g., Kselman) argue that verses 12–21 give a positive answer to the questions of verses 9–10. Remembrance of the great Exodus redemption provides assurance that God's loyal love/compassion has not ceased.

---

5. Broyles, *The Conflict of Faith and Experience in the Psalms*, 155–6.

6. Frank-Lothar Hossfeld and Erich Zenger, *Psalms 2: A Commentary on Psalms 51–100*, trans. Linda M. Maloney, Hermeneia (Minneapolis, MN: Fortress Press, 2005), 280.

7. Compare: "a God compassionate and gracious (אל רחום וחנון), slow to anger (ארך אפים) and great in steadfast love (חסד) and faithfulness, keeping steadfast love (חסד) for thousands, forgiving iniquity" (Exod 34:6-7) with "Has his [God's] steadfast love (חסד) ceased forever? Has God (אל) forgotten to be gracious (חנות)? Has he shut up his compassion (רחמיו) in anger (אף)?" See Kselman, "Psalm 77 and the Book of Exodus," for discussion. See also Adam D. Hensley, *Covenant Relationships and the Editing of the Hebrew Psalter*, LHBOTS 666 (London: Bloomsbury T&T Clark, 2018), 214–17. As mentioned in Chapter 3, the foundational nature of this credo is indicated by the many echoes of it in the Hebrew Bible. For only a few, see Num 14:18; 2 Chr 30:9; Neh 9:17; Pss 86:5, 15; 103:8; 111:4; 112:4; 116:5; 145:8; Joel 2:13.

8. See Walter Brueggemann, *The Psalms and the Life of Faith*, ed. Patrick D. Miller (Minneapolis, MN: Fortress, 1995), 258–67; Kselman, "Psalm 77 and the Book of Exodus," 51–8; Lawrence Boadt, "The Use of 'Panels' in the Structure of Psalms 73–78," *CBQ* 66 (2004): 544–6; Millard does not speak of "resolution" but clearly understands these closing verses as primarily creating the anticipation of God's future saving intervention. Matthias Millard, *Die Komposition des Psalters: Ein Formgeschichtlicher Ansatz*, FAT 9 (Tübingen: Mohr Siebeck, 1994), 101. The same is true of Weber: "Ps 77 schliesst mit der Zuversichtsaussage, dass Jahwe sein Volk wie eine Herde durch die Vermittlung von Mose und Aaron führ(t)e." Weber, *Psalm 77 und sein Umfeld*, 289.

But the remembrance of God's past wonders (vv. 12–13) and the hymn recalling the Exodus event (vv. 14–21) more likely continue "the painful reflection of vv. 4–11 on God's failure to duplicate his great works in the present."[9] The repetition of vocabulary from these earlier verses supports this point (זכר and שיח in vv. 12–13 [see v. 7]). These closing verses are better interpreted as a shift in appeal rather than mood.[10] The psalmist shifts from speaking primarily *about* God (vv. 2–11) to speaking directly *to* God (vv. 14–21).

So, while this section certainly moves in the direction of resolution and a corresponding change in mood/understanding/perspective, this movement is not completed within the psalm itself. The reflection on God's past deeds in verses 12–21, therefore, "does not eliminate or solve the discrepancy between divine activity in the past and the lack of intervention in the present."[11] Consequently, as the psalm comes to a close, the searching questions of verses 8–10 are left open-ended and unanswered. The psalmist stands "at the threshold of a new understanding but has not entered."[12]

Broyles helpfully observes that the entirety of Psalm 77 functions as an appeal. The psalm has no formal petition, and lament is only directly addressed to God in verse 5. But, as Broyles points out, the turn to God in the closing verses indicates that the psalm as a whole has been uttered in God's presence. In this way, the *entire psalm* functions as an appeal for Yahweh to actualize the "praise" recounted in verses 14–21.[13]

Psalm 78

Richard J. Clifford has offered a compelling structural analysis of Psalm 78.[14] The major contours of his study are followed here with minor modifications. Clifford

---

9. Tate, *Psalms 51–100*, 275.

10. Broyles, *The Conflict of Faith and Experience in the Psalms*, 156. Others also detect no shift in mood in these verses. See, for example, Tate, *Psalms 51–100*, 275–6.

11. Hossfeld and Zenger, *Psalms 2*, 280.

12. Tate, *Psalms 51–100*, 276.

13. Broyles, *The Conflict of Faith and Experience in the Psalms*, 157.

14. See Richard J. Clifford, "In Zion and David a New Beginning: An Interpretation of Psalm 78," in *Traditions in Transformation: Turning Points in Biblical Faith*, ed. B. Halpern and Jon D. Levenson (Winona Lake, IN: Eisenbrauns, 1981), 121–41. Many studies have adopted Clifford's structuration, though with minor modifications. For example, Tate, *Psalms 51–100*, 287–8; James L. Mays, *Psalms*, Interpretation (Louisville, KY: Westminster/John Knox Press, 1994), 201; Stephen Dunn, "Wisdom Editing in the Book of Psalms: Vocabulary, Themes, and Structures" (PhD diss., Marquette University, 2009), 87, accessed August 21, 2018, https://epublications.marquette.edu/cgi/viewcontent.cgi?article=1012&context=dissertations_mu. Unlike Clifford, however, Dunn believes that Ps 78 is using Israel's history as "wisdom instruction." Dunn, "Wisdom Editing in the Book of Psalms," 88.

shows that the psalm consists of an introduction followed by two parallel historical recitals. Both climax in "a sequel in which divine merciful response is depicted":[15]

Introduction to Psalm (vv. 1–8)[16]	
First recital:	Second recital:
Preface to first recital (vv. 9–12)	Preface to second recital (vv. 40–43)[17]
Wilderness events (vv. 13–32)	From Egypt to Canaan (vv. 44–64)
Gracious act (vv. 13–16)	Gracious act (vv. 44–55)
Rebellion (vv. 17–20)	Rebellion (vv. 56–58)[18]
Divine anger and punishment (manna and quail) (vv. 21–32)	Divine anger and punishment[19] (destruction of Shiloh) (vv. 59–64)
Sequel (vv. 33–39)	Sequel (vv. 65–72)

The psalm opens with an authoritative Mosaic-esque command to God's people (v. 1): "Hear (האזינה), O my people, my teaching; incline your ear to the words of my mouth!"[20] This teaching is what the psalmist and his generation have received

---

15. Clifford, "In Zion and David a New Beginning," 129.

16. Clifford contends that the introduction consists of vv. 1–11. But the rebellion of the "sons of Ephraim" in vv. 9–11 is better taken as the opening verses of the first recital. The parallels between vv. 9–12 and the opening verses of the second recital (vv. 40–43) confirm this point: וישכחו עלילותיו ("they forgot his deeds") (v. 11) and לא זכרו את ידו ("They did not remember his hand") (v. 42); מצרים ... שדה צען ("Egypt ... field of Zoan") (see vv. 12, 43). Thus, vv. 9–12 and vv. 40–43 function as prefaces to the two parallel recitals aimed at accomplishing the purpose set forth in the introduction of vv. 1–8: encouraging later generations to not respond "like their fathers" to God's great deeds but rather look to these deeds as a basis for confident trust in (and so obedience to) God. The many parallels in vocabulary between vv. 1–8 and the two recitals confirm this point (e.g., "so that ... they [i.e., later generations] might not forget the deeds of God" [ולא ישכחו מעללי אל] [v. 8]; "They [i.e., earlier generations] forgot his deeds" [וישכחו עלילותיו] [v. 11]; "They [i.e., earlier generations] did not remember his hand" [לא זכרו את ידו] [v. 42]).

17. Various lexical repetitions highlight the parallel nature of these sections. See the previous footnote and the following discussion for examples.

18. Lexical repetitions between the opening verses highlight the parallel nature of these sections. See מרה ("to rebel") and נסה ("to test"), and עליון ("Most High") in vv. 17–18, 56.

19. The parallel nature of these sections is indicated by the exact repetition of the same sentence in their opening verses. See שמע יהוה ויתעבר ("God heard and became angry") in vv. 21 and 59.

20. Clifford rightly notes that this command, and the wisdom-like elements that follow (see "parable"; "riddles of old"), does not indicate that the speaker of Ps 78 is a wise man or that Ps 78 is a "wisdom psalm." A better comparison is with the book of Deuteronomy, and in particular the "Song of Moses" in Deut 32:1–43 (cf., Ps 78:1–2 and Deut 32:1–3): "The speaker of the psalm, then, is not a wise man solving riddles or merely teaching a lesson from history. He authoritatively restates the traditions so that Israel will be able to decide for Yahweh." Clifford, "In Zion and David a New Beginning," 131. See also Weber, *Psalm 77 und sein Umfeld*, 289–90. In light of these observations, Millard's classification of Ps 78

from previous generations of Israelites. They are to pass it on to subsequent generations who are to do likewise (vv. 4 and 6). In terms of content, the instruction consists of two parallel accounts of the God–Israel relationship: God performs great deeds for Israel (vv. 12–16; 44–55); the people respond with rebellion (vv. 17–20; 56–58); God's anger is provoked and the people are punished (vv. 21–31; 59–64); God's response is ultimately one of compassion (vv. 38–39; 65–72).

Verses 5–8 show that this teaching has a definite goal, namely, that later generations trust and obey God on the basis of his wonders—not forget them like their rebellious and unbelieving forefathers (vv. 6–8). The psalmist achieves this goal largely by showing how the unbelieving response of this "stubborn and rebellious generation" (v. 8) kindled God's anger/wrath and led to their punishment. Each recital, however, does not climax in God's anger. They instead culminate in God's compassionate response to Israel in accordance with the foundational credo of Exodus 34:6–7.

The first "recital" (vv. 13–32) contains traditions from the Pentateuch but restructures them. It recounts God's gracious acts in the Exodus event, God's leading the people in the wilderness, and his miraculous provision for them there (vv. 12–16). The next two sections (vv. 17–32) form a structural unit, which explains that, despite the "wonders" (v. 4) just recounted, the people "sinned again." They consequently incurred God's anger and judgment (vv. 21–32). The heart of the matter is that God's people rebelled and failed to trust in his salvation (vv. 17, 22, 32; see v. 8).[21] The message is clear: later generations should respond by placing their trust in God and obeying him (vv. 4–8).

The concluding verses of the first recital (vv. 33–39) are a "sequel" that represent a break in the narrative. As mentioned earlier, they climax in God's compassionate response to his people despite their persistent infidelity:[22]

But he is compassionate (רחום); he atones for iniquity (עון)
    and he does not destroy.
He holds back his anger (אף) often,
    and he does not arouse all of his wrath. (Ps 78:38)

---

as a "*weisheitspsalm*" ("wisdom psalm") (Millard, *Die Komposition des Psalters*, 90) misses the mark.

21. See אמן ("to believe/trust") in vv. 8, 22, and 32; מרה ("to rebel") in vv. 8, 17.

22. The clause type heading v. 38 indicates a break in the narrative. The verbless/nominal clause (on this issue, see Cynthia L. Miller, ed., *The Verbless Clause in Biblical Hebrew: Linguistic Approaches*, LSAWS 1 [Winona Lake, IN: Eisenbrauns, 1999]) והוא רחום does not describe a narrative event. It gives a static description of God: "But/yet he is compassionate." Like Clifford, Hossfeld and Zenger (*Psalms 2*, 283, 297), and others, I take the *yiqtols* of v. 38 (יכפר, ישחית, and יעיר) as generalizing statements about God: "He *atones* for iniquity … he *does not destroy* … he *does not arouse* all of his wrath." Another option is to take them as past frequentive. See S. R. Driver, *A Treatise on the Use of the Tenses in Hebrew and Some Other Syntactical Questions* (Grand Rapids, MI: Eerdmans, 1998), 127–8.

This verse gives "a thematic description of God's nature, in stylistic and lexical dependence on the credo in Exod 34:6–7"[23] ("The Lord, the Lord, a compassionate [רחום] God ... slow to anger [אף] ... forgiving iniquity [עון] ..."). Thus, like the psalmist of Psalm 77 (vv. 9–10), the psalmist of Psalm 78 alludes to Exodus 34:6–7 at a pivotal structural location in the psalm. Here the point of the allusion is to indicate that, in showing Israel compassion, God had acted in accordance with his self-revelation to Israel in Exodus 34:6–7. For this reason, God did not utterly destroy his people but held back the full force of his wrath.

A second recital parallels the first (vv. 40–64). Clifford observes that verses 44–55 are arranged after the pattern found in Exodus 15:1–18. They describe God's gracious acts of redeeming Israel from Egypt, bringing them to his "holy territory (i.e., Canaan)," and deciding to dwell with them at the Shiloh sanctuary (i.e., "this mountain your right hand bought" [v. 54]).[24] Israel's "rebellion" (vv. 56–58) and the resultant "Divine anger and punishment" (vv. 59–64) correspond to that of verses 17–32. The consequence of Israel's rebellion was that God forsook his dwelling place at Shiloh ("the tent where he dwelled with man [אהל שכן באדם]") (v. 60) and gave his people over to the adversary (vv. 61–64). These negative consequences are intended to deter later generations of God's people from responding to God's great wonders in the same way (vv. 4–8).

A second "sequel" parallel to the first (vv. 33–39) follows (vv. 65–72). It pulls double duty as the climax of both the second recital and the psalm as a whole. This sequel likewise recounts God's compassionate decision to continue in relationship with his wayward people, emphasizing that God does not *permanently* remove his presence from them. As Clifford notes, verses 33–39 spoke in general terms about God's mercy toward Israel. But here in verses 65–72, God's mercy is specified in the selection of Judah, Zion, and David.

Significantly, this parallel with the first recital reveals that God's compassionate response described in verses 65–72 is a further, more specific, outworking of the foundational credo of Exodus 34:6–7 (see vv. 38–39). Thus, the structural location and corresponding literary function of allusions to Exodus 34:6–7 demonstrate this credo's significant role in Psalm 78: it is presented as the foundation for God's merciful decision to continue in relationship with his rebellious people from their inception to the time of David.

The closing verses explain that, in spite of Israel's persistent rebellion, God "awoke" to defeat their adversaries. He chose the tribe of Judah (not the tribe of Ephraim [v. 67]) and Mount Zion. Here, God set up a new dwelling place that was more firmly established than the Shiloh sanctuary (v. 69). The language here (i.e., vv. 68 and 71) evokes that of verses 52, 54, and 55, which describe God's former dwelling place at Shiloh (135).

---

23. Hossfeld and Zenger, *Psalms 2*, 297. Hensley also highlights the allusion to Exod 34:6–7 in 78:38. Hensley, *Covenant Relationships and the Editing of the Hebrew Psalter*, 216.
24. Clifford, "In Zion and David a New Beginning," 133.

The purpose of these verses is not to stress that God had rejected northern tribes in favor of the southern (and their respective sanctuaries), as has commonly been claimed. The point is instead that "the destruction of one shrine does not mean that God will not choose another" (135). This "sequel" is not about God's choice of one tribe over another; it is about God's willingness to continue to dwell among "all Israel"—despite their persistent sinfulness and disobedience. Clifford summarizes this point well:

> The first [sequel] ... spoke in general terms of Yahweh's merciful intent to forgive sin and not destroy, his willingness to live with a persistently sinful people. Here [i.e., the second "sequel"], that same merciful intent is specified in the selection of Judah, Zion, and David. The destruction of Shiloh does not mean the end of the sanctuary in Israel's midst. God begins a fresh mercy in Zion-Jerusalem.[25]

Clifford argues that the psalm's overall intent is to celebrate "God's merciful choice of Zion and David as the continuation today of the ancient shrine celebrating the exodus and conquest tradition. It unites the old sacred epic with the new religious tradition of the choice of Zion and David" (137). He therefore suggests that the closest parallels in the MT Psalter in terms of genre are other psalms that celebrate Zion (e.g., Pss 2, 46, 48, and 76) (137).

Clifford's observations here are helpful; he is right to ascribe such importance to God's choice of David and Zion in the psalm's overall purpose. But, at the same time, the introduction (vv. 1–8) suggests that Psalm 78 also has a more general purpose in view: to encourage later generations to trust in God on the basis of his unwavering faithfulness to a persistently rebellious people, from their inception to the time of David. And, as we have seen, this unrelenting faithfulness traces back to God's gracious character as revealed in Exodus 34:6–7.

Before leaving the discussion of Psalm 78, an important aspect of Clifford's analysis deserves to be reiterated given the history of this psalm's interpretation: Psalm 78 is not about a specific tribe. Clifford rightly points out that the Ephraimite defeat is an instance of *all* Israel's infidelity. Further, the destruction of God's dwelling place at Shiloh "is a punishment dealt to all Israel. The tribe of Ephraim/Joseph is no longer the site of the shrine. Judah is the new location. The northern tribes per se are not rejected."[26] Psalm 78 is about God's remarkably merciful choice to continue dwelling among *all* Israel in light of their continual sin and rebellion.

---

25. Ibid., 136–7.

26. Ibid., 132. Clifford rightly points out here that "their forefathers (אבותם)" in v. 8 has in view all of the Israelite tribes, and that "in vv. 21, 31, 33, 55, 59, and 72, Jacob/Israel designates the whole people, not only the northern tribes."

Table 5.1 Analogous Literary Progression of Psalm 73 and Psalms 77–78

Core aspect of Israelite "faith" challenged	Confrontation with a severe conflict of faith and experience	Radical shift in perspective on God's posture/involvement
God's goodness Exodus 34:6–7	Psalm 73:1–16 Psalm 77	Psalm 73:18–28 Psalm 78

Formal Correspondence with Psalm 73: Evidence

The evidence offered here mirrors that which was presented for Psalms 74–76 in Chapter 4.

Analogous Literary Progression

The major literary progression of Psalm 73 is repeated for a second time in the sequence of Psalms 77–78. In Table 5.1, Psalm 77 corresponds to the first part of this progression (73:1–16) and Psalm 78 to the second (73:18–28).

Like Psalm 74, Psalm 77 centers on the same fundamental theological dilemma as Psalm 73 (column 2): the focus is that God's prolonged inactivity has resulted in the perception of a severe conflict between faith and experience. In Psalm 77, the psalmist/community experiences the prolonged absence of God's saving activity (experience) as suggesting that the gracious and compassionate God, the One who keeps steadfast love to *all* generations, who does not reject forever or remain *permanently* angry (faith), has changed (77:8–11). This disorienting experience posed a severe threat to the core Israelite credo of Exodus 34:6–7 (column 1).

The transition to Psalm 78 marks a radical shift in perspective that mirrors the inner-psalm progression to verses 18–28 in Psalm 73 (column 3). In stark contrast to the community's perception of God in Psalm 77, the Divine profile promoted in Psalm 78's didactic historical recital is a God who *is*—not merely *was*—gracious and compassionate (v. 38), a God who *restrains* his anger (v. 38) and who does *not* permanently reject his people (vv. 59–72). Whereas in Psalm 77 Israel's "experience" appeared to undermine the theology of Exodus 34:6–7 (vv. 8–10), in Psalm 78 Israel's "faith" (i.e., the history of God's dealings with his people) aims to generate confidence in its enduring reliability among all generations (vv. 38; 65–72).[27]

---

27. In this connection, the reader should recall that both psalms contain an intertextual reference to this credo (i.e., 77:8–9; 78:38). Further, it should be remembered that God's gracious act in 78:65–72 is portrayed as a specific outworking of this credo in Israel's history. See the earlier brief exegesis of these psalms for details.

Thus, like Psalms 74–76 before it, this psalm sequence also mirrors the major literary progression of Psalm 73 in terms of the distinctive conceptual/semantic relationship between the psalm's two main halves.

Analogous Network of Parallels

Notably, we find in this sequence as well a group of repetitions following the same pattern as those McCann detected in Psalm 73. As observed in relation to Psalms 74–76, this finding is particularly noteworthy in light of the conceptual/semantic correspondence with Psalm 73 already discovered. Consider Table 5.2.

Table 5.2 shows that a group of linguistic features occurring in Psalm 77 is repeated in Psalm 78. These repetitions resemble the rhetorical device in Psalm 73

Table 5.2 Parallels between Psalm 77 and Psalm 78

Parallel	Psalm 77	Psalm 78
Theme of God's past deeds	Focuses on discrepancy between God's past saving activity and present inactivity (vv. 8–10)	Central purpose is to pass down God's past deeds as basis for confidence in God and obedience to him (vv. 4–8)
The Divine title אדון ("Lord")	"Will the *Lord* reject forever?" (v. 8)	"The *Lord* awoke from sleep … and smote his adversaries." (vv. 65–72)
דור ("generation")/motif of "the connection of generations"	"Has his promise ended for all *generations*?" (lit. for generation and generation") (v. 9)	"… declaring to a later *generation* the praiseworthy deeds of God, his strength and the wonders he has done." (v. 4); "He (i.e., God) commanded our fathers to make them known to their sons so that a later *generation* … might rise up and declare them to their sons, that they might set their confidence in God." (vv. 5–7); "that they not be like their fathers, a stubborn and rebellious *generation*, a *generation* whose heart was not established. …" (vv. 7–8)
The antonyms שכח ("to forget")/זכר ("to remember") (*God as subject)	"Has God *forgotten* to be gracious?" (v. 10)	"He (i.e., God) *remembered* that they are flesh." (v. 39)
ימין יד / יד ("right hand"/"hand")	"My sickness is this: the changing of the *right hand* of the Most High." (v. 11)	"He brought them to the border of his holy land, the mountain that his *right hand* acquired." (v. 54); "They did not remember his *hand*, the day he redeemed them from the adversary." (v. 42)
רחם ("compassion")/אף ("anger")	"Has he shut up his *compassion* in *anger*? (v. 10)	"But he is *compassionate* … he holds/held back his *anger* often." (v. 38)
The credo of Exodus 34:6–7	Enduring reliability severely undermined by lived experience (77:8–11)	Enduring reliability established from Israelite history (78:38–39; 65–72)

by marking the radical shift in perspective observable in the progression to Psalm 78. A brief consideration of each bears this point out.

1. In Psalm 77 the prolonged absence of God's saving deeds *undermines* the community's confidence in God (vv. 8–11). On the other hand, the central purpose of Psalm 78's didactic retelling of Israelite history is to *evoke confidence* in God and obedience to him on the basis of such deeds (vv. 4–8).
2. In Psalm 77 the psalmist perceives that the Lord (אדון) has rejected Israel *forever* in anger (v. 8). But Psalm 78 recounts how the Lord (אדון) rejected Israel *only temporarily* in anger. The Lord then reestablished his presence among Israel more firmly than before (i.e., in the choice of David/Zion) (v. 65; see vv. 59–72).
3. The psalmist of Psalm 77 perceives that God's promise has ended with the present generation (דור) (v. 9). However, Psalm 78 sets forth God's past deeds as the basis for confidence in God among all generations (דור) (vv. 4, 6, 8).
4. In Psalm 77 God's absence results in questioning whether God has *"forgotten"* (שכח) to be gracious to Israel (v. 10). Psalm 78 recounts how God graciously stayed his anger because, time and again, he *"remembered"* (זכר) Israel's frailty and mortality (v. 39).
5. In Psalm 77, God's prolonged absence implies that his "right hand" (ימין) has changed (v. 11). By way of contrast, Psalm 78 emphasizes the great wonders that God's mighty "right hand" (ימין) (v. 54)/"hand" (יד) has accomplished (v. 42) for Israel throughout her history, and despite her unfaithfulness (i.e., the Exodus and conquest/settlement).
6. Psalm 77 laments that God's compassion (רחמים) has been shut up in his anger (77:10) (אף). Psalm 78, however, reminds the reader that Divine compassion (רחום)—not anger (אף)—(v. 38) has had the final word throughout Israel's history.
7. Psalm 77 centers on the psalmist's perception that God's prolonged absence was *severely undermining* the enduring reliability of Exodus 34:6–7 (see vv. 8–10). Psalm 78, however, *establishes* this credo's reliability throughout Israel's history; its theology is set forth as the basis of God's continued relationship with Israel from their inception to the time of David (see vv. 38–39; 65–72).[28]

The above seven links thus follow the consistent pattern observed in both Psalm 73 and the grouping of Psalms 74–76. Each marks the radical shift in the psalmist's perspective on God from the preceding literary unit, which in this case is Psalm 77. It is, therefore, unsurprising that these repetitions point to the

---

28. Even though the words רחם and אף just discussed reflect this link in both psalms (i.e., the credo of Exod 34:6–7), I list it separately because the influence of the credo is not limited to these two words in Ps 78. As we have seen, the psalm's parallel structure indicates that God's gracious act recounted in vv. 65–72 is meant to be seen as a specific outworking of this credo in Israel's history.

same conclusion reached in the last chapter: their number and consistent pattern suggest intentionality and thus further corroborate a deliberate relationship with Psalm 73.[29]

Further support for this point comes from evaluating the links in light of the principles/criteria of Chapter 1. Each is discussed in the order presented above.

1. The theme of God's past saving deeds in Israel's history predominates in both Psalms 77 and 78. This emphasis is noticeably absent from the following Psalm 79. Psalm 77 centers on the disparity of God's past saving activity and present inactivity. Psalm 78, the second largest psalm in the MT Psalter (next to Ps 119), is a massive recital of God's past saving deeds in history (78:4). This theme is arguably the major conjunctive feature between these adjacent psalms.
2. Corroborating the intentionality of the above theme is the observation that it is articulated with similar roots, words, phrases, and motifs in both psalms. Each contains (but is not limited to) the following:[30] the Exodus motif (77:14–21; 78:12–13; 42–55); the phrase "from of old (מקדם/מני קדם)" (77:6, 12; 78:2); the phrase "deeds of God/Yah" (see מעללי יה in 77:12, מעללי אל in 78:7);[31] the noun עלילה ("deed") (77:13; 78:11);[32] words built from the root עזז ("to be strong") (77:15; 78:4, 26, 61);[33] words built from the root פלא ("to be wonderful") (77:12, 15; 78:4, 11, 12, 32).[34] In both psalms this root also occurs in a description of God containing the verb עשה ("to do/make"): "You are a God who works wonders" (77:15) (עשה פלא); "His [God's] wonders that he has done" (פלאותיו אשר עשה in 78:4); references to God's "right hand (ימין)" as effecting deliverance (77:11; 78:54);[35] use of the root גאל ("to redeem") to refer to God as "redeeming" Israel or as Israel's "redeemer" (77:16; 78:35 [see also פדה in 78:42]).[36]
3. The occurrences of the Divine title אדון ("Lord") in these adjacent psalms (Pss 77:3, 8; 78:65) account for three of the six total in Psalms 73–83. Further

---

29. In the present case as well "amount of links" is considered a mark of intentionality, since all conform to the same pattern.

30. For other potentially significant links in this connection, see Hossfeld and Zenger, *Psalms 2*, 293.

31. These phrases (or the noun מעלל ["deed"]) occur nowhere else in Pss 73–83.

32. These are the only two occurrences of the noun in Pss 73–83.

33. Words built from this root only occur two other times in Pss 73–83 (74:13; 81:2).

34. These instances account for six of the seven total occurrences of the root פלא in Pss 73–83 (the other being 75:2).

35. References to God's "right hand" only appear in two other Asaph psalms (74:11; 80:16, 18).

36. This verb only occurs once elsewhere in Pss 73–83 (74:2). Outside of the Asaph psalms, it only appears in seven other psalms in the MT Psalter (Pss 19:15; 69:19; 72:14; 103:4; 106:10; 107:2 [2×]; 119:154).

suggesting intentionality is the observation that this title (1) occurs only once in the lengthy Psalm 78, and (2) appears at structurally and theologically significant locations in each psalm: the questions articulating the major theological dilemma of Psalm 77 (vv. 8–10 [see v. 8]); the second "sequel" of Psalm 78 (vv. 65–72).

4. The motif of "the connection of generations" is central in both psalms.[37] In each case, it is reflected in the noun דור ("generation") (77:9; 78:4, 6, 8). This motif is absent from the surrounding psalms, only appearing in two others in the collection (see 73:25 and 79:13).
5. The question "Has God forgotten (שכח) to be gracious?" (77:10) occurs at the structural and theological center of Psalm 77 (vv. 8–11). The semantically related statement that "God remembered" (v. 39) Israel on account of their frailty occurs at an analogous location in Psalm 78 (i.e., the psalm's prominent first "sequel").
6. After Psalm 78, there are only two other references to God's mighty "hand" (יד) (78:42) in the collection, and these come in adjacent psalms (80:17; 81:15). Only one other remaining psalm contains a reference to God's "right hand" (80:15, 17; cp. 77:10; 78:54). Strengthening this parallel's intentionality is: (1) its occurrence at the prominent structural center of Psalm 77 (v. 10); and (2) two other groupings in the collection contain a similar link (i.e., 74–76; 80–81). As noted in relation to Psalms 74–76, such consistency in the collection suggests intentionality.
7. Apart from these adjacent psalms, a word built from the root רחם (see Pss 77:10; 78:38) appears only one other time in the collection (79:8). Further, in both psalms, רחם and אף are part of an allusion to Exodus 34:6–7. Finally, these links also occur at a structurally and theologically significant location in each psalm (77:8–11; the first "sequel" of Ps 78).
8. Both psalms not only contain an intertextual reference to Exodus 34:6–7, but this allusion also shapes each psalm in a significant way: in Psalm 77 the central theological dilemma is articulated in terms of this credo (so Kselman; see the exegesis above); in Psalm 78 its theology is set forth as the basis of God's compassion toward Israel from the Sinai desert to David (see the exegesis above).

These observations further corroborate the intentionality of the repetitions in Table 5.2. As such, they provide deeper roots for the deliberate literary correspondence I am arguing for with Psalm 73.

I should point out that I am not claiming that these are the *only* links reflecting the deliberate juxtaposition of Psalms 77 and 78. My argument is that these are the most valuable for understanding the collection's distinctive design since they tacitly reveal a deliberate correspondence with the opening Psalm 73. As noted in Chapter 1, the goal here is not simply to amass links between psalms, even

---

37. Hossfeld and Zenger, *Psalms 2*, 293.

apparently deliberate ones. It is to identify those most significant for bringing the contours of the collection's shape into focus.

That being said, other significant links are still relevant. While these are more peripheral in terms of their ability to establish a deliberate relationship with Psalm 73,[38] they nevertheless further evince the deliberate juxtaposition of Psalms 77 and 78. Consider, for example, the following connections:

1. Four of the five occurrences of the verb נחה ("to lead") in Psalms 73–83 appear in these adjacent psalms (77:21; 78:14, 53, 72).
2. These adjacent psalms contain three of the four occurrences of the root אזן ("to hear") in Psalms 73–83 (77:2; 78:1 [2×]). More specifically, each contains a verb in the *hip'il* stem built from this root (האזין in 77:2; האזינה in 78:1). The remaining occurrence of the root comes in 80:2 (האזינה).
3. Confirming the first two links as likely intentional is the observation that they are part of a striking structural parallel. Psalms 77 and 78: (1) both have the verb אזן in the *hip'il* stem in their opening verses (77:2; 78:1); and (2) the final verse of each (77:21; 78:72) is a statement containing the verb נחה ("to lead") in the context of a shepherd metaphor. In both cases, God "leads" his people by the "hand(s)" of one or more prominent figures from Israel's past ("You [God] led [נחה] your people like a flock by the hand [יד] of Moses and Aaron" [77:21]; "He [David] shepherded them with an upright heart, and led [נחה] them with the skillfulness of his hands [78:72] [כפיו]").[39]
4. As Weber points out, Psalm 77 ends with a reference to Moses (v. 21), and Psalm 78 begins with a clear reference (*deutlichen Bezug*) to the Song of Moses in Deuteronomy 32 (78:1).[40] This type of "tail-head linkage" clearly resembles (and is, consequently, corroborated by) the technique used to link two distinct but related narratives.[41]
5. The only two occurrences of the noun שנה ("year") in Psalms 73–83 are in these adjacent psalms (77:6; 78:33). Surprisingly, this common Hebrew noun only occurs in six other psalms in the MT Psalter (Pss 31:11; 61:7; 65:12; 90:4, 9, 10 [3×], 15; 95:10; 102:25, 28).

---

38. This is not technically true of נחה. It actually performs both functions. See the discussion in the next section.

39. Others have observed this structural parallel as well. See Weber, *Psalm 77 und sein Umfeld*, 289; Robert L. Cole, *The Shape and Message of Book III (Psalms 73–89)*, JSOTSup 307 (Sheffield: Sheffield Academic Press, 2000), 60.

40. Weber, *Psalm 77 und sein Umfeld*, 290.

41. For example, the clause אחרי מות יהושע ("after the death of Joshua") in Judg 1:1 and the reference Joshua's death in Josh 24:29 (וימת יהושע ["And Joshua died"]) binds the narrative of Judges to that of Joshua. A similar technique between Deut 34 and Josh 1 links those books. Later we will see an even closer analogue to this narrative technique in the progression from Ps 78 to 79.

6. These two psalms contain the only two uses of the verb מאן ("to refuse"/"reject") in the entire MT Psalter (Pss 77:3; 78:10).
7. The only two instances of the verb יסף ("to add"/"do again") in Psalms 73–83 are in these psalms (77:8; 78:17). This verb only appears six other times in the MT Psalter (Pss 10:18; 41:9; 61:7; 71:14; 115:14; 120:3). Further, in both 77:7 and 78:17 the verb occurs with the adverb עוד ("again"). This adverb is only used in two other Asaph psalms (Pss 74:9; 83:5). Strengthening the intentionality of this link is its presence at the most structurally and theologically significant location of Psalm 77 (vv. 8–11).
8. Both psalms contain references to the patriarch "Joseph" (77:16) (יוסף and 78:67). His name only appears twice elsewhere in the MT Psalter (Pss 80:2, 6; 105:17).

Thus, considered collectively, the significant links between these psalms (i.e., those in Table 5.2 and those just discussed) mount a compelling argument for their deliberate juxtaposition. Indeed, the ties are so strong that Weber has plausibly suggested that one psalm may have been composed in light of the other.[42]

To return to the main point: the significant links displayed in Table 5.2 are a second area of significant literary correspondence with Psalm 73, pointing to deliberate design.

Linguistic Parallels with Psalm 73

In the case of this psalm sequence as well, correspondence with Psalm 73 is reflected in direct linguistic parallels:

1. Like the grouping of Psalms 74–76, the sequence of Psalms 77–78 also contains an expression closely resembling the clause "recounting all your works" (לספר כל מלאכותיך) in Psalm 73:28: "recounting (ספר) the praises of God; his strength, and his wonders (נפלאותיו) that he has done" (78:4; cp. 75:2) (see also ספר in vv. 3 and 6). Outside of Psalms 73–78, the verb ספר only occurs in one other Asaph psalm (79:13).
2. Zion theology plays a significant (constructive) role in the grouping of Psalms 77–78 and Psalm 73 (see v. 17). Psalm 78 climaxes in God's merciful choice of David/Zion (vv. 65–72), which includes God's building of the Jerusalem sanctuary (78:69) (מקדש). The turning point of Psalm 73 is the psalmist's entrance into the temple (see מקדשי אל in 73:17).[43]

42. Weber, *Psalm 77 und sein Umfeld*, 290. Thus, in the case of Pss 77–78, the high degree of literary correspondence is an argument for intentionality; these adjacent psalms appear to share many *non-incidental* ties. Other significant parallels could be listed, such as the verb דרש ("to seek"), which only occurs in these adjacent psalms in the collection (77:3; 78:34).

43. In this connection, the reader should recall Clifford's claim that the closest generic parallels to Ps 78 are other psalms celebrating Zion, such as Ps 76. Clifford, "In Zion and

3. The motif of God's leading Israel is important in both Psalm 73 and Psalms 77–78 (73:24; 77:21; 78:14, 53, 72), where it manifests in the verb נחה ("to lead") in each case.[44]
4. Both share an important concern for the faith of future "generations" (דור) (73:15; 77:9; 78:4, 6, 8 [2×]).[45]
5. While Psalms 73 and 77 both have the nation in view (73:1; 77:12–21), the psalms themselves are decidedly *individual* in focus, something not true of any other psalms in the collection. This individual focus is reflected in the high number, and near-equivalent amount, of first-person verbs having the psalmist as subject (sixteen in Ps 73 and fifteen in Ps 77).[46] These account for thirty-one of the thirty-five first-person verbs in the collection (nearly 91%).[47] Only three other psalms in the collection even contain first-person verbs with the psalmist as subject (75 [3×]; 78 [2×]; and 81 [2×]).[48]
6. In both cases a reflective tone accompanies the individual focus just described—also something not characteristic of other psalms in the collection. There is virtually no address to God in the first half of these psalms (73:1–16; 77:1–11) (but see 73:15; 77:5). Rather, their first half consists of personal reflections or musings on God's prolonged inactivity amid circumstances in which God "should" be acting. Significantly, such reflection leads to a perceived conflict between faith and experience in each case (73:1–16; 77:8–11).

Formal Correspondence with Psalm 73: Interpretation

This striking literary correspondence with Psalm 73 suggests intentionality: like the grouping of Psalms 74–76, the sequence of Psalms 77–78 appears to *deliberately* parallel Psalm 73. The key to grasping the significance of this relationship is again the close connection between structure and meaning. To recall Greenstein's observation noted in the last chapter, the similar form of these "discrete materials"

David a New Beginning," 137. Outside of these two psalms, the noun מקדש ("sanctuary") only occurs one other time in Pss 73–83 (74:7).

44. The verb נחה occurs nowhere else in Pss 73–83.

45. This noun only occurs in one other psalm in the collection (Ps 79:13 [2×]).

46. Pss 73:3 (2×), 13 (2×), 14, 15 (3×), 16, 17 (2×), 21, 22 (2×), 25, 28; 77:2, 3, 4 (3×), 5 (2×), 6, 7 (2×), 11, 12 (2×), 13 (2×).

47. Pss 73:3 (2×), 13 (2×), 14, 15 (3×), 16, 17 (2×), 21, 22 (2×), 25, 28; 75:5, 10 (2×); 77:2, 3, 4 (3×), 5 (2×), 6, 7 (2×), 11, 12 (2×), 13 (2×); 78:2 (2×); 81:6 (2×); alternatively, these could have God as subject.

48. In addition, apart from Ps 73, only one other psalm contains a first-person singular subject pronoun (either אני or אנכי) with the psalmist as subject (75:10). The first-person pronoun is rare in these psalms. The form אני is used four times in this way in Ps 73, and אנכי once in 75:10.

Table 5.3 The Semantic Relationship between Psalm 73 and Psalms 77–78

Psalm/psalm group	Confrontation with a severe conflict of faith and experience	Resolution to the conflict of faith and experience	Core Israelite belief challenged/promoted
Psalm 73	vv. 1–16	vv. 18–28	"God is good to Israel" (v. 1)
Psalms 77–78	Psalm 77	Psalm 78	The theology of Exodus 34:6–7

(i.e., Psalm 73 and the sequence of Psalms 77–78) leads us to find a "meaningful correlation" between them: Psalms 77–78 are a second distinct and deliberately arranged psalm group that develops Psalm 73's topic on an inter-psalm level (Table 5.3).

Such an interpretation is once again not immediately apparent since the core Israelite belief challenged/promoted is different in each case (column 4). But here too a closer look brings clarity. In this case, clarity comes from the original context of Exodus 34:6–7, undoubtedly known to the collection's editor(s).[49] We saw in Chapter 3 how Exodus 33:19 explicitly states that God's self-revelation in 34:6–7 was, more fundamentally, a manifestation of God's *goodness* (טוב). This shows that the challenge posed to the credo in Psalm 77 is ultimately a threat to God's goodness *even apart from a deliberate parallel relationship with Psalm 73*. That such a relationship does exist (Table 5.3, column 4) tacitly confirms what is already implicit in Psalm 77 itself: the fundamental issue in the psalm group of Psalms 77–78 is God's goodness (טוב) (73:1). The characteristic movement of many poetic lines is thus a fitting analogue in the case of this second grouping as well: the "movement" from Psalm 73 to Psalms 77–78 is one of general to specific; from a focus on God's goodness (Ps 73) to a specific, and extremely important, manifestation of it (i.e., the credo of Exod 34:6–7) (Pss 77–78).

The shape of this second grouping also reflects an editorial concern to *resolve* the crisis lamented.[50] The deliberate juxtaposition of Psalm 78 directs the reader/ singer to that psalm's didactic retelling of Israel's history for resolution to the crisis over Israel's core credo in Psalm 77 (and God's goodness more fundamentally) (Table 5.3, columns 3 and 4). Such is the paratextual function for Psalm 78 that both the semantic/conceptual correspondence with 73:18–28 (Table 5.3, column 3) and the significant repetitions from Psalm 77 tacitly signal.

Regarding the latter, we saw in Chapter 4 how Psalm 73 clarified the significance of the parallels between Psalm 74 and Psalms 75–76: these links reflect deliberate literary correspondence with the rhetorical device at work in the collection's

---

49. This is implied in the allusions to the credo in Pss 77 and 78.
50. Thus, contra Kselman, Brueggemann, and others (see the exegesis of Ps 77 above), it is Ps 78 (not 77:12–21) that completes the reversal in perspective/understanding that begins within Ps 77 itself.

opening psalm. Since Psalms 77–78 share the same parallel relationship with Psalm 73, this rhetorical device also reveals the significance of the repetitions in Table 5.2: they are used to highlight the resolution that Psalm 78 is promoting in relation to the crisis of faith in Psalm 77. Thus, the rhetorical device at work within Psalm 73's two halves appears to have been replicated on an inter-psalm level between the "two halves" of both groupings considered so far.

Here too the specific nature of the resolution resembles the one the psalmist of Psalm 73 reached. We have seen that both Psalms 77 and 78 feature the core Israelite credo of Exodus 34:6–7. However, Psalm 78 promotes a radically different perspective on its enduring truthfulness than what the psalmist experiences in Psalm 77. The deliberate sequencing of these psalms thus encourages singers/readers to trust the enduring truthfulness of the very credo (Ps 78) that the crucible of lived experience had threatened to consume (Ps 77). This observation implies that the editorial purpose behind the arrangement was to shore up the deep-seated commitment to the "God of belief" (i.e., the "God of Exod 34:6–7") reflected (but severely shaken) in Psalm 77 itself. Thus, like Psalm 73 and the first grouping, resolution consists in promoting confidence in a deeply held belief that nearly fractured under the weight of lived experience. Like the first grouping, confidence is grounded in God's own self-revelation in history (78:38; 65–72).[51]

Thus, if the questions of Psalm 77:8–10 read as a point-by-point refutation of the theology of Exodus 34:6–7 (so Kselman), the adjacent Psalm 78's didactic retelling of Israelite history essentially offers a point-by-point editorial rebuttal in the collection's final form.[52]

God does not *permanently* reject his people (78:56–72; cf. 77:8); God's promise does *not*, in fact, come to an end (78:1–4; cf. 77:9); God does not *ultimately* "forget" to be gracious, and does not shut up his compassion *indefinitely* (78:38–39; cf. 77:10); God's mighty "right hand" does *not*, in fact, change (78:42, 54; cf. 77:10)—despite conflicting evidence (77:8–10).

If the proposed interpretation is correct, the primary rationale behind Psalm 78's placement was to resolve the faith crisis voiced in 77:8–11. The latter verses thus occupy a central place in my interpretation. So far, the evidence for this view has been the deliberate parallel relationship with Psalm 73. A closer look at the psalms themselves, and the links they share, provides further support for the proposed interpretation.

---

51. The reader should recall here that the psalmist conceives of God's compassionate acts in both "sequels" of Ps 78 (i.e., vv. 33–39; 65–72) as historical displays of God's self-revelation in Exod 34:6–7.

52. In this connection, the reader should remember that Ps 78 is a *didactic* retelling of history (like virtually all history); the whole point of recounting the past is to shape the reader's/singer's outlook on the future. The link between Pss 77:1 and 78:1 supports the view that Ps 78 should be read as a response/rebuttal to Ps 77. As others have noted (e.g., Cole, Hossfeld and Zenger), the exhortation for God's people to "Hear! (האזינה)" in 78:1 reads like a direct address to the requests for God to "hear (האזין)" in 77:1.

First, the exegesis of Psalm 77 indicated that verses 8–11 are the structural and theological center of the psalm. It is here that the psalmist voices the vexing conflict of faith and experience confronting the community. Thus, on the assumption that the collection's editor(s) did not juxtapose psalms for trivial reasons, it is most reasonable to conclude that the primary rationale behind Psalm 78's sequencing was to address these questions—the location where the psalm's major theological dilemma is articulated. As we have seen, this is precisely the interpretation that formal correspondence with Psalm 73 tacitly signals (Table 5.3, columns 3 and 4).

Second, confirming this line of reasoning is the following observation: 77:8–11 is where each parallel in Table 5.2 appears. That Psalm 78 would share such deliberate links with the most theologically significant location of Psalm 77 supports the claim that the dilemma voiced in those verses explains the psalm's juxtaposition. In this connection, the reader should recall the methodological point made in Chapter 1 that even significant parallels needed "weighing." We saw above that the links in Table 5.2 are not the only significant ties between Psalm 77 and Psalm 78; others appear to reflect their deliberate juxtaposition. But the considerations offered here highlight those in Table 5.2 (i.e., those occurring in 77:8–11) as the most significant for understanding the rationale behind that editorial decision.

The interpretation offered here suggests that, contrary to the claims of some, the resolution Psalm 78 promotes is *not* theodical in nature; the psalm is not positioned to "deuteronomistically" explain the dismal circumstances of Psalm 77 in terms of Israel's sin.[53] And neither does Psalm 78's juxtaposition signal that those

---

53. A number of interpreters have taken such a view. For instance, consider Cole's comments: "In 77.10 the poet wonders if God has forgotten (חשכח) to be gracious. In reality it is not God who has forgotten but Israel in general (78.42) (לא זכרו), and the sons of Ephraim in particular (וישכחו), in spite of the fact that they were commanded not to forget (78.7) (ולא ישכחו)." Cole, *The Shape and Message of Book III*, 66. This is a major characteristic of Cole's understanding of Ps 78's placement, namely, that the sin/rebellion of the people in Ps 78 explains God's anger in Ps 77 (Cole, *The Shape and Message of Book III*, 63–76). However, I would suggest that Cole has made a "fruit purée" at this point. Psalm 78 does give a theodicy for God's punishment of the forefathers (i.e., disobedience and unbelief). But this point is not relayed to explain the reason that future generations find themselves in similar dismal circumstances (how Cole uses them on a "canonical level"). It is rather to encourage/exhort future generations not to be like the forefathers but trust and obey (vv. 7–8). Cole, therefore, proposes a "canonical interpretation" that goes "against the grain" of Ps 78. As discussed in Chapter 1 (see pp. 18–20), such interpretations are rejected here. A similar critique applies to Weber's view that the defeat of the northern tribes in Ps 78 explains the judgment upon "Jacob" and "Joseph" in Ps 77. See Weber, *Psalm 77 und sein Umfeld*, 290. Weber's view is also unpersuasive, I would suggest, since it is based upon the (faulty) assumption that Ps 78 is about the northern tribes, not "all Israel." For this point, see the exegesis of Ps 78 above. I would suggest that theodical interpretations also fail at the level of Ps 77. According to Ps 77, sin is *no longer* the problem; *God* is. It is thus unlikely an editor/author would use Ps 78 in the way Weber and Cole propose.

dismal circumstances have changed. The psalm is, after all, a didactic retelling of Israel's *history*. Rather, if the arguments presented above are sound, what we see is an editorial concern to reinforce faith's foundations in the face of circumstances whose prolonged duration had threatened to erode them.

Notably, the hope that Psalm 78 cultivates vis-à-vis Psalm 77 is rooted in—not directed away from—God's choice and establishment of Zion.[54] As we have seen, the climax of both the second "recital" in Psalm 78 and the psalm as a whole is a celebration of God's merciful choice of *David and Zion* (vv. 65–72). This celebration may only cultivate a general hope in God's continued faithfulness. However, an alternative interpretation suggests itself in light of two factors: (1) the prominent and constructive role of Zion theology in the first grouping (Ps 76), and (2) the promises of Israel's restoration and renewal that contain references to "David" and/or Zion in various texts from the exilic/postexilic period (e.g., Jeremiah; Ezekiel).[55]

These factors raise the possibility that the present shape of this sequence promotes a more *specific* demonstration of Divine faithfulness: David and Zion were not only an important part of Israel's *history* but will also factor significantly in Israel's *future*. Though, as in the case of the preceding grouping, there are no specifics regarding how, when, or to what extent, this might happen.

The Theological Message of Psalms 77–78

The similarity with the design of the previous grouping reveals an analogous theological message: "Faith sticks to God's self-revelation [i.e., the credo of Exodus 34:6–7, more fundamentally "God is good to Israel"] amid conflicting evidence." This message is tacitly implied by the findings that (1) the grouping's shape encourages resolute commitment to the enduring truthfulness of Exodus 34:6–7 in the face of conflicting evidence (77:8–11); and (2) the parallel relationship with Psalm 73 (see Table 5.3) is a tacit paratextual indicator that God's goodness is the ultimate issue at stake. Thus, while the particular manifestation of the crisis differs in this second grouping (i.e., the conflict involves a different core belief [Exod 34:6–7]), the same basic theological message has emerged.

Given that Psalm 77's historical setting is vague and unspecified ("the day of my distress" [יום צרתי]) (v. 3), at first glance it seems that the message is *not* contextualized within specific historical circumstances like the first grouping. In the next chapter, however, I consider evidence that this grouping should be read against the same historical setting as the first: the aftermath of the temple's destruction in 586 BCE (74:1–11). In fact, there we will see that the vague and unspecified setting of Psalm 77 is actually one of the clues to this interpretation.

---

54. Recall the similar emphasis in the grouping of Pss 74–76.
55. That is, the general period during which this collection likely achieved its present shape. This point will be discussed further later.

Structural Implications for Psalms 73–83

Four important structural implications emerge from the foregoing analysis, the fourth more provisional than the first three. There are others, but they will be taken up and developed in the next chapter. First, the analysis has identified Psalms 77–78 as a second internally coherent, self-contained, literary unit—a distinct and deliberately arranged psalm group that *resolves* the theological crisis it addresses. If valid, the conclusions reached here call into question structural proposals (or aspects of them) that separate Psalm 77 from 78.[56]

The analysis also suggests that the literary unity of Psalms 73–76 extends to Psalms 77–78: the sequence of Psalms 73–78 represents two related, but distinct, psalm groups (Pss 74–76; 77–78), each developing the topic of Psalm 73 on an inter-psalm level. The literary unity of Psalms 73–78 is the subject of much closer investigation in the next chapter.

A third implication is this: the conclusions reached tacitly establish the psalm boundary between Psalms 76 and 77 as another significant location of editorial division. Chapter 2 showed that some (e.g., Hossfeld and Zenger; Weber) have reached a similar conclusion based upon the fact that Psalm 77 shares much stronger links with Psalm 78 than with Psalm 76. This observation is not insignificant and is valid as far as it goes.

But the combined conclusions of Chapters 4 and 5 have revealed even stronger evidence for a literary caesura or break at this juncture: the sequences of Psalms 74–76 and 77–78 are both distinct, internally coherent, literary units. Such unity *within* each grouping tacitly indicates a higher-level literary boundary *between* them (i.e., one level above the individual psalm). Consequently, whatever significant links Psalms 76 and 77 may share, this important indicator of editorial separation indicates that these links should not be mistaken for evidence that Psalms 76 and 77 belong to the same psalm group.[57] Weber is, therefore, correct to conclude that "Ist die Relation von Ps 77 zu Ps 76 disjunktiv/zentrifugal, so die zu Ps 78 konjunktiv/zentripetal."[58]

---

56. Especially noteworthy in this regard is the popular view that divides the collection in half at Ps 78 (73–77; 78–83), thereby separating Pss 77 and 78. See the survey of the studies of Millard, Leuenberger, and Ho in Chapter 2.

57. There are several links that could possibly be significant: נגינה ("song") (76:1; 77:7); statements about God's self-revelation using the verb ידע (76:2; 77:15); predications that God is "great (גדול)" (76:2; 77:14); the verb אור ("to light up"/"shine") with reference to God in (76:5; 77:19); rhetorical questions with מי ("who?") used as indirect assertions about God's power/greatness in (76:8; 77:14). Cole characteristically interprets these parallels as indicating that Pss 76 and 77 belong to the same psalm group. See Cole, *The Shape and Message of Book III*, 54–62. But significant parallels alone are insufficient to establish that psalms belong to the same psalm group. Disjunctive factors, such as those discussed here, must also be taken into account.

58. Weber, *Psalm 77 und sein Umfeld*, 289.

Finally, there are implications for where Psalm 79 "fits" in the collection's structure. Many studies agree with the conclusion here that the sequence of Psalms 77–78 represents a deliberate arrangement. But quite a few disagree with my decision to exclude Psalm 79 from these psalms in the collection's structure (e.g., Millard; Hossfeld and Zenger; Leunberger; Jones). Hossfeld is particularly forceful on this point: "If we survey the triad of Psalms 77–79, we observe equivalent linkages between Psalm 78 and its predecessor and successor, *without any possibility of placing a caesura between the three psalms*" (emphasis added).[59]

Notwithstanding Hossfeld's certainty, this chapter has presented evidence for a tacit boundary between Psalms 78 and 79, namely, that Psalm 78 *concludes* a psalm group. This implies that Psalm 79 does not belong with Psalms 77–78 in the collection's structure but begins a third grouping. Chapters 6–8 offer considerably more support for this interpretation.

---

59. Hossfeld and Zenger, *Psalms 2*, 294. While Cole does not make such a direct statement, his analysis is consistent with it. Characteristic of his study, Cole detects strong conjunction but no element of disjunction between Pss 78 and 79. See Cole, *The Shape and Message of Book III*, 79–86.

Chapter 6

THE LITERARY UNITY OF PSALMS 73–78

So far in this study I have presented evidence that the sequences of Psalms 74–76 and 77–78 both deliberately parallel the opening Psalm 73, and have traced out some implications of this formal correspondence.[1] In the process, the literary unity of the first six psalms (Pss 73–78) has become apparent. This chapter delves deeper into this unity and explores its implications for the design of the collection as a whole.

Psalms 74–76 and Psalms 77–78 as Parallel Psalm Groups: Evidence

It has become clear in the course of analysis that the groupings established so far are strikingly similar in design. This finding is unsurprising since both, as argued, deliberately parallel the same psalm (i.e., Ps 73). What is of interest here is that such symmetry shows that the groupings also parallel each other. Consider the findings of previous chapters: (1) each progresses from a "God-lament" (Pss 74; 77) to one or more psalms positioned to resolve the faith crisis at its center (Pss 75–76; 78); (2) an analogous network of parallels is used to highlight this resolution in both; (3) the specific nature of the resolution is the same; (4) as a consequence of these two observations, the basic theological message of each grouping is the same; and (5) in both cases, Zion theology factors importantly in the resolution promoted (Pss 76; 78:65–72).

These five areas of structural and semantic correspondence clearly evince the parallel nature of these groupings. Closer investigation yields further evidence. This consists primarily in the striking similarity of the initial psalms (Pss 74 and 77). We already noted the significant thematic correspondence between these "laments": both center on a disorienting conflict between faith and experience, in which Israel's faith is in a position of extremity. Here I point out that this thematic correspondence manifests itself in the interrogative "God-lament" in both psalms (74:1, 10–11; 77:8–11). Additionally, in each case complaint over the prolonged

---

1. This chapter is a revised and expanded version of Stephen J. Smith, "The Shape and Message of Psalms 73–78," *CBQ* 83 (2021): 18–37. I would like to thank the Catholic Biblical Association for permission to reprint material from that article here.

and enigmatic inactivity of God's mighty "hand"/"right hand" (ימין) (Pss 74:11; 77:11) (i.e., saving/judging activity) is either part of these questions or closely related to them.² Further, the interrogatives reflect the psalmist's outlook that such Divine inactivity is a sign of God's wrathful (אף) rejection (זנח) (74:1, 11; 77:8, 10).³

Additional parallels in vocabulary, motif/theme, and structure further demonstrate the parallel nature of these psalms. Some overlap in language/form is to be expected given the stereotypical nature of psalmic language. But these God-laments are *strikingly* similar:

1. Both are concentrically arranged with multiple God-laments at the prominent central location (74:10–11; 77:8–10).⁴
2. The complaint over the prolonged inactivity of God's mighty "hand/right hand" (77:11; ימין) noted above comes at the central structural location in both psalms.
3. Both contain mythopoetic imagery relating to the chaotic "waters (מים)" (see 74:13–14; 77:17, 18, 20). Such imagery is rare in Psalms 73–83.
4. Psalms 74 and 77 share a slew of similar vocabulary. The most significant are as follows: גאל ("to redeem") (74:2; 77:16);⁵ זכר ("to remember") (74:2, 18, 22; 77:4, 7, 12); שכח ("to forget") (74:19, 23; 77:10);⁶ זנח ("to reject") (74:1; 77:8) with temporal adverbial modifier (נצח; עולמים); ימין ("right hand" [i.e., God's]) (74:12; 77:11); לילה ("night") יום ("day") (74:16, 22; 77:3, 6, 7); צאן ("flock") (74:1; 77:21); נצח ("forever") (74:1, 3, 10, 14; 77:9; in God-laments in 74:1, 10 and 77:9), which reflects the same important time motif in both psalms (74:1, 3, 9, 10, 19, 23; 77:6, 8, 9); עז ("might") (74:13; 77:15); the root פעל ("work" [of God]) (74:12; 77:13);⁷ קדם ("of old") (74:2, 12; 77:6, 12);⁸ קדש (holiness/holy) (74:3; 77:14).⁹

---

2. In this connection, the reader should recall that while 77:11 is not a question, it is essentially the climactic conclusion to the questions in vv. 8–10.

3. These are the only two occurrences of the verb זנח in Pss 73–83. The verb only appears eight other times in the MT Psalter (in six psalms) (Pss 43:2; 44:10, 24; 60:3, 12; 88:15; 89:39; 108:12). In both 74:1 and 77:8 the verb comes in a God-lament with a similar temporal adverb or adverbial phrase ("Why do you reject forever [74:1]?" [זנחת לנצח]; "Will the Lord reject forever?" [הלעולמים יזנח]). The verb only occurs with a similar phrase one other time in the MT Psalter (Ps 44:24).

4. See the discussion of the structure of these psalms in Chapters 4 and 5 respectively.

5. This verb only occurs one other time in Pss 73–83 (78:35).

6. These two psalms account for three of the five instances of this verb in Pss 73–83. The other two come in Ps 78 (vv. 7, 11).

7. This root occurs nowhere else in Pss 73–83.

8. This noun occurs only once elsewhere in the collection (78:2).

9. There are only two other occurrences of this noun in Pss 73–83 (78:54; 79:1).

In addition to the striking resemblance of their initial psalms, a few noteworthy correspondences exist between the "second half" of each grouping, Psalms 75–76 and 78 respectively. These further reflect the parallel nature of the groupings:

1. Both share a similar concern to "recount" (ספר) God's "wonders" (נפלאות) (75:2; 78:3, 4, 6).[10]
2. As we have seen, Zion theology plays an important role in both Psalms 76 and 78. In this connection, the reader should recall Clifford's conclusion that the closest generic analogues to Psalm 78 are Zion psalms like Psalm 76. Notably, in both groupings this thematic link manifests in the common expression "Mt. Zion" (הר ציון) (see 74:2; 78:68), which occurs nowhere else in the collection.
3. The proximate Psalms 75 and 78 contain three (75:1; 78:38; 78:45) of the MT Psalter's nine total occurrences of the verb שחת in the *hipʿil* (the others appear in 14:1; 53:2; 57:1; 58:1; 59:1; 106:23).
4. Both have the motif of God's mighty "hand" (75:9; 78:42, 54) as a deliberate repetition with the preceding lament. After Psalm 78, this motif appears only in the adjacent Psalms 80 and 81 (80:18; 81:15).

The striking literary symmetry between these groupings, which we have seen consists in structural, semantic, and linguistic correspondence, suggests intentionality; these groupings stand in a deliberate parallel relationship.

Psalms 74–76 and Psalms 77–78 as Parallel Psalm Groups: Interpretation

Different levels of structure reveal themselves as (deliberate) parallels are discerned at different "levels" in the collection. The parallel nature of these adjacent groupings indicates that together they form a larger structural unit consisting of Psalms 74–78. Two additional parallels corroborate this conclusion.

The first is their titles. The psalms at the extremities (i.e., Pss 74 and 78) are the only two Asaph psalms with the superscription משכיל לאסף ("a Maskil of Asaph").[11] Further, the first element in the superscription of each intervening psalm (Pss 75–77) is the same, למנצח ("To the choirmaster"?).[12] Thus, the structuration

---

10. Similar statements in Pss 73–83 only appear in 73:28 (on which, see below) and 79:13.

11. There are only twelve other psalms in the MT Psalter so designated (Pss 32; 42; 44; 45; 47; 52–55; 88–89; 142).

12. Even if למנצח + an optional prepositional phrase in Pss 76:1 and 77:1 was originally a postscript to the preceding psalm as Waltke has suggested, it stands in the superscript *heading* of Pss 76 and 77 in the form of the text that has been preserved. See Bruce K. Waltke, "Superscripts, Postscripts, or Both," *JBL* 110 (1991): 583–96.

proposed here results in (but is not *based* upon) clear symmetry among the superscriptions of these psalms.[13]

Such symmetry may be incidental. Alternatively, it may further reflect (not create) the editorial unity of these five psalms, given (1) such unity has been established on other grounds (i.e., the parallel relationship of their constituent groupings); and (2) though disputed by some, Wilson and many others have advanced arguments that "type designations" (i.e., משכיל) and "indications of use" (i.e., למנצח) in superscriptions reflect editorial intentionality.[14] If so, the paratextual feature משכיל heading Psalms 74 and 78 is an instance of "distant parallelism" and serves as the most prominent feature demarcating Psalms 74–78 as a distinct unit.

Additional support for the claim that משכיל may perform an organizing function is the observation that ten of the twelve remaining occurrences in the MT Psalter are in superscriptions of *consecutive* psalms (see Pss 42–45 [Pss 42 and 43 are a unity]; Pss 52–55; 88–89) (the exceptions are in Pss 32:1 and 142:1). In light of such consecution, Willgren cites the two nonconsecutive משכיל psalms under discussion (Pss 74, 78) as evidence against Wilson's view that this "type designation" serves an organizing function.[15] But if my analysis is correct, such nonconsecution is explained by the fact that משכיל performs a bracketing role here. Thus, though

---

13. I would suggest that the symmetry among the superscriptions of Pss 74–78 (and a similar symmetry detected among those of Pss 79–82; see Chapter 8) on the structuration offered here is more obviously an *organized pattern* than what we see on Ho's proposal. See Peter Ho, *The Design of the Psalter: A Macrostructural Analysis* (Eugene, OR: Pickwick, 2019), 144. For the details of Ho's proposal, see the summary of his work in Chapter 2 of this study (pp. 58–60). Ho's attempt to find an organized pattern among the superscriptions on his structuration seems forced.

14. A well-known example from Wilson's seminal work is the "softening" role he attributed to the type designation מזמור in Pss 47–51 and למנצח (with others, including מזמור) in Pss 62–68. See Gerald H. Wilson, *The Editing of the Hebrew Psalter*, SBLDS 76 (Chico, CA: Scholars Press, 1985), 163. For other arguments that superscriptions (both their presence and absence) serve an organizing function, see Jamie A. Grant, *The King as Exemplar: The Function of Deuteronomy's Kingship Law in the Shaping of the Book of Psalms*, SBLABib 17 (Atlanta, GA: SBL Press, 2004), 227–9; Michael G. McKelvey, *Moses, David and the High Kingship of Yahweh: A Canonical Study of Book IV of the Psalter*, Gorgias Biblical Studies 55 (Piscataway, NJ: Gorgias Press, 2013), 259–60, 265, 268–9, and 271. For arguments to the contrary, see David Willgren, *The Formation of the "Book" of Psalms*, FAT II. Reihe 88 (Tübingen: Mohr Siebeck, 2016), 172–95. It should be noted that my argument here is not that למנצח is being used to "soften" abrupt breaks as Wilson proposed elsewhere. I am only suggesting that למנצח may further reflect the deliberate grouping of these psalms. Thus, while not playing a "softening" role, למנצח would still serve an organizing function in the collection's present form. I am borrowing "type designations" and "indications of use" from Willgren, *The Formation of the "Book" of Psalms*, 178, 183.

15. Willgren, *The Formation of the "Book" of Psalm*, 181.

nonconsecutive, משכיל would still have an organizing function: it reflects the boundaries of the unit composed of Psalms 74–78.

So, while not the basis of their deliberate grouping, these aforementioned elements in the superscriptions of Psalms 74–78 may further reflect it.[16]

Second, an inclusion formed by Psalms 74:1–3 and 78:67–72 (another instance of distant parallelism) works in tandem with the "type designation" משכיל as a boundary marking feature. Suggesting its intentionality is the clustering of the same (or synonymous) group of words and themes/imagery at these extremity locations (i.e., at the boundaries of what appears to be a deliberate unit on other grounds): synonymous verbs for "reject" (78:6; 74:1) (זנח/מאס);[17] the phrase הר ציון ("Mt. Zion")[18] (74:2; 78:68); references to the Jerusalem sanctuary containing the root קדש ("holy place/sanctuary") (74:3; 78:69); shepherd imagery, reflected in similar vocabulary (i.e., צאן [flock] [74:1; 78:70]); the root רעה (["to shepherd/pasture"][19] [74:1; 78:71]); and references to God's people as a "tribe (שבט)"[20] and "inheritance (נחלה)"[21] (see 74:2; 78:67, 68, 71).

In light of the evidence presented for the unity of Psalms 74–78, the clustering of the same (or very similar) group of linguistic features at these extremity locations is striking; it suggests the presence of a deliberate literary inclusion. As such, this "distant parallel" corroborates the claim that, while the sequences of Psalms 74–76 and 77–78 are separated on one literary level (i.e., the psalm group), they are joined on another (i.e., a larger unit consisting of Pss 74–78).

Psalms 74–78, then, constitute a second literary level above the individual psalm in Psalms 73–83, what we may call the "unit." And tacitly signaling its

---

16. In my view, it is not "all or nothing" when it comes to the question of whether superscriptions have an editorial function; sometimes they appear to, sometimes they do not.

17. The verb מאס only occurs elsewhere in Pss 73–83 at 78:59 (and in the MT Psalter at 15:4; 36:5; 53:6, 8; 89:39; 106:24; 118:22). The verb זנח only appears elsewhere at 77:8 (and elsewhere in the MT Psalter at 43:2; 44:10, 24; 60:3, 12; 88:15; 89:39; 108:12). Interestingly, this connection is even clearer in the LXX Psalter, which has the same verb (ἀπωθέω) in both places (cf., Pss 73:1; 77:67). It would require a much more thorough study to determine whether this observation reflects the translator's awareness of the connection being proposed here.

18. This phrase occurs nowhere else in Pss 73–83. The exact phrase only occurs elsewhere in the MT Psalter in two other psalms (see 48:3, 12; 125:1). The plural הררי ציון ("mountains of Zion") appears in 133:3.

19. This root only occurs elsewhere in Pss 73–83 at 79:13; 80:2, 14.

20. The only other place this term occurs in the collection is at 78:55, where it also has the sense of "tribe." The noun שבט is used in the sense of "tribe" in only two other psalms in the MT Psalter (105:37; 122:4 [2×]).

21. Psalms 78:55, 62, and 79:1 are the only other occurrences of this noun in the collection.

boundaries are the following two parallels: (1) the "type designation" משכיל (74:1; 78:1); and (2) an inclusion formed by 74:1–3 and 78:67–72.[22]

The Unit of Psalms 74–78: A Dual Response to the Sixth-Century Crisis

The above conclusion raises an important question: what editorial purpose is associated with the joining of these groupings into a larger literary unit? The answer is found in significant semantic *differences* between their initial psalms. For all of their similarity discussed above, Psalms 74 and 77 differ in orientation, setting, focus, the psalmist's/community's posture, and in terms of the effects of God's inactivity.

Regarding Psalm 74, notice that (1) the predominant orientation is communal; (2) the setting is concrete (i.e., the aftermath of the Temple's destruction [vv. 2–9]); (3) the focus is on an enemy of the nation/God (see vv. 3–8, 18–23); (4) the posture is decidedly Godward;[23] and (5) the psalm emphasizes the effects of God's prolonged inactivity upon God himself (i.e., God's "name" or reputation [see especially vv. 4, 7, 10, 13–17, 18, 19, 21–23]).

On the other hand, in Psalm 77 we see that: (1) the orientation is not communal but individual; (2) the setting is not concrete but vague and unspecified ("the day of my distress" [v. 3]); (3) the focus is not on an enemy but solely on the God–Israel relationship (i.e., no third party is in view); (4) the posture is not predominantly Godward but selfward;[24] and (5) the emphasis is on the effects of God's enigmatic inactivity on God's people, not God's reputation.[25]

---

22. Editorial critics have argued for inclusions bracketing a number of groups of psalms in the MT Psalter. For example, see Grant, *The King as Exemplar*, 61; Michael K. Snearly, *The Return of the King: Messianic Expectation in Book V of the Psalter*, LHBOTS 624 (New York: Bloomsbury, 2016), 110; McKelvey, *Moses, David and the High Kingship of Yahweh*, 272.

23. Reflected in the following features: (1) the imperatives addressed to God (see vv. 2, 3, 11, 18, 20, 22 (3×)]; (2) the predominance of the second-person singular pronominal suffix referring to God (25× in fourteen verses); (3) the cluster of second-person masculine singular pronouns in addresses to God in the "praise" section of vv. 12–17 (seven occurrences); and (4) the many second-person singular verbs addressed to God (seventeen in ten verses).

24. Reflected in the following features: (1) the sparsity of any address to God in the first half of the psalm (only in v. 5). The psalmist only begins to address God in v. 12; (2) the use of real third-person questions in vv. 8–10, rather than the usual rhetorical questions addressed to God; (3) the sixteen first-person singular verbs (in nine verses) referring to the psalmist; (4) the statements focusing on the distress caused to the psalmist (vv. 3–5).

25. Reflected in the direct statements focusing on the distress caused to the psalmist (vv. 3–5), the third-person questions in vv. 8–10, and the absence of an explicit concern for the effects of God's inactivity upon his reputation.

Additionally, while the fundamental nature of the theological dilemma is the same in both groupings (i.e., a conflict of faith and experience), we have seen that the core belief challenged/promoted differs. Psalm 74 has in view God's reputation as the Great King, while Psalm 77 focuses on the theology of Exodus 34:6–7.

These considerations bring into focus the organizing principle used to structure these two groupings: progressive repetition. These adjacent groupings offer two different (progressive), but complementary, perspectives on one and the same crisis (repetition). Pointing in this direction is the observation that the parallel relationship between these groupings consists of both striking similarities and differences.

The grouping of Psalms 74–76 introduces the crisis: the conflict of faith and experience precipitated by God's prolonged absence in the temple's destruction (74:1–11). Whatever the original setting of Psalm 77, two observations jointly suggest that it (and the grouping to which it belongs) has been (re)contextualized within this more specific setting in the collection's final form: (1) the grouping of Psalms 77–78 closely parallels and is deliberately joined to Psalms 74–76; and (2) the vague and unspecified nature of Psalm 77's historical setting mentioned earlier ("the day of my distress" [v. 3]) makes the psalm particularly adaptable for (re)use in a more specific setting. Together these observations suggest that the unit's first grouping (Pss 74–76) provides an important literary context for the second, namely, the specific crisis lamented in Psalm 74:1–11. The unit of Psalms 74–78, therefore, has a singular topic/crisis in view: God's prolonged absence in the Temple's destruction.

Using progressive repetition to organize these parallel groupings enables the collection's editor(s) to develop this topic in a "three-dimensional manner" or in "surround sound."[26] The grouping of Psalms 74–76 offers a communal, external (i.e., enemy focus), and Godward perspective on this crisis. This grouping emphasizes the effects of God's absence upon God's own character/reputation, and establishes that such Divine behavior appeared to undermine Israel's profile of God as the Great King who vanquishes all chaotic forces that threaten Zion and its inhabitants (vv. 12–17). And it reflects an editorial concern to resolve this crisis by the placement of Psalms 75–76. The sequencing of these psalms shores up the reader/singer's confidence that, despite conflicting evidence (74:1–11), Yahweh is *still* the Zion's Great King.[27]

---

26. Both analogies for progressive repetition come from Peter Gentry. See Peter J. Gentry, *How to Read & Understand the Biblical Prophets* (Wheaton, IL: Crossway, 2017), 42, and Peter J. Gentry, "The Literary Macrostructures of the Book of Isaiah and Authorial Intent," in *Bind Up the Testimony: Explorations in the Genesis of the Book of Isaiah*, ed. Daniel I. Block and Richard L. Schultz (Peabody, MA: Hendrickson, 2015), 230–1.

27. To reiterate the point made in Chapter 4, the community of Ps 74 does not abandon this belief. But confidence in it is clearly shaken. Psalms 75–76 function to shore up that belief, with all of its implications for God's people, in their current location.

Like the second of so many parallel lines, the adjacent grouping (Pss 77–78) does not move to a different topic but treats the same topic differently. The "sound" coming from this "left speaker" offers a complementary perspective on the sixth-century crisis by focusing on the individual, internal (i.e., God–Israel focus), and selfward effects of God's prolonged absence in the temple's destruction. This grouping emphasizes that the crisis also posed an especial threat to the theology of arguably Israel's most foundational credo, Exodus 34:6–7 (77:8–11). And the juxtaposition of Psalm 78 points the singer/reader to a lengthy didactic retelling of Israel's history to find resolution to this crisis. The message that emerges is that, despite conflicting evidence (77:8–11), singers/readers can bank on the enduring truthfulness of this credo (78:38; 65–72). This second grouping also gives a positive, constructive role to Zion theology ("repetition") but adds another dimension to it ("progressive"), namely, David (cf. Pss 76; 78:65–72).

Notably, the inclusion formed by Psalms 74:1–3 and 78:67–72 encapsulates the dilemma of the unit it brackets (Pss 74–78), as well as the unit's perspective on resolving it: lived experience mounts a compelling argument that the great Shepherd's rejection of his flock is permanent (74:1–3). But God's past dealings with Israel offer the hope that, in his sovereign timing, God will reestablish his (benevolent) presence in Israel even more firmly than before (78:67–72).

Implications for Previous Scholarship

The conclusions reached here challenge previous scholarship at a number of points. In Chapter 5 I suggested that recognizing progressive repetition as the principle governing the sequencing of Psalms 73 and 74 indicated that interpretations of this sequence based upon linear, narrative-like principles were misguided. The above considerations have similar implications for the entire sequence of Psalms 73–78. As we have just seen, the analysis has suggested that this principle also structures the unit of Psalms 74–78.

The reader will recall from Chapter 2 that a number of interpretations based upon a linear, narrative-like principle resulted in the postulation of an "ebb and flow"-type editorial strategy at work in the sequencing of Psalms 74–78, between waves of lament (Pss 74; 77:1–11) and waves of hope (Pss 75–76; 77:12–21; 78).[28] On this view, the laments (here Pss 74, 77) "temper" the hope reflected in the non-laments (here Pss 75–76), and there is no resolution to the faith crises of Psalms 74 or 77; the cry of lament "resumes" once again in a narrative-like fashion following the intervening hopeful psalms (e.g., Pss 75–76 and 78).

But if progressive repetition is the principle at work, Psalm 77's lament is not to be understood as "resuming" one voiced "earlier" in Psalm 74 or "tempering" the hope reflected in Psalms 75 or 76. As argued, these psalms belong to *distinct* psalm groupings, neither of which is "open-ended," and both of which have their

---

28. See the summary of the works of Cole, Jones, and (to some extent) McCann in Chapter 2.

own internal literary unity. As a consequence, we have seen that: (1) Psalms 74 and 77 instead offer complementary perspectives on a singular crisis: the disorienting effects of God's absence in the Temple's destruction (74:1–11); and (2) Psalms 75–76 and 78 are editorially positioned as *resolutions* to this crisis in their respective groupings. Thus, if the conclusions reached here are sound, "ebb and flow"-type interpretations are misguided because they are predicated upon a misunderstanding of the organizing principle at work in the sequencing of Psalms 73–78.

Another analogy Gentry uses to elucidate progressive repetition (i.e., in addition to "stereo sound") may help clarify the interpretation offered here and further distinguish it from a linear/narrative approach. The groupings to which Psalms 74 and 77 belong (Pss 74–76; 77–78) may be thought of as two distinct "conversations" on the same topic.[29] Psalms 74–76 begin a "conversation" on the sixth-century crisis, develop it in a particular direction (Ps 74), and then end that conversation (Pss 75–76). Psalms 77–78 begin a second "conversation" on that same topic, develop it in a different (though complementary) direction (Ps 77), and likewise end that "conversation" (Ps 78).

There is, therefore, continuity in terms of the topic being "discussed" (the conflict of faith and experience precipitated by the sixth-century crisis) but discontinuity in terms of the "conversation" about that topic (i.e., the distinct manifestations of this crisis in Pss 74 and 77 respectively). Only the former is "resumed" from Psalms 74–76 in the grouping of Psalms 77–78. I argue in Chapters 7 and 8 that the sequence of Psalms 79–82 is based upon the same organizing principle, though it takes a more complex form (i.e., chiasmus).

The above conclusions also challenge an interpretation that has gained traction since McCann's important study of Book III (MT). I am referring here to the view that the sequence's arrangement points singers/readers *away* from Zion theology as a basis for hope. The analysis of Chapters 4–6 has pointed in precisely the opposite direction: both groupings identified so far direct readers *toward* such theology as a basis for hope (Pss 74; 76; 78:65–72).

McCann's interpretation, I would suggest, breaks down at both the level of the individual psalm and the editorial strategy at work. As earlier chapters pointed out, the community of Psalm 74 *engages* but does not *accept* the apparent failure of this theology. Like Psalm 76, Psalm 74 reflects an inflexible commitment to this theology. At the individual psalm level, then, both psalms cultivate a robust hope in what McCann refers to as "the traditional Davidic/Zion theology." As a result, the view that either psalm contributes to an editorial strategy aimed at pointing readers *away* from this theology does violence to their individuality (albeit

---

29. See Gentry, "The Literary Macrostructures of the Book of Isaiah and Authorial Intent." I do not mean to suggest any sort of narrative-like "dialogue" by using the analogy of a "conversation." My purpose in using this analogy is to clarify the following point: for all of the literary continuity between Pss 74–78, an important element of *discontinuity* should be recognized between its constituent groupings (74–76; 77–78).

unintentionally) and should be discouraged.[30] In terms of the editorial strategy at work, we have observed (so far) a sustained commitment to this theology and a consistent appeal to it as a basis for future hope.

Also challenged are interpretations locating the collection's major division (or any division) between Psalms 77 and 78.[31] Chapter 5 already presented evidence against this view: (1) Psalms 77–78 form a distinct, internally coherent, psalm grouping, revealing strong literary continuity between them; and (2) Psalm 78 concludes a grouping. These observations strongly argued against positing *any* type of editorial separation between Psalms 77 and 78—especially the collection's major structural division. The conclusions reached in this chapter reinforce this interpretation: Psalm 78 also tacitly marks the closing boundary of the collection's first major unit (Pss 74–78). This observation simultaneously implies that (1) no break should be posited between Psalms 77 and 78; and (2) the major break in the collection falls between Psalms 78 and 79.[32]

Relatedly, these structural observations suggest that views ascribing a central theological and/or literary position to Psalm 78 are also misguided. In Chapter 2 we saw that Hossfeld and Zenger posited such a role for Psalm 78, both with respect to its "microcontext" (i.e., Pss 77–79) and the collection as a whole.[33] The basis of this view is that Psalm 78 is the numerical center of the collection, with five psalms on each side,[34] and shares equivalent links with the flanking psalms.[35] Similarly, we noted that Beat Weber (who likewise thinks Ps 78's numerically central location is significant) also believes that Psalm 78 plays a central theological role in the collection. Judith Gärtner's position was similar, suggesting that Psalm 78 is the theological center specifically of Psalms 74–79.[36]

But if the analysis so far is sound, such importance should not be ascribed to Psalm 78 in the collection's design. As we have seen, Psalms 74–78 consist of two distinct groupings (Pss 74–76; 77–78) that stand in the same parallel relationship with Psalm 73, developing its topic in different directions. Psalm 78 is given no particular prominence on this structuration. Thus, numerical centrality does not appear to correspond to either structural or theological centrality in this case.

---

30. I refer the reader to the methodological discussion on pp. 18–20 for this point.

31. E.g., Millard, Leunberger, Ho. See Chapter 2.

32. This point will receive further corroboration in Chapters 7 and 8, where I argue the literary unity of Pss 79–82.

33. Frank-Lothar Hossfeld and Erich Zenger, *Psalms 2: A Commentary on Psalms 51–100*, trans. Linda M. Maloney, Hermeneia (Minneapolis, MN: Fortress Press, 2005), 294.

34. It is also the numerical center of the MT Psalter in terms of verses. See חצי הספר ("half of the book") in the margin of BHS at Ps 78:36. In terms of letters, the Jewish scribes locate Ps 80:14 as the middle letter of the Psalter.

35. Hossfeld and Zenger, *Psalms 2*, 293–4. In Chapter 8, I explore the significance of the links that Ps 78 shares with Ps 79.

36. See the literature survey in Chapter 2 for further details of the views of both Weber and Gärtner.

The analysis of Psalms 79–82 in the following chapters will further bear out this conclusion. The view that emerges there is that Psalm 78 is neither the structural nor the theological center of the collection. Rather, in addition to simultaneously marking two closing boundaries, Psalm 78 is something of a bridge that connects the collection's two major structural units (Pss 74–78; 79–82).

The Literary Relationship between Psalm 73 and Psalms 74–78

What remains to be considered is the literary relationship between the unit of Psalms 74–78 and the opening Psalm 73. Table 6.1, which summarizes the study's conclusions so far, brings this relationship into focus.

Table 6.1 displays the two-part macrostructure of Psalms 73–78: Psalm 73 and the unit of Psalms 74–78. Psalm 73 orients the reader/singer to the fundamental theological dilemma that Psalms 74–78 proceed to develop (i.e., the conflict between God's goodness and Israel's experience) (column 2). This unit develops the dilemma: (1) within the specific historical context of the temple's destruction (column 4); and (2) in two specific, complementary directions: this crisis jeopardized God's goodness (column 5) by challenging both his status as the Great King (column 5) and the foundational credo of Exodus 34:6–7 (column 5).

But Table 6.1 also shows that, like Psalm 73 itself, the parallel unit aims to provide *resolution* to the theological dilemma it addresses (column 3). It consequently sends the message that "God is *still* good to Israel" (73:1, 18–28; 75–76; 78) (column 6)—despite the conflicting evidence of the sixth-century crisis (73:1–16; 74; 77). Finally, Table 6.1 reveals how Psalm 73 anticipates the basic two-part structure of the unit's constituent groupings, conflict (73:1–16; 74/77) (column 2)/resolution (73:18–28; 75–76/78) (column 3), and fundamental theological message (column 6).

Table 6.1 The Literary Relationship between Psalm 73 and the Unit of Psalms 74–78

Psalm/Psalm group	Confrontation with a severe conflict of God's goodness and Israel's experience	Resolution to the conflict of faith and experience	Historical setting	Core Israelite belief challenged/ promoted	Theological message
Programmatic introduction: Psalm 73					
Psalm 73	vv. 1–16	vv. 18–28	----------	"God is good to Israel"	"God is good to Israel"
The Unit of Psalms 74–78					
Psalms 74–76	Psalm 74	Psalms 75–76	the Temple's destruction	God's status as the Great King	----------
Psalms 77–78	Psalm 77	Psalm 78	----------	Exodus 34:6–7	----------

Note: The broken dotted line indicates that the relevant cell agrees with the occupied cell in the same column.

These observations suggest that Psalm 73 functions as a programmatic introduction to the unit of Psalms 74–78: this opening psalm encapsulates the following unit's structure, the theological dilemma it addresses, and the overarching theological message it communicates.[37] It therefore becomes apparent that Psalm 73 functions as something of a hermeneutical lens for the singer/reader of Psalms 74–78. In this connection, it should not go unnoticed that Psalm 73:1 succinctly summarizes not only the main message of Psalm 73 (see Chapter 3) but Psalms 73–78 as a whole: God *is* good to Israel.

Notably, the conclusions reached so far reveal consistency in the organizing principle used to structure the collection: progressive repetition is the sole principle used so far. And it operates at two different levels of Psalms 73–78: (1) between the introductory Psalm 73 and the unit of Psalms 74–78 (Chapters 4 and 5); and (2) within that unit itself (Chapter 6). Such consistency suggests intentionality.

An Overarching Editorial Strategy for Psalms 73–78

The foregoing analysis has revealed that the design of Psalms 73–78 has a singular focus: addressing, and resolving, a multidimensional collision between "faith" (i.e., various core Israelite beliefs about God) and "experience" (the individual/community's current experience of God) precipitated by God's prolonged absence in the Temple's destruction (*c*.586/587 BCE).[38] This observation points to an overarching editorial strategy uniting Psalms 73–78. And, though not this study's focus, it is worth pointing out that it may also provide a window into the formation of their present configuration.

We saw in Chapter 2 how more than one scholar (e.g., Weber; Gärtner) believes that the present configuration (of the collection, and so this sequence) was the result of multiple redactional stages. However, the analysis of Psalms 73–78 offered here suggests an alternative theory. *If* it is valid to infer the collection's history from a synchronic analysis, I would suggest that a single synchronic act in response to the sixth-century crisis better accounts for the nature of the design detected.[39]

---

37. Not a few others have argued for the introductory function of initial psalms. See Gerald H. Wilson, *The Editing of the Hebrew Psalter*, SBLDS 76 (Chico, CA: Scholars Press, 1985), 204–7; Jerome F. D. Creach, *Yahweh as Refuge and Editing of the Hebrew Psalter*, JSOTSupp 217 (Sheffield: Sheffield Academic Press, 1996), 74; McKelvey, *Moses, David, and the High Kingship of Yahweh*, 39; Hossfeld and Zenger, *Psalms 2*, 237.

38. I should remind the reader here that this interpretation does not require that Ps 74 was composed for the sixth-century crisis, though I believe it was (contra Weber). It only requires that it is being used for this purpose in the collection's present form. Chapter 8 provides evidence that, whatever its origin, Ps 74 is being used to respond to the sixth-century crisis in the collection's present shape.

39. See Chapter 8 for further support of this view. This theory is not at odds with the linguistic evidence suggesting a northern origin for this sequence and the collection as a

In my view, the remarkable literary unity and sustained focus of this psalm sequence point in this direction. But even if a more complex diachronic process was involved, I hope it has become clear that grasping the structure, message, and purpose of this sequence's present form is not dependent upon reconstructing this process. A careful synchronic literary analysis has proved sufficient.

On the proposed interpretation, the final form of Psalms 73–78 would have aided the exilic/postexilic communities in navigating the disorienting conflict between "the God of Israel's faith" and the "God of experience" that God's prolonged absence in the temple's destruction precipitated.[40] In such a case, this group of psalms would have served a critical function for those communities as the very foundations of their faith were being shaken. It would have strengthened those foundations by fostering a renewed hope in the "God of Israel's faith" amid a jarring collision with the "God of experience."

At this point some may raise the question of whether we find support from the Second Temple period for reading Psalms 73–78 in the way I am suggesting. In this connection, the reader should recall the third of Willgren's three questions from Chapter 1: Can support for the proposed readings be found in the ancient contexts (i.e., the Second Temple period)?[41] Willgren concedes that this question is usually difficult to answer. Nevertheless, he maintains that it is important to ask because it can "shed light on possible anachronisms in suggested intentions behind the compilations and situate the formation process more firmly in the ancient material and scribal cultures."[42]

---

whole. For this point, see Gary A. Rendsburg, *Linguistic Evidence for the Northern Origin of Selected Psalms*, SBLMS 43 (Atlanta, GA: Scholars Press, 1990), 69–81. The point I am making concerns the collection's final form. As we will see in Chapter 8, Ps 79 was almost certainly composed in response to the sixth-century crisis. Thus, the terminus post quem for the collection's present form is shortly after that event, whatever the origin of the other psalms. A northern origin for most of the psalms/sequences (if correct) would mean that the "single act" I am proposing consisted of their reappropriation for this later purpose, whatever that might have involved (e.g., reuse of entire sequences; rearrangement of psalms, etc.). In this sense, the proposal here is similar to Weber's views. Though, as noted in Chapter 2, Weber does not conceive of formation as a "single act." It is worth pointing out in connection with these comments that Ps 79 is absent from Rensburg's discussion of linguistic evidence for the northern origin of Pss 73–83.

40. I say "exilic/postexilic" because we cannot be absolutely certain when this grouping reached its present form. The presence of Ps 79 in the collection (see Chapter 8) helps us identify the exilic period as the terminus post quem for this process. But it is difficult to be much more precise.

41. See the discussion on pp. 7–8.

42. David Willgren, "A Teleological Fallacy in Psalms Studies? Decentralizing the 'Masoretic' Psalms Sequence in the Formation of the 'Book' of Psalms," in *Intertextualität und die Entstehung des Psalters: Methodische Reflexionen—Theologiegeschichtliche*

I know of no textual evidence from the Second Temple period that confirms the reading argued over the past four chapters (summarized in Table 6.1). That is, I know of no textual evidence *other than the design reflected in the shape of the sequence itself*. Given that (1) the collection reflects an exilic/postexilic setting; and (2) there is no textual evidence that the collection ever existed in a substantially different form, it is reasonable to conclude that its present shape has its origins in the Second Temple period. Thus, to the extent that it is compelling, the evidence for *deliberate* design (recall here the author-/editor-oriented approach of this study) presented over the past four chapters is *itself* ancient support for the proposed reading. For we see in this evidence the editorial (and so hermeneutical) "footprints" of the community that gave this sequence its present shape.[43] I would therefore suggest that confirmation of the reading I am proposing is "built into," so to speak, the text itself.

The Exclusion of Psalm 79

Before concluding this chapter, I revisit the question of Psalm 79 from Chapter 5. Having argued the literary unity of Psalms 73–78, we can now better address this issue. I noted in Chapter 2 that a number of scholars include Psalm 79 with one or more *preceding* psalms in the collection's structure (e.g., Millard; Leunberger; Hossfeld and Zenger; Jones; Ho). This view is not without foundation. Psalm 79 does, for instance, share a number of significant links with the preceding Psalm 78.[44]

The following set of links is commonly pointed out. Psalm 78 ends (vv. 68–72) with the psalmist recounting God's choice of Mt. Zion (הר ציון), his building of the sanctuary (מקדש) like the heavens (רמים) and earth (ארץ), and bringing (בוא) David to shepherd his inheritance (נחלה). Psalm 79 opens (vv. 1–2) by lamenting that nations have come (בוא) into God's inheritance (נחלה), defiled his holy (קדש)

Perspektiven, ed. Alma Brodersen, Friederike Neumann, and David Willgren, FAT II 114 (Tübingen: Mohr Siebeck, 2020), 42.

43. I borrow the analogy of "footprints" from Nancy L. DeClaissé-Walford, *Reading from the Beginning: The Shaping of the Hebrew Psalter* (Macon, GA: Mercer University Press, 1997), vii. Along similar lines, Michael Goulder has noted, "The oldest commentary on the meaning of the psalms is the manner of their arrangement in the Psalter: that is, the collections in which they are grouped, the technical and historical notes they carry, and the order in which they stand." Michael D. Goulder, *The Psalms of the Sons of Korah*, JSOTSup 20 (Sheffield: JSOT Press, 1980), 1.

44. See Hossfeld and Zenger, *Psalms 2*, 293–4; Robert L. Cole, *The Shape and Message of Book III (Psalms 73–89)*, JSOTSup 307 (Sheffield: Sheffield Academic Press, 2000), 77–87; J. Clinton McCann, "Books I–III and the Editorial Purpose of the Psalter," in *The Shape and Shaping of the Psalter*, ed. J. Clinton McCann, JSOTSup 159 (Sheffield: Sheffield Academic Press, 1993), 99.

temple, turned Jerusalem (ירושלם) to ruins, and given the corpses of God's servants to the birds of the heavens (שמים) and beasts of the earth (ארץ). In light of such links, scholars have understandably detected a deliberate relationship between these psalms.[45]

More specifically, scholars draw attention to the thematic–historical connection between the ending of Psalm 78 and the beginning of Psalm 79 that these links highlight: the sequential progression from Psalms 78 to 79 mirrors the historical progression from the establishment of Jerusalem, David, and the temple (78:65–72) to their dissolution in the sixth century BCE (Ps 79:1–3). Psalm 79 seems to "pick up" right where Psalm 78 leaves off.

By way of response, it first needs pointing out that adjacent psalms may share significant links and not belong to the same low-level psalm group (i.e., one level above the individual psalm). This can be shown by considering the many links that Psalms 105–107 share.[46] This example is particularly apropos since (1) Psalms 105–107 occur at what most editorial critics would consider a clear structural boundary in the MT Psalter (i.e., a location of clear literary disjunction), the one demarcating Books IV and V; and (2) these psalms exhibit a "tail-head" linkage resembling the connection between Psalms 78:68–72 and 79:1–2.

Barry C. Davis has observed that the first three verses of Psalm 107 (the first psalm of Book V) "echo lexically and respond thematically to the terminology and issues presented in the concluding five verses of Psalm 106 [the final psalm of Book IV]. Of the 15 lexeme families of Ps 107:1–3, 7 (47 percent) are replicated in Ps 106:44–48 [sic]."[47] In addition to this observation, Davis explains that

> the beginning of Psalm 107 also provides a thematic response to the plea recorded in Ps 106:47 for the LORD to deliver (ישע) his people from distress and to gather (קבץ) them from exile among the nations (גוי). Psalm 107:2–3 reports that the people of God have been redeemed (גאל) out of their disastrous situation and gathered (קבץ) from the lands (ארץ) to which they had been dispersed.[48]

These and other links suggest to some that the boundary between Books IV and V is a "soft" one, with Psalms 105–107 forming a psalm group (e.g., Egbert Ballhorn).[49]

---

45. See especially Cole, *The Shape and Message of Book III*, 80.

46. I realize that scholars who question the MT Psalter as a base text for analysis might not find this example persuasive. As will become clear, however, my argument stands whether or not one accepts this as a legitimate example.

47. Barry C. Davis, "A Contextual Analysis of Psalms 107–118" (PhD diss., Trinity Evangelical Divinity School, 1996), 68. Quoted from Michael K. Snearly, *The Return of the King: Messianic Expectation in Book V of the Psalter*, LHBOTS 624 (New York: Bloomsbury, 2016), 106–7.

48. Davis, "A Contextual Analysis of Psalms 107–118," 68. Quoted from Snearly, *The Return of the King*, 107.

49. Snearly, *The Return of the King*, 106.

But despite these significant connections (i.e., literary continuity), Snearly points out that Davis (with the majority of editorial critics) nevertheless affirms the traditional "hard" book boundary between Books IV and V (i.e., literary discontinuity).[50] Snearly summarizes the evidence for this view: (1) the similarity between the doxologies at the end of the books; (2) arguments for the cohesion of Book IV; (3) arguments for the cohesion of Book V (i.e., Snearly's own study); (4) in addition to the many parallels, there are also significant differences between Psalm 105 and Psalms 106–107. For example, the distribution of the phrase הללו יה ("Praise the Lord!"); (5) the key root זכר ("to remember") in Psalms 105–106 (105:5, 8, 42; 106:4, 7, 45) is absent from Psalm 107; (6) Psalms 105–106 seem to address the exilic crisis (106:47), while Psalm 107 is "written from the perspective of restoration (104.3; see also 7, 14, 20, 30)."[51]

This example illustrates an important principle already utilized considerably in this study: in addition to evidence of editorial joining, editorial-critical investigation must also take into account evidence of editorial separation. As noted in Chapter 1, the very idea of structure implies *both* literary continuity and discontinuity. For present purposes, this means that factors tacitly suggesting editorial separation between Psalms 78 and 79—not *only* the connections they share—must be factored into discussions on Psalm 79's place in the collection's structure.

We can now summarize these factors, some of which were mentioned in Chapter 5. The first is the inner literary cohesion of the sequence of Psalms 77–78 argued in Chapter 5, which implies a break between Psalms 78 and 79. In this connection, it is worth recalling a particular structural parallel that distinguishes these psalms from Psalm 79: the verb אזן ("to hear") in the *hip͑il* stem occurs at the beginning of both (77:2; 78:1), and the verb נחה ("to lead") occurs at their conclusion in connection with a prominent figure from Israel's past (77:21; 78:72).[52] Third, a significant difference between Psalms 77–78 and Psalm 79 is often not pointed out. Absent from Psalm 79 is a focus on the major conjunctive feature binding Psalms 77–78 together, the theme of God's saving deeds in history.

A fourth factor is the substantial evidence that Psalms 74–78 are a distinct literary unit, corroborating a hard break after Psalm 78. Fifth is the parallel relationship of Psalms 74–76 and 77–78, and that which each shares with the opening Psalm 73. These relationships are an argument for the distinct nature of each sequence, and so the exclusion of Psalm 79 from the latter. Sixth, the observation that the first two groupings begin with a God-lament psalm (Pss 74 and 77) creates the expectation that Psalm 79—also a God-lament (see Chapter 8)—will likewise *begin*

---

50. Ibid.
51. Ibid., 109.
52. It is true that the shepherd metaphor also appears at the end of Ps 79 (see v. 13). But there is a significant difference often not pointed out. Unlike both Pss 77:21 and 78:72, in 79:13 this metaphor is not connected to a prominent figure from Israel's past.

a (third) psalm grouping.⁵³ The consistent pattern emerging is that God-laments, and so Psalm 79, begin psalm groups in the collection. Chapter 8 will further bear this point out. Finally, the literary unity of Psalms 79–82 argued in that chapter is further evidence that the collection's major break falls between Psalms 78 and 79.

I would suggest that these seven considerations collectively establish a tacit editorial break between Psalms 78 and 79. As mentioned above, once the analysis of Psalms 79–82 has been carried out, the view that emerges is that this is a "hard" break, separating the collection's two major units (Pss 74–78; 79–82). Though, as we shall see, these distinct units are closely related.

If this assessment is correct, whatever the significance of the links between Psalms 78 and 79, they should not be mistaken for evidence that the two psalms belong to the same low-level psalm group. Later I present evidence that studies grouping Psalm 79 with Psalm 78 in the collection's structure have misunderstood the literary level at which the significant links between these psalms operate. These parallels do not, as is supposed, link *two psalms within a group* (i.e., Pss 78 and 79) but *two groups of psalms* (i.e., the larger psalm units of Pss 74–78 and 79–82). As we shall see, this point has important interpretive implications.

---

53. The strong parallels that Ps 79 shares with both Pss 77 and 74 (especially the latter) add considerable weight to this point. I discuss these parallels in Chapter 8.

Chapter 7

PSALMS 80-81: GOD WILL HEAR AND DELIVER—
DESPITE CONFLICTING EVIDENCE

The final two chapters are a combined argument for the literary unity of Psalms 79–82. This psalm sequence, I contend, represents a second major literary unit that closely resembles the design of the first (Pss 74–78). At the same time, its structure is more complex, taking the form of chiasmus (A1 [Ps 79], B1 [Ps 80], B2 [Ps 81], A2 [Ps 82]). Nevertheless, as we shall see, progressive repetition still governs psalm sequencing.

This chapter focuses on Psalms 80–81, arguing that these adjacent psalms are a third psalm sequence that deliberately parallels the initial Psalm 73. The reason for departing from a sequential analysis of the collection will become clear as the analysis progresses.

Analysis of Psalms 80 and 81

As has been our practice, the first task is a concise analysis of Psalms 80 and 81.

Psalm 80

Psalm 80 is a communal lament. And, like Psalms 74 and 77, Psalm 80 is a God-lament psalm.[1] As seen below, the conflict of faith and experience confronting the community is articulated at length in verses 5–16. The psalm's unclear setting has been the subject of lively debate.[2] The clearest structural indicator is the refrain of verses 4, 8, and 20. This refrain consists of a petition for Yahweh to "restore" (*hipʿil* of the verb שוב ["to return"]) the community in language reminiscent of the Aaronic benediction (Num 6). Broyles points out (correctly in my view) that this petition may exploit the various meanings of the verb שוב (i.e., "restore"/"repent")

---

1. See Craig C. Broyles, *The Conflict of Faith and Experience in the Psalms: A Form-Critical and Theological Study*, JSOTSup 52 (Sheffield: Sheffield Academic Press, 1989), 161–5.
2. See the concise summary of views in Marvin E. Tate, *Psalms 51-100*, Word Biblical Commentary (Nashville, TN: Thomas Nelson, 1990), 309–13.

to imply an admission/acknowledgment of past failure.[3] It is clear that the refrain marks the conclusion of a section given its appearance at the end of the psalm (v. 20). Consequently, verses 4 and 8, also instances of the refrain, mark the closing boundary of a subsection.

Three considerations suggest that verses 15–16 also mark a closing boundary:[4] (1) verse 15 resembles the psalm's refrain, which concludes a section;[5] (2) verses 17–20 witness a shift to volitives that continue throughout the rest of the psalm;[6] and (3) the verb נטע ("to plant") and the noun גפן ("vine") are repeated in verses 15–16 from the unit's opening verse (v. 9). This repetition signals an inclusion around the section focusing on the vine metaphor.

A four-part structure emerges from these observations:

A1. Prayer for Deliverance (six volitives) (vv. 2–4)[7]
    B1. God-lament ("How long?"): transformation of Shepherd metaphor (vv. 5–8)
    B2. God-lament ("Why?"): transformation of vineyard metaphor (vv. 9–16)
A2. Prayer for Deliverance (five volitives) (vv. 17–20)[8]

Verses 2–4 form an opening plea for deliverance. The community appeals to God as the "Shepherd of Israel," "the one who drives Joseph like the flock," and "the one who dwells upon the cherubim." These appellations recall God's care for the community in the Exodus and conquest, as well as his royal military prowess associated with the ark of the covenant. The community desperately implores God with six volitives: "Hear!," "Shine forth!," "Rouse your strength!," "Come to our salvation," "Restore us!," and "Shine your face!" (v. 3). The latter two occur in the

---

3. Broyles, *The Conflict of Faith and Experience in the Psalms*, 163–4. The community's acknowledgment of past failure is also implied in v. 19: "then we will not turn back (נסוג) from you." See Pss 44:18; 53:4; Isa 50:5; 59:13; Zeph 1:6. See below for discussion.

4. The *vav* fronting v. 16 (see וכנה אשר נטעה ימינך ["even the stock that your 'right hand' planted"]) indicates the grammatical dependency of v. 16 on v. 15. The two verses, therefore, should not be separated.

5. Compare אלהים צבאות שוב נא הבט משמים וראה ("O God of Armies, turn! Look from heaven, and see!") in v. 15 with אלהים השיבנו והאר פניך ("O God of Armies, restore us! [lit. "cause us to return"] Let your face shine!") (v. 4); אלהים צבאות השיבנו והאר פניך ("O God of armies, restore us! [lit. "cause us to return"] Let your face shine!") (v. 8); and יהוה אלהים צבאות השיבנו האר פניך (O Lord God of Armies, restore us! [lit. "cause us to return"] Let your face shine!") (v. 20).

6. See the discussion below for this point.

7. האזינה ("give hear!"); הופיעה ("shine forth!"); עוררה ("stir up!"); and לכה ("come!"). השיבנו ("restore us!"); האר פניך ("shine your face!").

8. יאבדו ("may they perish!") (v. 17); תהי ("may it be") (v. 18); תחינו ("revive us!") (v. 19); השיבנו ("restore us!") (v. 20); האר פניך ("may your face to shine!") (v. 20).

initial instance of the psalm's refrain, which marks the conclusion of the first section: "O God, restore us (השיבנו); shine your face upon us, that we might be saved!"

Sections B1 and B2 (vv. 5–16) are the heart of the appeal. Verses 5–8 take up the shepherd metaphor from verses 2–4 but transform it to draw attention to a conflict between faith and experience:[9]

> O Lord, God of Hosts, how long will you smoke against the prayers of your people?
> > You have fed them the bread of tears,
> > and have given them tears to drink in great measure. (Ps 80:5–6)

These verses accuse God of having fed his flock with tears instead of bread. The basis for this charge is the community's perception that God has—for a prolonged duration—failed to answer their prayers. The implication is that such Divine behavior contradicts Israel's traditional profile of God as a *good* shepherd.[10] In verse 7 the community laments that this situation has resulted in mocking from Israel's neighbors. The first section of the central unit closes with a second instance of the refrain (v. 8).

The second half of this central section (vv. 9–16) transforms another of Israel's conventional metaphors, that of the vine. Hee Suk Kim has pointed out that the psalmist here takes up an image used elsewhere in scripture to critique Israel of unfaithfulness (e.g., Isa 5:1–7; Jer 2:21; 12:10; Ezek 15:1–8; Hos 10:1) and shockingly turns it on its head to critique God.[11] In verses 9–12 God is portrayed as a benevolent gardener or vinedresser. With much care he uprooted his "vine" from Egypt, drove out many nations to protect it (i.e., the conquest), firmly planted it in the promised land, and caused it to flourish under David and Solomon.

However, like the "praise" motif in Psalm 74:12–17 discussed in Chapter 4, verses 9–12 are not "straight praise." They have as their goal the God-lament that follows in verse 13: "Why have you broken down its walls so that every passerby plucks it?" This "praise" section works with the God-lament to draw God's attention to an inconsistency between his past praiseworthy conduct (vv. 9–12) and his present behavior (v. 13). As a whole, verses 9–13 point out the absurdity

---

9. Hee Suk Kim, "A Critique against God? Reading Psalm 80 in the Context of Vindication," in *Why? … How Long? Studies on Voices of Lamentation Rooted in Biblical Hebrew Poetry*, ed. LeAnn Snow Flesher, Carol J. Dempsey, and Mark J. Boda, LHBOTS (London: Bloomsbury T&T Clark, 2014), 103. See also the discussion in Broyles, *The Conflict of Faith and Experience in the Psalms*, 161–2.

10. By "traditional" I do not mean to suggest that this metaphor belongs to certain stratum of religious tradition in ancient Israel. I only mean that, when used of God, the shepherd metaphor is used consistently in the Hebrew Bible to depict God as a good rather than negligent shepherd (e.g., Pss 23; 77:21; 28:9).

11. Kim, "A Critique against God?," 105.

of a gardener destroying the protective walls of a vine—thereby exposing it to danger—for which he has taken so much time and care to cultivate.[12]

The petitionary verse 15 that follows and closes the section indicates the rhetorical nature of the question: the psalmist seeks not an explanation but change. The psalm concludes in verses 17–19 as it began, with petitions for deliverance/restoration. This section, and the psalm as a whole, concludes with a final instance of the refrain (v. 20). The conclusion also contains a communal pledge of renewed faithfulness to God ("may your hand be upon the man of you right hand ... then we will not turn away from you [ולא נסוג ממך]").[13] As noted above, this pledge seems to "betray an awareness that the people have defected from God."[14] Thus, in conjunction with Broyles's observations on the key word שוב noted above, this pledge paints the picture of a repentant community, one acknowledging the justness of God's initial anger, and who desires to remain faithful upon Divine deliverance.

Psalm 81

Psalm 81 is in two major sections. Verses 1–6 are a hymnic introduction, and verses 7–16 constitute an extended Divine oracle.[15] The first four verses are a congregational summons to worship at a festal gathering. The congregation is summoned to "sing" and "shout for joy" to the "God our strength" (אלהים עוזנו) and the "God of Jacob" (v. 2). Goldingay rightly notes that "vv. 6–16 [Heb. 7–17] will spell this out."[16] For, in these verses God himself recounts how he manifested his

---

12. Broyles, *The Conflict of Faith and Experience in the Psalms*, 162.

13. The verb סוג ("to turn away/back") is often used to express the idea of unfaithfulness. It most often occurs in the *nipʿal* when it has this meaning (Isa 50:5; 59:13; Jer 38:22; Zeph 1:6; Ps 44:19). But it is also used this way, as here, in the *qal* (Ps 53:4; Prov 14:14). Significantly, the verb is used elsewhere in Pss 73–83 in the sense of unfaithfulness (Ps 78:57), though there the verb is in the *nipʿal*.

14. Hieke overstates his case when he claims that "Psalm 80 does not contain a confession of sin or guilt, and there is *no trace* of any explanation for the immense distress or any solution of the problem" (emphasis added). Thomas Hieke, "Psalm 80 and Its Neighbors in the Psalter: The Context of the Psalter as a Background for Interpreting Psalms," *BN* 86 (1997): 40. Verse 19 contradicts this claim.

15. As was the case with Ps 75 (see Chapter 4), I follow Jacobson here in using the term "oracle" for the extended God-quotation in vv. 7–16 "with the greatest care." Rolf A. Jacobson, *Many Are Saying: The Function of Direct Discourse in the Hebrew Psalter*, LHBOTS 397 (New York: T&T Clark, 2004), 92. As noted in Chapter 4, "oracle" implies present communication from God. But God-quotations in psalms like Ps 81 are best understood as "either a quotation of words of God that had been communicated in the past ... or as artistic liturgical compositions that drew upon the theological traditions of Israel's past." Jacobson, *Many Are Saying*, 112. See Jacobson's discussion on ibid., 92–93, 111–12.

16. John Goldingay, *Psalms 42–89*, Baker Commentary on the Old Testament: Wisdom and Psalms (Grand Rapids, MI: Baker, 2008), 548.

great strength on Israel's behalf by delivering them from Egyptian bondage (vv. 7-8, 11).[17]

God also, and most importantly, promises to continue protecting and providing for his people—if they would only "listen" to his voice (i.e., obey) (vv. 16-17). Further, the congregation is summoned to "lift up a song" and "blow the horn" "on the day of our feast (ליום חגנו)" (vv. 3-4). The prepositional phrase ליום חגנו in verse 4 is usually understood as a reference to the Festival of Tabernacles. But it is possible that another festival is in view (e.g., Passover). Verses 5-6 give the reason for the summons to praise: God decreed it as a statute to Israel and made it "a testimony in Joseph" "when he [God] went out against the land of Egypt" (v. 6).[18] Thus, the joyous festal gathering has its origins in God's great Exodus redemption. It celebrates God's great acts of deliverance, which God himself recounts at length in the oracle of verses 7-17.

Scholars have proposed various interpretations for the final (and difficult) clause of verse 6 (שפת לא ידעתי אשמע).[19] I take a view similar to that of Michael Goulder;[20] these are the words of a psalmist leading the gathered congregation (vv. 1-5). They are specifically leading in a renewed commitment to "hear (שמע)"[21] (i.e., obey) the voice of God (lit. "lip of" [שפת]). And it is a voice that God's people have not steadfastly obeyed in the past ("... that I [i.e., God's people] had not known [לא ידעתי] [i.e., obeyed])."[22] In the psalm, the "voice of God" is heard at length in the oracle of verses 7-17.

---

17. God is referred to as "my strength (עזי)" in the opening lines of the so-called song of Moses (see Exod 15:2). This observation supports the view that "God, our strength (עוזנו)" in Ps 81:2 has in view God's Exodus redemption.

18. The MT of the first half of v. 6 reads as follows: עדות ביהוסף שמו בצאתו על ארץ מצרים ("A statute in Joseph he made it when he [i.e., God] went out over/against the land of Egypt."). The LXX has μαρτύριον ἐν τῷ Ιωσηφ ἔθετο αὐτὸν ἐν τῷ ἐξελθεῖν αὐτὸν ἐκ γῆς Αἰγύπτου· ("a testimony in Joseph he made it when he [i.e., Joseph] went out from the Egypt"). The MT makes good sense here in light of the emphasis on God's Exodus deliverance in the following God quotation (vv. 7, 8, 11 ["I am the Lord, your God, who brought you out of the land of Egypt."]). Also, the parallel with "Israel" and "Joseph" in vv. 5-6 argues for seeing Joseph as the recipient of the command rather than the subject of the verb "to go out" in v. 6.

19. For a concise summary, see Tate, *Psalms 51-100*, 319-20.

20. See Michael D. Goulder, *The Psalms of Asaph and the Pentateuch*, The Library of Hebrew Bible/Old Testament Studies 233 (Sheffield: Sheffield Academic Press, 1996), 153-4.

21. As is commonly the case, the *yiqtol* אשמע ("I will hear") does not express future tense but emphasizes the volition of the speaker: "I *will* hear."

22. I take the verbs ידע ("to know") and שמע ("to hear") here to mean "heed" or "obey." Both are used in this way in Ps 95, with which Ps 81 is commonly compared: "if only you would obey/hear his voice (אם בקלו תשמעו)" (v. 7); "They have not known (i.e., obeyed) my ways (לא ידעו דרכי)" (v. 10). For other examples of שמע in this sense, see Gen 26:5; Deut 21:18; Lev 26:21; Neh 9:17). The nomen regens שפת ("lip of") is understood to be in construct to an asyndetic relative clause: שפת (אשר) לא ידעתי ("Speech [*that*] I did not

This interpretation makes good sense in light of the content of the oracle. Verses 7–13 consist of God's account of/lament over the failure of the Exodus generation to "listen (שמע)" to his voice (v. 12) and the judgment received for not complying (v. 13). Verses 14–17, on the other hand, consist of a Divine promise of protection and blessing for future generations, provided that they "listen (שמע)" (v. 14). Thus, the gathered congregation, and every generation thereafter who sings/utters the words of the psalm, resolves to respond differently than the forefathers. Consequently, they are positioning themselves to receive God's promise of protection and blessing.

I understand the oracle of verses 7–17 to be in four parts of two to three verses each (vv. 7–8; 9–11; 12–13; 14–17). "Selah (סלה)" at the end of verse 8 marks the conclusion of the first part. The other sections are marked by the occurrence of the key word שמע ("hear"/"obey") at or near their beginning (see vv. 9, 12, 14). An analysis of the oracle supports this division.

In verses 7–8, Yahweh recounts how he answered his people's cry to be freed from Egyptian bondage, delivering and putting them to the test in the wilderness. Verses 9–11 form a unit that consists of an "oracle within an oracle, which represents the oracle by which God tested the Israelites at Meribah (8c)."[23] Here God longs that his stubborn people would heed his voice (v. 9), a response to the great deliverance they received (v. 11). If only they would listen, God declares, he would abundantly "fill" their mouths (v. 11). In verses 12–13, however, God laments the disobedient response of his people: Israel was not willing to "listen/obey." Consequently, God sent them away in the stubbornness of their heart to follow their own desires.

The final section of the oracle (vv. 14–17) shifts the focus from past generations to present/future ones. It contains God's most direct address to the gathered congregation and subsequent hearers/readers of the psalm. These verses are, therefore, in one sense the most important of the psalm. Significantly, they reveal that this oracle, while solemn, is a *hopeful* exhortation to obedience.

The verses that have preceded (vv. 7–13) were primarily a solemn Divine warning for the gathered congregation to avoid the disobedient response of the forefathers. Continuing that tone of lament, God expresses his desire that present/future generations of his people would "listen to/obey (שמע) me" and "walk in my ways" (v. 14). Graciously attached to this exhortation is the Divine promise that compliance will result in (1) God's swift deliverance ("Quickly I would subdue their enemies, and turn my hand against their foes");[24] and (2) God's abundant

---

know"). See the discussion in R. D. Holmstedt, "The Restrictive Syntax of Genesis i 1," *VT* 58 (2008): 59–63.

23. Tate, *Psalms 51–100*, 323–4.

24. As others have noted (e.g., Goldingay, *Psalms 42–89*, 555), this statement need not presuppose a life setting of national subjugation by an enemy. It may simply be a general promise for when God's people find themselves in such a situation because of their disobedience.

Table 7.1 Analogous Literary Progression of Psalm 73 and Psalms 80–81

Core aspect of Israelite "faith" challenged	Confrontation with a severe conflict of faith and experience	Radical shift in perspective on God's posture/involvement
God's goodness	Psalm 73:1–16	Psalm 73:18–28
A God willing to hear and deliver	Psalm 80	Psalm 81

provision for his people ("He would fill them [lit. "him"] with the best of wheat ...") (vv. 15–16). The language here recalls God's response/promise to past generations, described in verses 8 ("You called out in distress, and I delivered you") and 11 ("Open your mouth wide, and I will fill it").

Thus, as Tate notes, "the preaching in Ps 81 lays before the congregation an open future of blessing" (vv. 14–17).[25] Despite the persistent unwillingness of God's people to obey, God nevertheless graciously holds out an abiding promise to protect and bless them—if they would "listen" to his voice.

Formal Correspondence with Psalm 73: Evidence

The same type of correspondence with Psalm 73 observed in the case of the first two psalm groupings suggests a deliberate parallel relationship here as well.

Analogous Literary Progression

Table 7.1 shows that the major literary progression of Psalm 73 is repeated for a third time in the collection in these adjacent psalms. The "lament" of Psalm 80 corresponds to Psalm 73:1–16 and Psalm 81 to 73:18–28.

Column 2 shows that, like the first "part" of each grouping we have considered, the appeal of Psalm 80 centers on the same basic theological dilemma as Psalm 73:1–16: the perception of a disorienting conflict between faith and experience. In Psalm 80 the psalmist's appeal paints the shocking portrait of God as a *bad* Shepherd (v. 6) and *malevolent* Vinedresser (vv. 9–13) (experience), a portrait that severely undermines Israel's core belief that God is willing to hear and deliver (faith) (column 1).[26]

---

25. Tate, *Psalms 51–100*, 327.

26. For the foundational nature of this belief (i.e., that God *will* hear and deliver his people when called upon), see: Pss 3:4; 4:4; 5:4; 7:11–14; 12:6, 8; 14:5–6; 17:6; 25:3, 5, 15; 27:10; 28:5; 31:6, 15, 20–21; 36:6–7; 38:16; 40:18; 41:2–4; 51:6; 54:6–7; 55:17–20, 24; 56:10–12; 57:3–4; 58:11–12; 59:11, 17–18; 61:6; 64:8–10; 70:6; 71:3, 5–8, 20; 86:5, 7; 106:44–46; 109:31; 123:2; 126:5–6; 130:7–8; 139:7–12; 137:8; 140:6–7, 13–14; 142:6–7; 143:12. In conjunction with these texts, see the discussion in Broyles, *The Conflict of Faith and Experience in the Psalms*, 122–4.

Like the second "part" of the previous groupings, the transition to Psalm 81 is marked by the same type of perspectival shift observable in Psalm 73:18–28. In sharp contrast to the community's experience of God in Psalm 80, the Divine profile that God's own self-revelation promotes in Psalm 81 (see vv. 7–17) is that of a *good* Shepherd who *is* willing to hear and deliver a repentant people (vv. 14–17). Thus, the truthfulness of the core belief that experience appears to severely threaten Psalm 80 is firmly established by God's own self-revelation in the adjacent Psalm 81.

Like the first two psalm groupings, then, this psalm sequence also mirrors the major literary progression of Psalm 73's two halves.

Analogous Network of Parallels

Here I draw attention to a second correspondence with Psalm 73 that has become familiar, namely, a group of repetitions mirroring those McCann discerned between that psalm's two halves.[27] A perusal of Table 7.2 reveals that the repetition of a group of words in Psalm 81, and the motifs some reflect, marks that radical shift in perspective observable in the progression to that psalm:

1. In Psalm 80 the cry to "Hear!" (האזינה) (80:2) is voiced by a community perceiving God as a "bad" Shepherd who seems unwilling to hear, "feeding" them only a steady diet of tears (v. 4). In Psalm 81 God's plea for Israel to "Hear" (שמע) reflects the good Shepherd's *willingness* to hear and deliver his people (v. 14), provided they do not rebel like their forefathers (vv. 9, 12).[28]

---

27. There are other links between these psalms not listed here, some of which may be significant. An example is the verb הלך ("to walk/come") in 80:3 ("Come to save us!") and 81:13 ("They were walking in their own counsels"), which Cole considers significant. Robert L. Cole, *The Shape and Message of Book III (Psalms 73–89)*, JSOTSup 307 (Sheffield: Sheffield Academic Press, 2000), 99. This verb occurs sixty-eight times in the MT Psalter, over 1,500 times in the Hebrew Bible, and in seven of the eleven total Asaph psalms. It also appears in all but one psalm in the string of Pss 77–83 [Ps 79]), within which Pss 80–81 appear. Thus, while it may be significant, it is excluded because it does not constitute the strongest evidence of deliberate design. I have excluded שלח ("to send") for similar reasons (cf. Pss 80:12; 81:13).

28. The reader should recall here that vv. 14–17 contain the psalm's most direct address to those appropriating Ps 81. For this reason, we noted that they are in one sense the most important verses of the Divine oracle. Thus, though the verb "hear" occurs earlier in the psalm in negative contexts (e.g., vv. 9, 12), reading "with the grain" of the text reveals that the focus for those appropriating the psalm is on God's *willingness* to hear in vv. 14–17. This aspect of the psalm therefore takes precedence in the interpretation here. See the exegesis above for further details.

Table 7.2 Parallels between Psalm 80 and Psalm 81

Parallel	Psalm 80	Psalm 81
Motif of God's "hearing" (אזן/ שמע)	"*Hear*! O Shepherd of Israel" (v. 2)	"*Hear*, O my people, I will admonish you! O Israel, if you would *listen* to me!" (v. 9); "But my people did not *listen* ..." (v. 12); "O, that my people would *listen* to me, that Israel would walk in my ways!" (v. 14)
Motif of "delivering (חלץ)/saving (ישע)"	"Come and *save* us!" (v. 3); "let your face shine that we might be *saved*" (cf., vv. 4, 8, 20)	"In distress you called out and I *delivered* you" (v. 8); "I brought you up from the land of Egypt" (v. 11); "Oh, that my people would listen to me ... Quickly I would subdue your enemies ...." (vv. 14, 15)
The motif of God "feeding (אכל)" his people	"How Long will you be anger with the prayers of your people? You have *fed* (them) with bread of tears" (v. 6)	"I am the Lord your God who brought you out from the land of Egypt. *Open your mouth wide and I will fill it*" (v. 11); "Oh, that my people would listen to me ... I would *feed* him [i.e., Israel] with the best of wheat." (vv. 14, 17)
The motif of "salvation history" (מצרים)	"You brought a vine out of *Egypt* ..." (v. 9) (used in "praise" section drawing attention to conflict of faith and experience)	"He made it a decree in Joseph when he went out over the land of *Egypt*" (v. 6); "I am the Lord your God who brought you out of the land of *Egypt* (v. 11); "I would quickly subdue their enemies ...." (vv. 15–16)
שוב ("to return"; "to restore" [hip'il])	"O God (of Hosts), *restore* us!" (vv. 4, 8, 20); "O God of Hosts, *turn*! Look down from heaven, and see!" (v. 15)	"Oh, that my people would listen to me ... I would *turn* my hand against their adversaries." (vv. 14–15)
איב ("enemy")	"Our *enemies* are mocking us" (v. 7)	"Oh, that my people would listen to me ... Quickly I would subdue their *enemies*." (vv. 14–15)
"right hand" (ימין)/"hand" (יד)	"have regard for ... the stock that your *right hand* planted" (v. 16); "may your hand be upon the man of your *right hand*" (v. 18)	"Oh, that my people would listen to me ... I would turn my *hand* against their adversaries." (vv. 14–15)

2. In Psalm 80 the motif of deliverance is tied to the portrait of a God perceived to be unwilling to "save" (ישע), despite continual cries for help (vv. 3, 4, 8, and 20). In Psalm 81:15–16, God's own self-revelation stresses his willingness to save present/future generations as he delivered (חלץ) in the past (vv. 8, 11, 14, 15).

3. In Psalm 80 the verb אכל is associated with the portrait of a "bad" shepherd who feeds the community bread of tears (v. 6). But in Psalm 81 it is associated with the image of God as a good Shepherd willing to "feed" (אכל) an obedient flock with good things (v. 17).
4. In Psalm 80 the community accuses God of virtually (and excessively) reversing the history of salvation that began with the Exodus from Egypt (מצרים) (v. 9; see vv. 9–12). In Psalm 81 God's own self-revelation promises to duplicate his saving activity that was so mightily displayed in that event (see מצרים) (v. 11; see vv. 15–17). God makes this promise despite his people's past waywardness (vv. 15–16), if they would obey him and walk in his ways (vv. 14–16).
5. The prominent refrain of Psalm 80 (and a line similar to it [v. 15]) repeatedly urges an enigmatically inactive God to become active once again and "restore (שוב)" the community (vv. 4, 8, 15, 20). By way of contrast, the Divine self-disclosure in Psalm 81:15 provides God's own assurance of his willingness to "turn (שוב)" his hand against the enemies of an obedient people.
6. In Psalm 80, the community laments that their enemies (איב) mock them (v. 6) while God, the "bad shepherd," continually shuts out their prayers (v. 7). Psalm 81:15, however, relates God's own promise to quickly subdue an obedient people's enemies (איב) (v. 15).
7. In Psalm 80 the community petitions God to once again put into action his mighty "right hand" (ימין)/"hand" (יד) (v. 16), perceived as enigmatically withheld at present. Psalm 81:15 contrastively characterizes God as ready to swiftly and mightily turn his "hand" (יד) against an obedient people's adversaries (v. 15).

It is thus clear that these seven repetitions conform to the pattern seen in Psalm 73: they consistently mark the radical shift in perspective in Psalm 81 to a Divine profile of a God who *is* willing to hear and deliver. And, as noted in relation to the first two psalm groups, the number and consistency of these repetitions suggest intentionality. In so doing, this network of repetitions provides further evidence of a deliberate relationship with Psalm 73.

Evaluation of these links in terms of the principles/criteria laid out in Chapter 1 corroborates their intentionality:

1. Words built from the root אזן ("to hear"), reflecting the motif of God's "hearing," only occur elsewhere in the collection at 77:2 and 78:1 (2×). Especially suggestive of this link's intentionality is that שמע is *the* keyword in the Divine oracle of 81:7–17 (see vv. 6, 9 [2×], 12, 14).[29] Further, the occurrences of שמע in Psalm 81 represent five of the nine total in Psalms 73–83.

---

29. Consider Jacobson's observation in this connection: "The call to 'obey/hear' is repeated in the God quotation to the point that it can be considered the quotation's 'unifying theme.'" Jacobson, *Many Are Saying*, 108–9.

2. The motif of "saving"/"delivering" is central to both psalms (80:3, 4, 8, and 20; 81:7–8, 11, 15–16), where it is reflected in partial synonyms (see ישע in 80:3, 4, 8, 20, and חלץ in 81:8). Its intentionality is strengthened by the observation that the verb ישע is a keyword (together with שוב ["to restore"]) in the prominent refrain of Psalm 80. It is also reinforced by the infrequency of the verb חלץ ("to deliver") in the MT Psalter. This verb only occurs eleven other times in total, and nowhere else within Psalms 73–83.
3. The motif of God "feeding" his people is also significant in both psalms (80:6; 81:11,[30] 17). This motif is reflected in the verb אכל ("to eat") in the *hipʿil* stem in each case (80:6; 81:17).[31] These are the only two occurrences of the verb אכל in the *hipʿil* stem in the MT Psalter. This verb only occurs, in any stem, in seventeen other psalms (Pss 14; 18; 21; 22; 27; 41; 50; 53; 59; 69; 78; 79; 102; 105; 106; 127; 128). Its presence in the crucial closing verses of the Divine oracle (see the analysis of Ps 81 above) supports its intentionality (vv. 14–17).
4. "Salvation history" is also an important motif in both psalms (80:9–12; 81:7–8, 11, 15–17).[32] This link is reflected in the proper noun מצרים ("Egypt") in each case (80:9; 81:6, 11). The noun only occurs in one other psalm in the collection, Psalm 78 (vv. 12, 43, 51).
5. The occurrences of the verb שוב ("to return") in these adjacent psalms represent five of the thirteen total in Psalms 73–83 (see 80:4, 8, 15, 20; 81:15). Three additional observations strengthen the likelihood of the verb's intentionality: (1) its high frequency;[33] (2) its recurrence as a keyword in the prominent refrain of Psalm 80 (and a line closely resembling it [i.e., v. 15]); and (3) its presence in the important closing verses of the Divine oracle (vv. 14–17).
6. The noun איב ("enemy") (80:7; 81:15) is common in the MT Psalter (seventy-four occurrences, seven times in Pss 73–83). But its presence in the important closing verses of the Divine oracle (vv. 14–17) with other significant links argues for its intentionality (i.e., שוב and אכל).
7. Two factors suggest the significance of references to God's powerful "right hand" (ימין)/"hand" (יד) (see 80:16, 18; 81:15): (1) as we have seen, the

---

30. Verse 11 reads: "I am the Lord your God who brought you up from the land of Egypt. Open your mouth wide and I will fill (מלא) it." The verb מלא ("to fill") here in 81:11 does also occur in Ps 80: "it [i.e., the vine] filled (מלא) the land" (80:9). This link may be significant. It is not listed because the occurrence of the verb in 81:11 is part of a more prominent connection between these psalms, the motif of God's feeding his people.

31. The verb אכל occurs in two of the collection's other psalms (Pss 78 [vv. 24, 25, 29, 45, 63] and 79 [v. 7]). It is not used of God's feeding his people in either.

32. Obviously, God's promised *future* deliverance in Ps 81:15–17 is not salvation *history*. But it reflects this motif since God's past and promised future deliverance are closely connected in the psalm.

33. Only one other psalm in the MT Psalter has more occurrences than Ps 80 (Ps 85 [5×]). And only one other is tied with it (Ps 78 [4×]).

Table 7.3 The Semantic Relationship between Psalm 73 and Psalms 80–81

Psalm/Psalm group	Confrontation with a severe conflict of faith and experience	Resolution to the conflict of faith and experience	Core Israelite belief challenged/promoted
Psalm 73	vv. 1–16	vv. 18–28	"God is good to Israel" (v. 1)
Psalms 80–81	Psalm 80	Psalm 81	The God who hears and delivers

collection's first two groupings contain similar references (cf. 74:11; 75:9; 77:11; 78:42, 54);[34] such consistency suggests intentionality; (2) this repetition appears with others in the prominent closing verses of the Divine oracle (i.e., vv. 14–17).

In corroborating the intentionality of links in Table 7.2, these observations support a deliberate correspondence with Psalm 73.

Formal Correspondence with Psalm 73: Interpretation

Recognition of this correspondence has the same basic interpretive implications for this sequence as the first two groupings considered. To avoid unnecessary repetition, the discussion here will be comparatively brief. I refer to the reader to the corresponding discussions in Chapters 4 and 5 for a more detailed justification of the conclusions reached here.

The nature of the formal correspondence uncovered once again suggests intentionality. And it leads us to posit the same meaningful relationship between these "discrete materials" (i.e., Pss 80–81 and Ps 73) that was suggested in the case of the first two groupings: Psalms 80–81 are a third sequence that develops the topic of Psalm 73 on an inter-psalm level.

The formal correspondence displayed in Table 7.3 tacitly indicates that the sequence of Psalms 80–81 is arranged to resolve the conflict of faith and experience in Psalm 80 (column 3). And the resolution once again resembles that of Psalm 73: encouraging confidence in a core belief that lived experience appeared to endanger. As we have seen, Psalm 81 reflects a radically different perspective on God's willingness to hear and deliver than that which is reflected in the appeal of Psalm 80. The sequencing of Psalm 81 encourages readers/singers to sing to the "God of strength" (81:2) who *is* willing to hear and deliver (a repentant people). Significantly, this third grouping also explicitly grounds such trust in God's own self-revelation (see especially 81:14–17). The arrangement of psalms, then, tacitly indicates that the underlying editorial purpose is to strengthen the commitment

---

34. See pp. 94 and 115.

to the "God of belief" (i.e., the God who is willing to hear and deliver) that is presupposed (but perceived to be under attack) in the appeal of Psalm 80 itself.[35]

It is interesting to note how the repetitions in Psalm 81 confirm this interpretation. On one level, the nature of the confirmation is the same as the other groups: these repetitions confirm the function assigned to Psalm 81 (i.e., to provide resolution to the crisis of Ps 80) because they reflect deliberate correspondence with the rhetorical device operating in the parallel Psalm 73.[36] In the present case, however, they also confirm this interpretation in another way.

The reader will no doubt have noted that five of the seven repetitions cluster in the concluding verses of the Divine oracle (vv. 14–17):

Oh, that my people would listen (שמע) to me!
  I would quickly subdue their enemies (איב)
  and turn (שוב) my hand (יד) against their adversaries …
He [i.e., God] would feed (אכל) you with the finest wheat. (Ps 81:14, 15, 17)

Such clustering gives prominence to God's self-revelation in these particular verses. This is significant because, as the exegesis above indicated, it is *these* verses that contain God's most direct promise to hear and deliver subsequent generations of Israelites who are repentant and willing to hear—such as those reflected in Psalm 80. Thus, if Psalm 81 does in fact function to resolve the faith crisis voiced in that appeal in the way being argued (i.e., to reassure readers/singers of God's *willingness* to hear and deliver), verses 14–17 are precisely the ones we would expect to receive the most prominence in this grouping's design.[37]

Consequently, in the face of the communal experience of God as a "bad shepherd" who "feeds" his people with the bread of tears (vv. 5–6) and a "malevolent vinedresser" who appears to have "reversed what he began in salvation history" (vv. 9–13),[38] the interpretive horizon of Psalm 81 provides reassurance that Israel's God is still a *good* Shepherd and that salvation history is *not* permanently reversed; God can (and is willing to) duplicate past actions of salvation and provision for a repentant people (vv. 14–17).

A Critique of the "Deuteronomistic" Interpretation

Given their prevalence in previous scholarship, it is necessary to provide a brief critique of "deuteronomistic" interpretations of Psalm 81's relationship to Psalm 80. A prevalent view among interpreters is that the Divine oracle in Psalm 81

---

35. The proposed interpretation, therefore, does no "violence" to either psalm in the sequence.

36. See the discussion on pp. 90–100 and 119–20.

37. In this connection the reader should recall the similar "weighing" of significant parallels in relation to Ps 77:8–11 in Chapter 5. See pp. 120–1.

38. Broyles, *The Conflict of Faith and Experience in the Psalms*, 162.

provides a theodical or "deuteronomistic" response to the community's "Why?" in Psalm 80 (v. 13); it explains God's harsh and apparently enigmatic behavior in terms of sin and disobedience (see 81:12–13).[39] Thus, on this view, God himself alleviates the conflict of faith and experience in Psalm 80 by shifting the blame back on the community, so to speak.

The following considerations cumulatively suggest that such an interpretation is mistaken. First, it fails to recognize the editorial prominence given to 81:14–17 in the grouping's design. This is a significant oversight since God's self-revelation here is *not* deuteronomistic in nature. It rather consists of God's promise to hear and deliver an obedient people. Thus, recognition of the editorial prominence that these verses receive points away from a deuteronomistic explanation of Psalm 81's placement.

Second, the deuteronomistic view does not sufficiently factor into interpretation the community's profile in Psalm 80. As the earlier exegesis showed, Psalm 80 appears to reflect a *repentant community that is ready and willing to be faithful*—not one unaware of, or unwilling to acknowledge, their role in their dismal circumstances. Given such a profile, it is unlikely that editors would appropriate Psalm 81's oracle in a deuteronomistic way, either to explain (1) God's initial anger; or (2) the continuance of God's anger in terms of the disobedience. Since the community had already (apparently) acknowledged their sin as the cause of the former and expressed a desire to be faithful, what would be the point of stressing the latter by adding the new context of Psalm 81? In other words, the deuteronomistic interpretation would be far more compelling if the communal posture reflected in Psalm 80 was more in line with the characterization of Israel in the Divine oracle of Psalm 81 (i.e., idolatrous and persistently stubborn).

I would suggest that this interpretation also fails at the level of Psalm 81; it goes "against the grain" of this psalm. The deuteronomistic reading is predicated upon an aspect of the oracle (i.e., vv. 5–13) that is intended to function as a *warning* for future singers/readers of Psalm 81—not, as the view's proponents appropriate it, as an *explanation* for the dismal circumstances of future generations. The Divine perspective of vv. 5–13, which highlights idolatry and stubbornness as the cause of Divine anger, has in view Israelite *history*. Later generations appropriating this psalm (such as the editor[s] responsible for Pss 73–83) are, therefore, to receive these verses as a strong deterrent against similar behavior and encouragement to

---

39. See Hieke, "Psalm 80 and Its Neighbors in the Psalter," 40–1; Cole, *The Shape and Message of Book III*, 98–101; Frank-Lothar Hossfeld and Erich Zenger, *Psalms 2: A Commentary on Psalms 51–100*, trans. Linda M. Maloney, Hermeneia (Minneapolis, MN: Fortress Press, 2005), 325–6; Kim, "A Critique against God? Reading Psalm 80 in the Context of Vindication," 113. This is not to say that such studies see the Divine oracle as *only* giving a deuteronomistic response. They also acknowledge God's promise to hear and deliver in 81:14–17. But, on these views, the conflict of faith and experience in Ps 80 is not resolved by such a Divine profile. It is resolved by the disobedience of the forefathers that God recounts in vv. 12–13.

obedience. But the deuteronomistic interpretation appropriates vv. 5–13 to *explain* a future generation's dismal situation (i.e., the community of Ps 80), an unlikely editorial move.

A final consideration is not so much a critique as it is indirect support for the interpretation argued in this chapter. The deuteronomistic interpretation does not comport with the nature of the editorial strategy discovered in the collection so far. In both Psalm 73 and the first two groupings, the resolution promoted was non-theodical in nature. We will see in the next chapter that the same is true of the collection's final psalm group.

It is true that each grouping must be evaluated on its own terms; a deuteronomistic interpretation should not be ruled out a priori on such grounds. However, an important aspect of interpretation involves revisiting (and revising) one's views of the "parts" in light of the emerging picture of the "whole." In light of the arguments given for a non-deuteronomistic interpretation in this chapter, attention to the emerging picture of this collection is illuminating. It both indirectly supports the view offered here and provides an additional argument against the popular deuteronomistic reading of previous studies.

Thus, the Divine oracle of Psalm 81 *is* used to resolve the conflict of faith and experience in Psalm 80—just not in a deuteronomistic way. God's promise to hear, deliver, and feed an obedient people with good things is what resolves the community's distorted perception of God as a "bad shepherd" reflected in the "How long?" question of 80:5. God's willingness to duplicate his past mighty acts of salvation (81:8, 11, 15–16) and compassionate acts of provision (see 81:11, 17) is what resolves the distorted image of God reflected in the "Why?" question of 80:13 (i.e., a malevolent vinedresser who has seemingly reversed salvation history [see vv. 9–16]). The resultant message? Faith clings to God's self-revelation amid conflicting evidence.

Chapter 8

THE LITERARY UNITY OF PSALMS 79-82 AND THE SHAPE AND MESSAGE OF PSALMS 73-82

This chapter turns to the remaining psalms of the unit I am arguing for in chapters 7 and 8 (i.e., Pss 79-82), Psalms 79 and 82. Though separated by two intervening psalms, I present evidence that Psalms 79 and 82 constitute a psalm group whose design closely resembles the first three. The explanation for their separation is the chiastic design of the unit to which they belong. Having made a case for this fourth and final psalm group, I argue the literary unity of Psalms 79-82 and explore its implications for the collection as a whole. The most significant finding is that the editorial strategy at work in Psalms 74-78 appears to extend to Psalms 79-82, revealing a uniform design and overarching purpose for Psalms 73-82. I conclude by considering Psalm 83's relation to Psalms 79-82, offering two possibilities.

Analysis of Psalms 79 and 82

We begin by considering Psalms 79 and 82 as individual psalms.

Psalm 79

Psalm 79 is another God-lament psalm, forming its appeal by drawing God's attention to a severe conflict between faith and experience.[1] Scholars have disputed that Psalm 79 has in view the destruction of Jerusalem and the Temple.[2] But the

---

1. See the discussion in Craig C. Broyles, *The Conflict of Faith and Experience in the Psalms: A Form-Critical and Theological Study*, JSOTSup 52 (Sheffield: Sheffield Academic Press, 1989), 157-60.
2. See the concise summary in Marvin E. Tate, *Psalms 51-100*, Word Biblical Commentary (Nashville, TN: Thomas Nelson, 1990), 298-9. After surveying objections raised against this view and alternative proposals, Tate concludes,

> In spite of all of these problems and theories, the time after the fall of Jerusalem in 587 seems to be best for the original setting of the psalm ... it seems most probable that Ps 79 belongs to the sizable corpus of OT literature (including Ps 74) which

evidence suggests that this is, in fact, the clear setting of the psalm. Hossfeld and Zenger point out that the psalm opens in verse 1 with an implicit citation of Micah 3:12.[3] The implication is that "the lamented catastrophe is interpreted as fulfillment of the destruction of the Temple and Zion announced in Mic 3:12."[4] This interpretation is confirmed by the fact that this same verse is quoted in the judgment discourse against the Temple in the book of Jeremiah (see Jer 26:18).[5] Further, in conjunction with this last observation, Psalm 79 as a whole reflects heavy influence of the book of Jeremiah.[6] Based upon these observations, Hossfeld and Zenger conclude, "the conclusion is inescapable: Psalm 79 engages with the destruction of the Temple and the fundamental crisis brought on in and by that event."[7] This is the view taken here.

The literature suggests that the psalm's structure can be analyzed in a number of ways. The following two-part division reflects the flow of the text well:[8]

I. The Community's complaint (vv. 1–5)
II. The Community's petition (vv. 6–13)

The first five verses are a foe-lament (vv. 1–4) that culminates in an interrogative God-lament (v. 5). The psalm opens in verse 1 with the complaint that nations (גוים) have come into "your inheritance (נחלתך)," defiled "your holy temple (היכל קדשך)," and turned "Jerusalem to ruins (ירושלם לעיים)." Verses 2–3 are a graphic description of the carnage wrought by the ruthless invaders upon "your servants"

---

emerged from the community which remained in Palestine during the exile and was used in penitential liturgies during that period. (Ibid.)

3. Frank-Lothar Hossfeld and Erich Zenger, *Psalms 2: A Commentary on Psalms 51–100*, trans. Linda M. Maloney, Hermeneia (Minneapolis, MN: Fortress Press, 2005), 304–5; The relevant portion of Mic 3:12 reads: ציון שדה תחרש וירושלם עיין תהיה ("Zion shall be plowed [as] a field; and Jerusalem shall become a heap of ruins"). Compare with Ps 79:1: באו גוים בנחלתך ... שמו את ירושלם לעיים ("nations have come into your inheritance ... they have turned Jerusalem into a heap of ruins"). Strengthening the likelihood that Ps 79:1 is an implicit citation of Mic 3:12 is the observation that the noun עי ("ruin") only occurs in two other texts in the Hebrew Bible outside of Ps 79:1, Mic 3:12, and Jer 26:18 (i.e., Mic 1:6; Job 30:24).

4. Ibid.

5. Ibid.

6. Zenger lays out the following evidence for this claim: 79:1: cf., Jer 26:18 = Mic 3:12; 79:2: cf., Jer 7:33; 16:4; 34:20; 79:3: cf., Jer 8:12; 14:16; 16:4, 6; 79:4: cf., Jer 19:8; 79:6–7: cf., Jer 10:25; 79:8: cf., Jer 11:10; 79:9: cf., Jer 24:9; 29:18; 42:18; 44:8, 12; 79:13: cf., Jer 23:1. Hossfeld and Zenger, *Psalms 2*, 305.

7. Ibid., 304–5.

8. Others have divided the psalm along these same lines. Tate, *Psalms 51–100*, 300; Rolf A. Jacobson, *Many Are Saying: The Function of Direct Discourse in the Hebrew Psalter*, LHBOTS 397 (New York: T&T Clark, 2004), 43.

and "your faithful ones" (e.g., "They have poured out their blood like water all around Jerusalem" [v. 3]). The goal is not merely to bemoan this tragedy or "inform" Yahweh of something he does not know but to move him to intervene.

The repetition of the second-person masculine singular pronoun referring to Yahweh in these verses depicts the nations as God's own enemies. Together with the picture of the carnage in Jerusalem, this depiction communicates that "the barbaric actions of the conquerors, for whom literally nothing is sacred, neither the Temple nor the corpses, are judged as such a fundamental offense against the order of law that YHWH, for the sake of his own divinity, can no longer accept."[9] In addition, the community complains, "we have become a taunt (חרפה) to our neighbors" (v. 4). The actual content of the taunt comes in verse 10 and is central to the psalm's argument for God to act.

The section's closing verses shift from foe-lament to God-lament:

How Long, O Lord? Will you be angry forever?
    Will your jealousy burn like fire? (Ps 79:5)

There may be a sense in which these questions are seeking information. But their main thrust is rhetorical. This point is indicated by the following barrage of petitions (vv. 6–12); it is action, not an answer, that the community seeks. The community acknowledges that Yahweh's anger is in some measure just (see "Do not remember our former iniquities!" [v. 8]). But the God-lament of verse 5 reveals their belief that it has "burned (בער)" beyond what they believe is warranted.[10] It needs to come to an end.

As just alluded to, petitions dominate the psalm's second section (vv. 6–13).[11] Verses 6–7 focus on redirecting God's wrath to the nations because of the harm done to God's people ("For he [i.e., the nations] has consumed Jacob" [v. 7]). Verses 8–9 aim at removing it from God's people, pleading for God to have compassion and atone for their sins. What is at stake, the community argues, is nothing less than God's great "name (שם)" (vv. 6, 9 [2×]) or honor/reputation. Verse 10 contains the content of the nation's taunt mentioned in verse 4: "Why should the nations

---

9. Broyles, *The Conflict of Faith and Experience in the Psalms*, 159; see also Hossfeld and Zenger, *Psalms 2*, 306.

10. Broyles, *The Conflict of Faith and Experience in the Psalms*, 157–8; John Goldingay, *Psalms 42–89*, Baker Commentary on the Old Testament: Wisdom and Psalms (Grand Rapids, MI: Baker, 2008), 523.

11. See שפך חמתך אל הגוים אשר לא ידעוך ("Pour out your wrath upon the nations who do not know you!") (v. 6); אל תזכר לנו עונת ראשנים ("Do not remember our former iniquities!") (v. 8); מהר יקדמונו רחמיך ("Let your compassion meet us quickly!") (v. 8); עזרנו ("Help us!") (v. 9); הצילנו ("Deliver us!") (v. 9); כפר על חטאתינו ("Atone for our iniquities!") (v. 9); תבוא לפניך אנקת אסיר ("Let the groans of the prisoners come before you!") (v. 11); הותר בני תמותה ("Preserve the sons of death!") (v. 11); השב לשכנינו שבעתים ("Return to our neighbors sevenfold.") (v. 12).

say, 'Where is their god?'" Jacobson has shown that this formulaic taunt characteristically occurs during a conflict between nations that is also understood to be a conflict between national gods. Importantly, this taunt is "directed as much toward the defeated nation's god as it is toward the nation itself... the victors speak the taunt because they interpret the defeat of the foreign nation as the defeat of the foreign god."[12]

Jacobson shows that within the psalm's overall argument this taunt is presented as the main reason that God should respond to the community's prayer.[13] The taunt is first mentioned in verse 4, but the actual content is given in verse 10 as motivation supporting the petition. Then, following the taunt, the psalmist petitions God as follows: "Return to our neighbors sevenfold to their laps, *their taunts with which the taunt you* (חרפתם אשר חרפוך)" (emphasis added) (v. 12). The taunt is nothing less than an assertion that Israel's God has been defeated with his people. Clear evidence for this view (at least according to the nations) is the destruction of both Jerusalem and the Temple, God's very own dwelling place (see v. 1). Jacobson explains the significance of this enemy quotation: "By quoting this enemy taunt, the psalmist names a pressing theological problem: Has the Lord been defeated, as some people believed? ... One may conclude that, as in previous psalms, the enemy quotation is the key element in the argument of the psalm."[14]

At the same time, Hossfeld and Zenger are correct in observing that this final section pleads for "the establishment of the order of law in the world of the nations by YHWH as the God of justice"[15] The taunt in verse 10 "makes unmistakably clear that this conflict between Israel and the nations is ... about YHWH's own, specific divinity [emphasis mine]. The question, 'Where is your God?' calls into question" Yahweh's Divine profile as "protector of life, savior of the oppressed, guarantor of law and justice."[16] As these scholars point out, the petitions in verses 10–12 (e.g., "let the vengeance of the blood of your servants that is poured out be known among the nations!") are pleading for the recovery of this particular Divine profile among both Israel and the nations.[17] As such, it becomes evident that the "fundamental God-crisis" that the psalm is concerned with is not only God's apparent defeat; it is his reputation as a righteous and just God. "The psalm

---

12. Jacobson, *Many Are Saying*, 42. These claims are based upon Jacobson's analysis of this formulaic taunt elsewhere (see Ps 42:3, 10; Ps 115:2) and taunts very similar to it found in Isa 10:9–10; 36:18b–20; Mic 7:10; Joel 2:17; and 1 Kgs 18:27. See Jacobson's excursus on this taunt on ibid., 40–2.

13. Ibid., 42.

14. Ibid. Jacobson's systematic analysis of enemy quotations that attack God reveals that they often articulate the psalm's central theological dilemma (e.g., Pss 3; 9/10; 11; 12; 14/53; 22; 59; 64; 71; 94; 115). See Jacobson, *Many Are Saying*, 28–49 for his detailed analysis of these quotations.

15. Hossfeld and Zenger, *Psalms 2*, 306.

16. Ibid., 307.

17. Ibid.

laments, above all that through these events YHWH's competence as a God of justice ... is hugely called into question."[18]

The psalm concludes on a surprisingly hopeful note. The community confidently affirms that they are "your people, and the flock of your pasture," and that they will praise God forever upon restoration (v. 13). The assumption is that praise will follow restoration. But the people's praise does not appear to be contingent upon deliverance: the community resolutely sticks to Yahweh even amid the catastrophic situation they are experiencing.

Psalm 82

This penultimate Asaph psalm centers on an important image in the collection: God as Judge and King (Pss 73–76). However, in Psalm 82 this image occurs in a unique setting, that of the "divine council" (עדת אל) (v. 1). In this short but highly debated psalm, God is pictured as the Most High of the earth who possesses all the nations (vv. 6, 8). He is thus able to stand authoritatively "in the midst of the [negligent] אלהים (בקרב אלהים)." He stands specifically as the accuser (vv. 2–4) and judge (vv. 6–7) of these אלהים, to whom he delegated authority for administering justice in these nations (see Deut 32:8–9 [LXX; Qumran]).

Lowell K. Handy's careful analysis of Psalm 82 shows that the psalm is divided into four units. These units are inversely parallel and are arranged around a central element:[19]

A1. Section I Assembly / God-rises (שפט) (v. 1)
   B1. Section II Address / gods confronted (vv. 2–4)
      C. Section III Address / chaos described (v. 5)
   B2. Section IV Address / gods confronted (vv. 6–7)
A2. Section V Assembly God rises (שפט) (v. 8)

Section one (v. 1) consists of a third-person description of God (אלהים) taking his stand (נצב) amid the "divine council" (עדת אל). The reference to the "divine council" in Psalm 82:1 reflects "Israel's version of the heavenly bureaucracy ... of divine beings who administer the affairs of the cosmos" that was common among the cultures of the Ancient Near East (ANE).[20] This divine council is found in a

---

18. Ibid., 304.

19. The following structure is adapted from Lowell K. Handy, "Sounds, Words and Meanings in Psalm 82," *JSOT* 47 (1990): 63. Others, such as Tate, have independently arrived at a similar concentric structure for the psalm. Whereas Handy sees God's address in vv. 2–4 and 6–7 as one section a piece, Tate divides them each into two (vv. 2 and 3–4, and 6 and 7), thus arriving at a seven-part concentric pattern. See Tate, *Psalms 51–100*, 334.

20. M. S. Heiser, "Divine Council," in *Dictionary of the Old Testament: Wisdom, Poetry, & Writings*, ed. Tremper Longman III and Peter Enns (Downers Grove, IL: IVP Academic, 2008), 113. See pp. 113–16 for a concise discussion of the concept of the "divine council" in Israel and the broader ANE. As Heiser points out, the most precise parallel to the "divine

number of other texts in the Hebrew Bible (e.g., 1 Kgs 22:19–20; Pss 89:5–7; 29:1; Job 1:6; 2:1; Deut 32:8–9, 43 [LXX; Qumran]). In Psalm 82:1 God is pictured as the undisputed leader of the divine council, who takes his stand "in the midst of the אלהים (בקרב אלהים)" to administer judgment upon them (שפט).[21]

The direct speech that immediately follows in section two (vv. 2–4) is best taken as the voice of the Most-High God.[22] Using language more at home on the lips of the psalmists, the Most High asks rhetorically "How long?" (עד מתי) the אלהים of verse 1 will judge unjustly (v. 2).[23] The clear implication is that it has been "too long" (cf. vv. 6–7). Verses 3–4 consist of a string of imperatives from the Most High. The Most High commands the אלהים to administer justice in the territories among the nations that he had assigned them.[24] These imperatives are a strong accusation of the אלהים for failing to administer justice among the nations.

---

council" in Ps 82:1 comes from the texts discovered at Ras Shamra. These texts indicate that "El" was the leader of the divine council in Ugarit, the same proper name found in 82:1 (see עדת אל). Heiser, "Divine Council," 113. There is no need, however, to postulate (as some do) a direct influence of the Ugaritic concept of a divine council. As Goldingay points out, the concept of a divine council was a common feature of the intellectual world of the ANE. Goldingay, *Psalms 42–89*, 560–1. The expression עדת אל in Ps 82:1 is, therefore, best understood as simply reflecting the Israelite version of this common cultural concept.

21. The use of the term אלהים in v. 1 to refer both to the Most High and the other members of the divine council should not be taken as evidence that Israelite religion was polytheistic or henotheistic at one time, with Ps 82 being a key text reflecting the transition to monotheism. As Heiser points out, the Hebrew Bible is replete with texts asserting Yahweh's utter uniqueness and supreme authority, many widely considered among the earliest in the Hebrew Bible. See the discussion in Heiser, "Divine Council," in *Dictionary of the Old Testament*, 114; based upon texts such as Exod 21:6; 22:7–8, and 27, not a few scholars over the centuries have understood the אלהים (plural) mentioned in v. 1 and throughout the psalm to be human Israelite judges. For the serious problems with this view and a refutation of it, see James M. Trotter, "Death of the אלהים in Psalm 82," *JBL* (2012): 228–30; Heiser, "Divine Council," in *Dictionary of the Old Testament*, 114–15.

22. Most understand the speech of vv. 2–4 as God's. For example, Tate, *Psalms 51–100*, 334; Hossfeld and Zenger, *Psalms 2*, 333–4; Jacobson, *Many Are Saying*, 113; Goldingay takes a minority view in seeing the entire psalm as on the lips of the psalmist. Goldingay, *Psalms 42–89*, 559–60.

23. This is the only instance in the Psalter where Yahweh asks this question. It is, however, attributed to Yahweh elsewhere in the Hebrew Bible (see Exod 10:3; Num 14:27; Jer 23:26).

24. As many have pointed out, the background here (seen more clearly in v. 6 ["You are gods, sons of the Most High"]) is provided by Deut 32:8: "When the Most High gave to the nations their inheritance, when he divided mankind, he fixed the boundaries of the peoples according to the number of the sons of God." The majority of text critics consider the text of the LXX and DSS, which reads "according to the number of the sons of God" (cf., the interpretive ἀγγέλων θεοῦ of the LXX) to be superior to the MT here. The MT reads "according to the number of the sons of Israel" (למספר בני ישראל). For a discussion of the

The third-person speech of section three (v. 5) could either continue God's words in verses 2–4 or reflect a switch to the speaker of verses 1 and 8: "They [i.e., the אלהים] do not know, they do not understand, they walk about in darkness; all of the foundations of the earth are shaken." This description of the אלהים "reveals the cosmic dimension of their failure," which has resulted in a chaotic situation that has shaken the very foundations of the earth (see Mic 6:2).[25]

Section four (vv. 6–7) is a second address of the Most High to the אלהים which parallels that of verses 2–4. It consists of the Most High's order-bringing response to the chaotic situation of verse 5: a death sentence for all of the אלהים ("You are gods, all of you. Therefore, you will die like men!"). Zenger observes,

> Verse 7 proclaims the end of these gods ... because they do not match the concept of God proclaimed by this psalm ... the "gods" and "sons of the Most High" are not what they pretend to be—namely, instances that guarantee justice and righteousness in the human world and in so doing make visible the face of the true God.[26]

The Most High's sentencing of the אלהים to death puts on display his Divine profile as the supremely Just One.

The psalm closes in a somewhat unexpected fashion (v. 8) (section five). It ends with a petition urging the Most High to "arise (קומה)!" and "judge (שפטה) the earth! For you possess all the nations (כי אתה תנחל בכל הגוים)."[27] In his important study of the divine council in ancient Israel, Michael Heiser draws upon B. Batto's research to shed light on this petition.[28] Batto's study focused on the "rising" of a deity in the ANE from his throne to take action. Heiser notes Batto's observation that the imperative קומה was "standardizing language for awakening God" and "stereotypical language" often found in "universal prayers for time of duress."[29] Further Batto observes that

> the motif of the sleeping deity is used to express Israel's belief in Yahweh's absolute kingship ... this conviction gives [Israel] the confidence to appeal

---

textual issues involved and defense of the LXX and Qumran readings over the MT, see Michael S. Heiser, "Deuteronomy 32:8 and the Sons of God," *BibSac* 158 (2001): 52–74.

25. Hossfeld and Zenger, *Psalms 2*, 335.

26. Ibid.

27. The reader will note the inclusion in vv. 1 and 8 formed by the verb שפט ("to judge").

28. See the discussion in Michael S. Heiser, "The Divine Council in Late Canonical and Non-Canonical Second Temple Jewish Literature" (PhD diss., University of Wisconsin-Madison, 2004), 79–81.

29. Cited from B. Batto, "The Sleeping God: An Ancient Near Eastern Motif of Divine Sovereignty," *Bib* 68 (1987): 169 in Heiser, "The Divine Council in Late Canonical and Non-Canonical Second Temple Jewish Literature," 80. Many interpreters point out that Ps 82 presupposes a time of duress.

Table 8.1 Analogous Literary Progression of Psalm 73 and Psalms 79/82

Core aspect of Israelite "faith" challenged	Confrontation with a severe conflict of faith and experience	Radical shift in perspective on God's posture/involvement
God's goodness	Psalm 73:1–16	Psalm 73:18–28
God's status as a God of justice/Zion's Defender	Psalm 79	Psalm 82

for help. Yahweh's reign is supreme and he can be counted on to "awaken" and maintain that right order which he decrees as creator and sovereign of all.[30]

Thus, Heiser rightly observes that in this closing petition the Most High is "not asked to arise to begin a new, heretofore unimagined governance of the nations; he is beseeched to maintain the order he decreed in ancient times. He is not asked to assume a new role; he is expected to act because he already is the eternally supreme king."[31]

Formal Correspondence with Psalm 73: Evidence

Though separated by two intervening psalms, Psalms 79 and 82 share the same parallel relationship with Psalm 73 as the three groupings considered so far.

Analogous Literary Progression

First, consider that the major literary progression of Psalm 73 is observable between these psalms as well. Psalm 79 corresponds to the first part (73:1–16), and Psalm 82 to the second (73:18–28) (Table 8.1).

Like the other laments in the collection, Psalm 79 centers on the same fundamental theological dilemma as Psalm 73, a severe conflict of faith and experience (column 2). The community perceives that God's prolonged absence amid the carnage wrought in Zion (experience) "hugely calls into question" (so Zenger) God's justice and ability to defend Zion (faith), even raising the question among the nations of whether Israel's God has been defeated.

Psalm 82 marks a radical shift in perspective on God from what we see in Psalm 79, resembling the progression to Psalm 73's second half (vv. 18–28) (column 3).

---

30. Batto, "The Sleeping God," 169.
31. Ibid. The final clause in the psalm, כי אתה תנחל בכל הגוים, is therefore best understood as introducing the grounds of the preceding petition, with the *yiqtol* תנחל stressing the ongoing nature of Yahweh's ownership of the nations, not Yahweh's future possession of them: "For (כי) you possess (תנחל) all the nations." The preposition ב prefixed to כל הגוים introduces the object of נחל.

The image of Israel's God as *the* just Judge of the universe dominates the psalm. And, far from being defeated, the Most High and Absolute Sovereign sentences the אלהים to death. Psalm 82 therefore establishes and affirms in no uncertain terms the very Divine profile that experience appeared to undermine in Psalm 79.

Thus, though flanking Psalms 80 and 81, Psalms 79 and 82 share the same semantic/conceptual relationship with Psalm 73's two halves as those intervening psalms.

Analogous Network of Parallels

Consider next that Psalms 79 and 82 also share a network of parallels resembling the rhetorical device operating in Psalm 73.

A perusal of Table 8.2 reveals that the repetitions displayed conform to the pattern of the rhetorical device in Psalm 73/the other groupings: each marks the radical shift in perspective observable in Psalm 82. In Psalm 79 every word, root, and motif is associated with the community's perception of the "God of experience," a God of questionable justice/a God apparently defeated by the gods of the nations. But in Psalm 82 these same linguistic features are associated with the Divine profile of God as *the* Just Judge who sovereignly rules and reigns. A few examples will suffice to make this point.

In Psalm 79 the root דלל ("to be low") comes on the lips of the community in cries for justice and rescue (v. 9). But in Psalm 82 it comes on God's "lips" in sovereign commands to the אלהים that reflect his justice: "Give justice to the *lowly/weak*!" (v. 3); "Rescue the *lowly/weak*" (v. 4). Or consider the question "How Long?" (עד מתי / עד מה). In Psalm 79 it appears in a rhetorical question implying that Yahweh's inactivity is unduly harsh, and so of questionable justice: "*How long*, O Lord? Will you be angry forever?" (v. 5). But when the question appears in Psalm 82, it comes on God's "lips" in a sovereign rebuke to the אלהים for failing to execute justice: "*How long* will you judge unjustly?" (v. 2). A final example is the root מות ("to die"). In Psalm 79 the root comes in a desperate plea in which the community portrays itself as "doomed/condemned to die" (lit. "sons of death" [בני תמותה]) because of Yahweh's inaction. In stark contrast, in Psalm 82 the root appears in Yahweh's condemnation of the אלהים to death for failing to execute justice: "Therefore, you (i.e., the אלהים) shall *die* like men" (v. 7). The remaining links follow the same pattern.

As noted in previous chapters, the presence of such repetitions is striking given the semantic/conceptual relationship already detected with Psalm 73. Here too their number and consistent pattern suggest intentionality and point to a deliberate connection with Psalm 73. Further corroborating the intentionality of these links (and so the parallel relationship with Ps 73) are the following observations based upon the criteria/principles discussed in Chapter 1:

1. The theme of God's justice is central in both psalms. Regarding Psalm 79, we noted Zenger's observation that God's absence in the face of the carnage wrought by the גוים "hugely" calls into question his profile as "a God of

Table 8.2 Parallels between Psalm 79 and Psalm 82

Parallel	Psalm 79	Psalm 82
Theme of the justice of God	Yahweh's profile as a God of justice is "hugely" called into question	Yahweh's profile as the Just Judge of all the earth firmly established
Motif of "defeat of the gods/God"	The nations taunt Yahweh as having been defeated by their god(s) (cf. vv. 4, 10)	Yahweh is depicted as the Most-High God who sentences the gods of the nations to death (cf. vv. 2–4; 7–8)
The root דלל ("to be low")	"Let your compassion meet us quickly, for we are brought very *low*" (v. 9) (community to Yahweh)	"Give justice to the *lowly/weak*." (v. 3); "Rescue the *lowly/weak*" (v. 4) (Yahweh to the אלהים)
נצל ("to deliver")	"*Deliver* us, and atone for our sins for the sake of your name" (v. 9) (community to Yahweh)	"*Deliver* (the weak and needy) from the hand of the wicked" (v. 4) (Yahweh to the אלהים)
"How Long?" (עד מה/עד מתי)	"*How long*, O Lord? Will you be angry forever? (v. 5) (community to Yahweh)	"*How long* will you judge unjustly? (v. 2) (Yahweh to the אלהים)
The root מות ("to die")	"Preserve the sons of *death*!" (v. 11) (community to Yahweh)	"Therefore, you (i.e., the אלהים) shall *die* like men" (Yahweh to the אלהים)
גוים ("nations")	"*Nations* have come into your inheritance." (v. 1); "Pour out your wrath upon the *nations*." (v. 6); "Why should the *nations* say, 'Where is their God?' Let the vengeance of the blood of your servants which is poured out be known among the *nations*!" (v. 10)	"Arise, O God, judge the earth; for you possess all of the *nations*!" (v. 8)
נחל ("to inherit/possess")	"O God, nations have come into your *inheritance*" (v. 1)	"Arise, O God, judge the earth; for you *possess* all of the nations!" (v. 8)

justice," within Israel and among the nations (see vv. 2–4, 10). In Psalm 82 *the* Divine profile that dominates is the Most-High Judge and King, the just and righteous אלהים among the nations (גוים) of the earth (v. 8). Notably, this focus on the relationship between God's justice and the גוים is absent from the intervening Psalms 80–81.
2. The motif "the defeat of the gods/God" is also not peripheral but significant in both psalms. In Psalm 79 the central claim of the taunt of the גוים (vv. 4, 10) is that Yahweh has been defeated along with his people ("Where is their God?" [v. 10]). In Psalm 82 this motif takes the form not of Yahweh's apparent defeat but of Yahweh's authoritative death sentencing of the gods of the nations (vv. 6–7). This significant link is also absent from the intervening Psalms 80–81.
3. The occurrences of words built from the root דלל ("to be low/poor") in these psalms account for three of the eight total in the MT Psalter (41:2; 72:13; 79:8; 82:3, 4; 113:7; 116:6; 142:7).
4. The occurrences of the verb נצל ("to deliver") in these psalms are the only two in Psalms 73–83. In both cases the form is a *hipᶜil* imperative.
5. The intentionality of the question "How long?" (82:2; 79:5) (עד מתי) is suggested by the fact that it does not occur on Yahweh's "lips" anywhere else in the MT Psalter.
6. The words built from the root מות ("to die") in these psalms (79:11; 82:7) account for two of the four occurrences in Psalms 73–83. Further suggesting the intentionality of this link is (1) the similarity of the forms themselves (see the noun תמותה in Ps 79:11 and verb תמותון in 82:7); and that (2) the noun תמותה in Psalm 79:11 only occurs one other time in the Hebrew Bible (Ps 102:21).
7. The occurrences of the noun גוים ("nations") in these psalms (79:1, 6, 10 [2×]; 82:8) account for five of the eight total in Psalms 73–83.[32] The importance of this noun in both psalms reinforces its intentionality: in Psalm 79 the havoc that the nations wreak in Jerusalem and its implications for Yahweh's reputation is a central theme. In Psalm 82 Yahweh's authority over all of the גוים of the earth is of central importance (v. 8).
8. Psalms 79 and 82 account for two of the nine occurrences of the root נחל ("to inherit/possess") in Psalms 73–83 (see נחלה ["inheritance"] in 79:1 and נחל ["to possess"] in 82:8). In both cases the root occurs in the same clause as the noun גוים ("nations"). This is only true once elsewhere in the collection (78:55). Notably, there are only two other occurrences of the verb נחל in the MT Psalter (Pss 69:37; 119:111).

---

32. The remaining three occurrences are in 78:55; 80:9; 83:5. The nations are also important in the adjacent Ps 83. But as argued below, Ps 83 is not part of the same psalm grouping as Pss 79 and 82. While the noun גוים occurs in the adjacent Ps 80 (1× [v. 9]), the nations clearly do not play as prominent a role in that psalm.

Table 8.3 The Semantic Relationship between Psalm 73 and Psalms 79/82

Psalm/psalm group	Confrontation with a severe conflict of faith and experience	Resolution to the conflict of faith and experience	Core Israelite belief challenged/promoted
Psalm 73	vv. 1–16	vv. 18–28	"God is good to Israel" (v. 1)
Psalms 79/82	Psalm 79	Psalm 82	The God of justice/sovereign Ruler over all nations

Formal Correspondence with Psalm 73: Interpretation

As in the last chapter, I offer an abbreviated discussion under this heading to avoid unnecessary repetition. Table 8.3 summarizes the interpretation tacitly indicated by formal correspondence with Psalm 73.

Table 8.3 displays that Psalm 82 is deliberately paired with Psalm 79 to develop the topic of Psalm 73 for a fourth (and final) time in the collection. Thus, like the parallel Psalm 73, Psalms 79 and 82 form a literary unit, a distinct and deliberately arranged psalm group (columns 2 and 3). Similar to the first three groupings, this pairing is structured to *resolve* the severe challenge to God's justice and sovereign rule over the nations (and God's goodness more fundamentally) that the community perceives in Psalm 79 (column 3). Psalm 82 promotes a radically different perspective on God's justice and sovereign rule over the nations than what we see in Psalm 79's urgent appeal. The deliberate pairing of Psalm 82 with Psalm 79 thus directs singers/readers to affirm the justice and absolute rule of the Most High (Ps 82) in the face of circumstances that appeared to contradict these realities (Ps 79).

The implication of such pairing is that Psalm 82 functions to undergird the deep commitment to the "God of belief" reflected in the appeal of Psalm 79 itself: God *is* a God of justice, indeed *the* God of justice; he has decidedly not been defeated by the gods of the nations but reigns as the sovereign Ruler over all nations (Ps 82)—despite conflicting evidence (Ps 79). He is *still* good to Israel (column 4). Resembling Psalm 73, then, the resolution that this pairing promotes is a shoring up of confidence in beliefs about Yahweh that lived experience threatened to severely undermine. Notably, this fourth grouping also anchors such confidence in God's own self-revelation (Ps 82:2–4, 6–7).

And, as explained in previous chapters, the significant parallels between these psalms (Table 8.2) confirm the proposed interpretation. In the present case, the repetitions in Psalm 82 are used to highlight the resolution this psalm promotes in relation to the conflict of faith and experience in the joined Psalm 79. Zenger's comments on Psalm 82 capture well the interpretation of this psalm pairing offered here: "the destruction of the Temple literally made the God of Israel placeless, so that in Psalm 79:10 the nations could say: 'Where now is your God?' … Our psalm

[Ps 82] attempts a radical answer: the God who is apparently the loser is in fact the one true God."[33]

Theological Message

The literary symmetry with the other three psalm groups points to the same basic theological message for the fourth: "Faith sticks to God's self-revelation (i.e., 'God of justice', 'the sovereign Ruler over the nations') amid conflicting evidence." Notably, this message is contextualized within the same historical circumstances as Psalm 74 (Ps 79). Though here the focus is broader, extending beyond the temple to Jerusalem as whole. Below we will see that this correspondence does not appear to be incidental.

The Unit of Psalms 79–82: Evidence

The combined conclusions of Chapters 7 and 8 reveal the literary unity of Psalms 79–82. We can now see that these four psalms provide an example of "editorial chiasmus":[34]

A1. Psalm 79
    B1. Psalm 80
    B2. Psalm 81
A2. Psalm 82

The inverted parallel arrangement of these psalms is a strong case for their literary unity, and so the unity of the two groupings they represent (Pss 79/82; 80–81).[35] Jan Fokkelman's broad criteria for identifying chiasmus are reasonable

---

33. Hossfeld and Zenger, *Psalms 2*, 336.
34. See n. 35 below.
35. This form of parallelism (i.e., chiastic and the closely related concentric pattern [A1, B1, X, B2, A2]) is well-documented at all levels of the text in Hebrew narrative and poetry. See John W. Welch, ed., *Chiasmus in Antiquity: Structures, Analyses, Exegesis* (Hildesheim, Germany: Gerstenberg Verlag, 1981). See also John Breck, *The Shape of Biblical Language: Chiasmus in the Scriptures and Beyond* (Crestwood, NY: St. Vladimir's Seminary Press, 1994). For other important (and more recent) studies on chiasmus, see Peter J. Gentry, "The Literary Macrostructures of the Book of Isaiah and Authorial Intent," in *Bind Up the Testimony: Explorations in the Genesis of the Book of Isaiah*, ed. Daniel I. Block and Richard L. Schultz (Peabody, MA: Hendrickson, 2015), 231 n9. Particularly relevant for inter-*psalm* chiasmus is Watson's observation that "*editors* have also used chiastic patterning when compiling books (and portions of books) of the OT" (emphasis mine). Wilfred G. E. Watson, *Traditional Techniques in Classical Hebrew Verse*, JSOTSup 170 (Sheffield: Sheffield Academic Press, 1994), 368. As an example of "editorial chiasmus" he cites the study of Walker and Lund, who argue that the entire book of Habakkuk has been

and legitimate the pattern detected here. Fokkelman suggests that such patterns are "valid if (1) demonstrable relations are present that (2) yield a better understanding of the text and point to new meaning. By 'relations' I mean correspondences."[36] The analyses of Chapters 7 and 8 show that both criteria are satisfied with respect to Psalms 79–82. That the proposed chiasmus meets the second criterion in particular receives further corroboration as this chapter progresses.

Interestingly, the two additional lines of evidence I presented for the literary unity of Psalms 74–78 in Chapter 6 (i.e., in addition to the parallel nature of its constituent psalm groups) also corroborate unity here.[37] First, as was the case with Psalms 74–78, the structure proposed for the second major unit also results in symmetry among superscriptions. Those at the extremities (Pss 79 and 82) are identical (מזמור לאסף ["a song of Asaph"]) (see Pss 79:1; 82:1), while those intervening begin with למנצח ("to the choir director/master"?) (see 80:1; 81:1).[38] This symmetry may be considered additional evidence for the unity of Psalms 79–82 given that (1) there are other grounds for considering Psalms 79–82 a unit (i.e., their chiastic structure); (2) others have observed the structuring function of superscriptions;[39] and (3) a similar symmetry exists in the titles of the first major unit in the collection (Pss 74–78). This last concern is relevant because such consistency in design suggests intentionality.

Thus, while not the basis for the deliberate grouping of Psalms 79–82, their superscriptions may further reflect it. If so, the superscription מזמור לאסף heading Psalms 79 and 82 would be an instance of distant parallelism, and the most prominent paratextual feature identifying the boundaries of this unit in the collection's final form.

Second, compare the first and last verses of this psalm sequence:

"O God, *nations* (גוים) have come into your *inheritance* (נחלה) …"
"Arise, O God, judge the earth; For you *possess* (נחל) all the *nations* (גוים)!"

(Ps 79:1; 82:8)

As noted earlier, the noun גוים and the root נחל only occur one other time in the same clause in this collection (78:55). It is therefore striking that the remaining two clauses appear at the extremity locations of a psalm sequence that appears to

---

so arranged. See A. Walker and N. Lund, "The Literary Structure of the Book of Habakkuk," *JBL* 53 (1934): 355–70.

36. J. P. Fokkelman, *Reading Biblical Narrative: A Practical Guide*, trans. Ineke Smit, Tools for Biblical Studies 1 (Leiden: Deo, 1999), 118.

37. Cf. pp. 127–30.

38. In the case of Pss 74–78 (Chapter 6), we saw that the psalms at the extremities (Pss 74 and 78) share an identical title (משכיל לאסף) (see Pss 74:1; 78:1), while the intervening Pss 75–77 all began with the prepositional phrase למנצח (see 75:1; 76:1; 77:1).

39. See p. 128n14.

constitute a literary unit on other grounds, Psalms 79–82. This observation suggests intentionality: the noun גוים and root נחל in 79:1 and 82:8 form a deliberate literary inclusion that works in tandem with the superscriptions of Psalms 79 and 82 to mark the boundaries of this unit.⁴⁰ That an inclusion also brackets the collection's first major unit supports this conclusion. Such consistency in design suggests intentionality.

Three additional observations indirectly support the literary unity of Psalms 79–82. First, those studying inverse parallel patterns at length have observed that inclusions very often bracket them, such as we find in 79:1 and 82:8.⁴¹ Second, we have seen that the inverse parallel arrangement is a prominent organizing principle at the highest literary level *within* the collection's psalms.⁴² It is therefore unsurprising to discover evidence that this same principle is used to create literary unity *between* the collection's psalms. The third, and most indirect, line of support comes from the observation that editorial critics have detected chiastic arrangements in other psalm sequences.⁴³

---

40. Reinforcing the deliberate nature of this inclusion is the reversal of the noun גוים and the root נחל in Ps 82:8: "nations (גוים) have come into your inheritance (נחלה) (79:1)"; "possess (נחל) all the nations (גוים) (82:8)". Others have noted that such reversal often characterizes inclusions. See D. Grossberg, "The Disparate Elements of the Inclusio in Psalms," *HAR* 6 (1982): 98. I am indebted to Cole's work for this source. Robert L. Cole, *The Shape and Message of Book III (Psalms 73–89)*, JSOTSup 307 (Sheffield: Sheffield Academic Press, 2000), 18. As Cole points out, such reversal characterizes the inclusion bracketing Ps 73: "… good (טוב) … God (אלהים) … . (73:1)"; "… God (אלהים) … good (טוב) … . (73:28)". Watson aptly labels this type of inclusio "chiastic inclusio." Watson, *Traditional Techniques in Classical Hebrew Verse*, 354.

41. For example, after examining these structures in detail for over three hundred pages, John Breck concludes that this is one of four "laws" governing chiastic and concentric patterns. Breck, *The Shape of Biblical Language*, 335–6. See also the discussion in Watson, *Traditional Techniques*, 376–80.

42. I have presented arguments for the chiastic or concentric arrangement of Pss 73, 74, 77, 80, and 82. See the exegesis of these psalms in Chapters 3, 4, 5, 7, and 8 respectively.

43. For example, scholars have advanced arguments for the chiastic or concentric arrangement of Pss 15–24 (Patrick Miller Jr., "Kingship, Torah Obedience, and Prayer: The Theology of Psalms 15–24," in *Neue Wege der Psalmenforschung*, ed. Klaus Seybold and Erich Zenger, HBS 1 [Freiburg: Herder, 1994], 127–42; Phillip Sumpter, "The Coherence of Psalms 15–24," *Bib* 94 [2013]: 186–209), 49–52 (O. Palmer Robertson, *The Flow of the Psalms: Discovering Their Structure and Theology* [Phillipsburg, NJ: P&R, 2015], 93–5), and 84–8 (Marcello Fidanzio, "Composition des Psaumes 84–88," in *The Composition of the Book of Psalms*, ed. Erich Zenger, Bibliotheca Ephemeridum Theologicarum Lovaniensium 238 [Leuven: Peeters, 2010], 468–83). Both David Mitchell and Peter Ho (among others) have contended that Books II (Pss 42–72) and III (Pss 73–89) of the MT Psalter have a chiastic arrangement. See David C. Mitchell, *The Message of the Psalter: An Eschatological Programme in the Book of Psalms*, JSOTSup 252 (Sheffield: Sheffield Academic Press, 1997), 71; Peter C. W. Ho, *The Design of the Psalter* (Eugene, OR: Pickwick, 2019), 95–6. My point

The Unit of Psalms 79–82: Interpretation

The first clue to interpretation comes from Hieke's observation that Psalm 80 should be read with the adjacent Psalm 79 as a "reaction to the destruction of Jerusalem and the Exile" in the collection's final form.[44] Pointing in this direction is the position of Psalm 80 adjacent to Psalm 79 and the nature of the links these psalms share. A number of scholars have pointed out that Psalm 80 reads like a "continuation" of Psalm 79's lament.[45] Psalm 79 concludes with the community's self-designation as "the flock (צאן) of your pasture (מרעית)" (v. 13). Psalm 80 opens by imploring the "Shepherd (רעה)" of Israel who leads Joseph "like a flock (צאן)" (v. 2). Further, like the adjacent Psalm 79:[46]

1. Psalm 80 is a God-lament centering on a severe conflict between faith and experience. In both psalms this crisis of faith is reflected in the God-laments "How long?" (עד מתי) (80:5; see 79:5) and "Why?" (למה) (v. 13) (see 79:10).
2. Psalm 80 is concerned that Yahweh's behavior has resulted in the "mocking/laughing (לעג)" of Israel's "neighbors (שכן)" (80:7; Ps 79:4).[47]
3. Psalm 80 also reflects a concern for God's "name" (שם) (80:19; see 79:6, 9 [2×]).

---

is not to affirm the validity of each of these proposals. It is simply to show that detecting inverse parallel arrangements at the inter-psalm level is not novel to this study.

44. Thomas Hieke, "Psalm 80 and Its Neighbors in the Psalter: The Context of the Psalter as a Background for Interpreting Psalms," *BN* 86 (1997): 39. See also Hossfeld and Zenger, *Psalms 2*, 317. Hieke suggests that the reference to the three tribes Ephraim, Benjamin, and Manasseh in v. 2 "might point to the last years of the Northern Kingdom" (late eighth century) for the original setting of this psalm. The psalm was then handed down in the tradition (with various redactional changes) and used by the "Asaph collectors" to lament the destruction of Jerusalem and the Exile. See the discussion in Hieke, "Psalm 80 and Its Neighbors in the Psalter," 39–40.

45. Hieke, "Psalm 80 and Its Neighbors in the Psalter," 39; Hossfeld and Zenger, *Psalms 2*, 317; Cole, *The Shape and Message of Book III*, 89. By "continuation," I am not suggesting a narrative-like relationship between the two laments. The point is that the links reflect the deliberate juxtaposition of these psalms for the purpose of lamenting one and the same crisis. See below.

46. What follows is not an exhaustive list of the links between these psalms, just enough to make the point.

47. These adjacent psalms contain the only three occurrences of the noun שכן ("neighbor") in Pss 73–83 (see Pss 79:4, 12; 80:7). This noun only occurs three other times in the MT Psalter (Pss 31:12; 44:14; 89:42). Words built from the root לעג ("to mock/laugh/deride") occur nowhere else in Pss 73–83 and only six other times in the MT Psalter (Pss 2:4; 22:8; 35:16; 44:14; 59:9; 123:4).

These correspondences are sufficient to establish that, in its present location, Psalm 80 is to be read against the same sixth-century setting as the adjacent Psalm 79. This relationship is analogous to that of Psalms 77 and 74 noted in Chapter 6. As pointed out there, Psalm 77 has been (re)used to lament the catastrophe of Psalm 74 in the collection's present form.

Psalms 79–82: A (Second) Dual Response to the Sixth-Century Crisis

Keeping in mind that Psalms 79–82 are a literary unit, the significance of the close correspondence between Psalm 79 and 80 becomes clear. It indicates that the two groupings these psalms head (Pss 79/82; 80–81)—and so the unit of Psalms 79–82 as a whole—offer *two complementary perspectives on the same theological crisis*: a conflict of faith and experience precipitated by the destruction of Jerusalem in the sixth century BCE (Ps 79:1). Thus, progressive repetition has been used to structure *both* of the collection's major units (Pss 74–78 and 79–82). The only difference is that, as already noted, it takes a more complex form in the chiastically arranged Psalms 79–82. The design of this second unit, therefore, bears a striking resemblance to the first.

The "music" coming from the "right speaker" (Pss 79/82) is that this crisis appeared to severely undermine God's justice and imply (at least to neighboring nations) his defeat by the gods of the nations (Ps 79).[48] In the face of such conflicting evidence, this grouping's shape leads readers/singers to nevertheless affirm that Israel's God remains the just Judge of the earth, and the Most-High God over all the gods of the nations (Ps 82).

The "music" coming from the "left speaker" (Pss 80–81) is that God's absence in Jerusalem's destruction seemed to severely challenge Israel's deep-seated belief in Yahweh as a *good* Shepherd who hears the prayers of his people (80:6–8). It also "sounds" the note that Yahweh, rather shockingly, appeared to reverse salvation history in his anger (80:9–13). The resolution that the placement of Psalm 81 promotes encourages continued trust that Yahweh is nevertheless willing to hear (i.e., he *is* a good Shepherd) and duplicate past saving acts (i.e., the people's situation is *not* irreversible). Since there may be an intended focus specifically on the northern kingdom in Psalm 80 (see vv. 2–3),[49] this second grouping may reflect the crisis from that perspective, and the first grouping from that of the southern kingdom (Ps 79). If so, hope for Israel's future reunification would be an important theme arising from the unit of Psalms 79–82.

If the above analysis is sound, then, like Psalms 74–78, neither a narrative-like organizing principle (e.g., Cole, Jones) nor the popular "compositional arc" approach (e.g., Millard; Hossfeld and Zenger; Gärtner) captures the structure of Psalms 79–82. Rather, the analysis has suggested that these psalms are structured

---

48. For the analogy of "stereo sound" to illuminate progressive repetition, see Gentry's comments on p. 36.

49. Hossfeld and Zenger, *Psalms 2*, 317.

chiastically (not concentrically as Ho has proposed).[50] Further, the analysis has revealed that the same organizing principle operating in Psalms 74–78 is also at work in Psalms 79–82: progressive repetition.

If valid, the implications of these structural observations are significant: this unit too—and so the entire sequence of Psalms 74–82—is organized to engage and resolve a singular crisis, namely, the devastating effects of God's absence in the aftermath of the Temple's destruction. Belonging to distinct, internally coherent, groupings, the laments of Psalms 79 and 80 do not "temper" the hope and confidence that the interpretive horizons of Psalms 81 and 82 respectively seek to foster in the reader.[51] The reader will recall the similar implications of the proposed structuration for the "laments" of Psalms 74 and 77.

Relatedly, the arrangement of Psalms 79–82 does not point readers *away* from Zion theology as a basis of hope. Psalm 82's pairing with Psalm 79 challenges readers not to accept its apparent failure, the very posture of the community in Psalm 79 itself (see especially v. 13). Here might also be mentioned the reference to the "son of man (בן אדם)" in Psalm 80:18, which may have in view Yahweh's promise to David.[52] The hopeful response that Psalm 81:14–17 provides to Psalm 80's lament suggests that this reference may anticipate some sort of future fulfillment of God's promise to David in the collection's final form.

However, as observed in the case of Psalm 78:65–72, here too we must exercise caution. At the very least, such an interpretation is consistent with (1) the conclusions reached in relation to Psalms 79–82 in general, and (2) the collection's positive perspective on Zion and David in particular. Either way, an important conclusion emerges from these observations: both of the collection's two major units reflect a unified perspective on David and Zion. Importantly, the *positive* and *constructive* role of Davidic/Zion theology that we have discovered in the collection's design challenges previous views (e.g., McCann's view).[53]

An Overarching Editorial Strategy for Psalms 74–82

As seen above, our findings have revealed a striking resemblance between the collection's two major units (Pss 74–78; 79–82). We have seen that each (1) focuses

---

50. See the discussion of Ho's work in Chapter 2. Though sometimes overlooked, an important distinction should be made between the "chiastic" and the "concentric" structure (Shimon Bar-Efrat, *Narrative Art in the Bible* [New York: T&T Clark, 2004], 98 n2). The former is symmetrical inverted parallelism, while the latter is asymmetrical. This difference in form corresponds to a difference in meaning or function. The concentric structure has a central element that does not correspond to another member in the structure, thereby highlighting its importance. Chiastic structures lack this central element, and so do not give prominence to any single member in the structure.

51. In this connection, the reader should consult the discussion on pp. 132–3.
52. See David Hill, "'Son of Man' in Psalm 80 v. 17," *NovT* 15 (1973): 261–9.
53. See pp. 133–4 of the present work.

on different, complementary, aspects of the same sixth-century crisis (i.e., different core Israelite beliefs it challenged); (2) consists of two psalm groups that parallel Psalm 73, consequently have the same basic two-part structure (conflict of faith and experience/resolution), and are organized by the same recursive principle; (3) communicates the same fundamental theological message; and (4) reflects a consistent perspective on David and Zion.

Further investigation brings into even clearer focus the resemblance of the collection's two major units. Note first the significant correspondences between their initial groupings, Psalms 74–76 and 79/82. Their initial laments (74; 79) are strikingly similar in the areas of setting, language, and imagery. In fact, their similarities even led Beat Weber to conclude that Psalm 74 served as a model for the composition of Psalm 79.[54] Consider the following selected correspondences between the two psalms:

1. Both are God-laments centering on a severe conflict of faith and experience. In each case this crisis is precipitated by God's absence in the destruction of Jerusalem/the Temple.
2. Both interpret this catastrophe in relation to God's anger (see אף in 74:1 and its denominative verb אנף in 79:5). Second, reference is made to Israel as God's inheritance (נחלה) at the beginning of both (74:2; 79:1).
3. These psalms contain the identical designation צאן מרעיתך ("flock of your pasture") for Israel (74:1; 79:13). This construct chain occurs only once elsewhere in the MT Psalter (Ps 100:3) (though צאן and מרעית are both used of Israel in Ps 95:7).
4. Both contain interrogative "Why?" (למה) (Pss 74:1; 79:10) and "How long?" (עד מתי or עד מה) God-laments (74:10; 79:5). Connected to the latter in both cases is the adverbial expression לנצח ("forever") (74:10 [see vv. 1, 3, and 19]; 79:5).[55]
5. Both reflect a concern that the catastrophe lamented is having a negative impact on God's "name (שם)" (see Pss 74:7, 10, 18, 21; 79:6, 9 [2×]).
6. Words built from the root חרף ("to reproach") play an important role in both psalms (see the verb חרף ["to reproach"] in Pss 74:10, 18, 22; 79:12 and related noun חרפה ["reproach"] in 74:22; 79:4, 12).[56]

I refer the reader elsewhere for a more comprehensive discussion of the similarities between these psalms.[57] Those mentioned here are sufficient to establish their close literary relationship.

Interestingly, significant correspondence also exists between the second "halves" of these same groupings (i.e., Pss 75–76 and 82). The image of God as the

---

54. Beat Weber, "Zur Datierung der Asaph-Psalmen 74 und 79," *Bib* 81 (2000): 521–32.
55. Outside of Pss 74 and 79, this phrase only occurs elsewhere at 77:9.
56. Words built from this root only occur once elsewhere in Pss 73–83 (78:66).
57. See Hossfeld and Zenger, *Psalms 2*, 305; Weber, "Zur Datierung der Asaph-Psalmen 74 und 79."

just Judge/King of all the earth is prominent in both (75:3–4, 5–11; 76:9–10; 82:1–8). In both halves this theme is reflected in the root שפט ("to judge") (see 75:3; 8; 76:10; 82:1, 2, 3, and 8). A word built from this root only occurs once elsewhere in the collection (see the noun משפט ["judgment/ordinance"] in 81:5). Similar ideas/motifs occur in connection with this theme in both cases: (1) references to "the wicked (רשעים)" (see 75:5, 9, 11; 82:2, 4);[58] (2) the motif of cosmic instability/stability ("When the earth totters, I make straight its pillars" [75:3]; "all of the foundations of the earth are shaken" [82:5; see also v. 8]); and (3) the distinctive image of God "arising (קום)" to judge (שפט)/for judgment (משפט) (Pss 76:10; 82:8).[59]

Next, note the significant correspondences between the remaining grouping of each major unit, Psalms 77–78 and 80–81. The most noteworthy are: (1) the initial God-lament of each grouping opens with an occurrence of the verb אזן ("to hear") in the *hipᶜil* stem. God is the addressee in both cases (see האזין in 77:2 and האזינה in 80:2);[60] and (2) the psalm linked to the God-lament (i.e., Pss 78 and 81 respectively) urges God's people to "Hear!" (see האזינה עמי ["Hear, O my people"] [78:1]; שמע עמי ["Hear, O my people"] [81:9; see also vv. 12, 14]).[61]

The following parallels are also noteworthy: (1) both Psalms 77 and 80 contain the similar image of God "leading" his people "like a flock": "You led your people like a flock (נחית כצאן עמך) (77:21); "... you who lead Joseph like a flock"[62] (נהג כצאן) (80:1); (2) the only four occurrences of the noun עדות ("testimony") occur in Psalms 78, 80, and 81 (78:5, 56; 80:1, 81:6); (3) both Psalms 78 and 81 share a similar salvation history motif that references the Exodus and the wilderness events (78:13–16; 81:7–8, 11); and (4) the lengthy recital of Psalm 78 and the extended Divine "oracle" of Psalm 81 reflect an analogous pattern of God's dealings with his people: God performs great deeds for his people (78:12–16; 44–55; 81:7–8, 11); the people respond not with faith and obedience but rebellion (78:17–20; 56–58; 81:12); God consequently punishes his people (78:21–31; 59–64; 81:13); God's response is ultimately compassionate and hopeful (78:38–39; 65–72; 81:14–17).

As the literature survey in Chapter 2 showed, the literary correspondence between Psalms 74–78 and 79–82 has not gone unnoticed in previous studies

---

58. References to "the wicked" only occur in one other psalm in the collection (Ps 73:3, 12).

59. In this connection, compare also the petitions of Pss 74:22 and 82:8: "Arise, O God, dispute your case (קומה אלהים ריבה ריבך)" (74:22); "Arise, O God, judge the earth (קומה אלהים שפטה הארץ)..."(82:8). Though not in the second "halve" of each grouping, the presence of this strikingly similar petition in both groupings supports the general point being made here: there is a significant correspondence between the groupings of Pss 74–76 and 79/82.

60. The verb אזן, in any stem, occurs nowhere else in Pss 73–83.

61. No other psalms in Pss 73–83 contain similar commands for God's "people" to "hear."

62. The phrase "like a flock [lit. the flock] (כצאן)" only occurs once elsewhere in Pss 73–83 (78:52).

(e.g., Millard; Leuenberger; Hossfeld and Zenger; Gärtner; Ho). But the conclusions reached here suggest that previous studies have not entirely grasped its significance. If the analysis is sound, the correspondence between these psalm sequences does not reveal the presence of two parallel linear progressions, parallel "compositional arcs" progressing linearly. Rather, in conjunction with the four major connections mentioned at the beginning of this subsection, the additional literary symmetry just pointed out suggests the following conclusion: the editorial strategy uniting Psalms 74-78 extends to Psalms 79-82, revealing a single overarching editorial strategy for Psalms 74-82. The collection's two major units recursively engage different aspects ("progressive") of the same sixth-century crisis ("repetition").

The first (74-78) focuses on certain core Israelite beliefs that the community perceived were being undermined by God's prolonged absence amid this crisis (see Pss 74 and 77). Like the second of two parallel lines, the second unit (79-82) returns to the same topic but develops it in a different direction: it shifts the focus to a different set of core beliefs that experience appeared to challenge (see Pss 79 and 80), and broadens the reader's perspective from the Temple's destruction (Ps 74) to the destruction of Jerusalem as a whole (Ps 79).[63] Thus, the recursive approach adopted for the structuring of Psalms 74-82 is an effective tool for developing the devastating impact of the sixth-century crisis in a "three-dimensional manner."[64]

Psalm 73 as Introduction to Psalms 74-82

The discovery of an overarching editorial strategy uniting Psalms 74-82 reveals the introductory role of Psalm 73 for the entire sequence:[65] Psalm 73 is a hermeneutical lens for the reading of Psalms 74-82. It signals readers/singers to interpret the sixth-century crisis as a severe threat to the thesis "God is good to Israel" at the most fundamental level (73:1). But, most importantly, this opening psalm signals the resolution that readers/singers are to reach with respect to that crisis (73:18-28; Pss 75-76; 78; 81, 82) and to discern in the following psalm sequence the overarching message that God is *still* good to Israel—despite the conflicting evidence that the sixth-century crisis represented (Pss 74, 77, 79, 80).

---

63. Broyles is correct that in Ps 74 the temple is a synecdoche for nation as a whole. Broyles, *The Conflict of Faith and Experience in the Psalms*, 150. But there is a clear focus on the Temple in Ps 74 absent from Ps 79.

64. Peter J. Gentry, *How to Read & Understand the Biblical Prophets* (Wheaton, IL: Crossway, 2017), 42.

65. For a more detailed description, see the discussion of Ps 73's introductory role on pp. 135-6. The general conclusions reached there apply equally here.

Significant Parallels between Psalms 78 and 79

Before turning to the collection's final psalm, it is necessary to briefly revisit a point discussed in Chapters 5 and 6. There we noted that Psalms 78 and 79 share a number of significant links. Parting ways with previous studies, I offered initial considerations supporting the following view: these links do not join two psalms within a group (e.g., Pss 78 and 79 within the grouping of 77–79 or 73–78) but two groups of psalms (i.e., Pss 74–78 and 79–82). This point can now be seen more clearly in light of the literary unity discovered for Psalms 79–82 in Chapters 7 and 8.

As scholars have pointed out (e.g., Cole; McCann; Hossfeld and Zenger), the "tail-head linkage" shown in Chapter 6 between the closing verses of Psalm 78 (vv. 68–72) and those opening Psalm 79 (vv. 1–2) highlights a clear semantic relationship between these psalms. The situation in Psalm 79 (i.e., the destruction of Jerusalem and the Temple) is a complete reversal of God's prior action in history (i.e., God's choice of David and Zion; God's building the Temple). Other significant links between these psalms highlight this same point. To cite only one, God's apparent unwillingness to "atone (כפר)" for his people's sin, evidenced by his withholding deliverance (79:9), appears to contradict his nature as a God who "atones (כפר)" for sin (78:38).[66] The number, location, and nature of the links between these psalms suggest rather clearly that the progression from Psalm 78 to 79 reflects deliberate design.[67]

However, I would suggest that the error of previous studies is the conclusion that this reversal or apparent contradiction is the *message* emerging from this psalm sequence. To recall McCann's thesis from Chapter 2, he argued that the above "tail-head linkage" *signals* the rejection of the David/Zion theology as a basis for hope. But the combined argument of Chapters 7 and 8 suggests that this interpretation is mistaken. The apparent failure of this theology is (as in the rest of the collection's psalm groups) the disorientated theological *starting point* of a grouping that Psalm 79 heads (i.e., Pss 79/82)—not the theological *message* it communicates.[68]

The additional (contrastive) context that Psalm 78 provides for Psalm 79, highlighted by the significant links they share, further underscores the severity of the crisis of faith lamented in Psalm 79 itself. But, as I have argued at length, Psalm 82 directs the reader to find *resolution* to this crisis. Consequently, the juxtaposition of the concluding verses of Psalm 78 and those opening Psalm 79

---

66. The root כפר occurs nowhere else in Pss 73–83. The root רחם in 78:38 and 79:8 highlights the same point. It only appears elsewhere in this collection at 77:10. See also זכר ("to remember") in 79:8 and 78:39.

67. For a fuller list of the links between Pss 78 and 79 than is provided here, see Hossfeld and Zenger, *Psalms 2*, 293–4; Cole, *The Shape and Message of Book III*, 77–87.

68. Similar to McCann's view is Jones's claim that the mention of David in 78:69–72 is "tempered by the arrangement of Psalms 78 and 79." Christine Dannette Brown Jones, "The Psalms of Asaph: A Study of the Function of a Psalm Collection" (PhD diss., Baylor University, 2009), 188. Similarly, see Cole, *The Shape and Message of Book III*, 79–80.

does not signal the rejection of the traditional David/Zion theology as a basis for future hope or "temper" it in any way; the pairing of Psalm 82 with Psalm 79 *fuels* the hope that Yahweh will "arise" and show himself to be Zion's great Sovereign once again. Thus, failure to recognize the organizing principle at work in Psalms 79–82 has (unintentionally) distorted the message scholars have detected in this sequence of psalms.

The significant links between Psalms 78 and 79 thus identify Psalm 78's function as something of a "bridge" or "hinge" connecting the first major unit (74–78) and the second (79–82).[69]

Psalm 83 as Conclusion to Psalms 73–82?

The literary unity of Psalms 74–82 raises an obvious question, namely, the relationship that Psalm 83 shares with Psalms 79–82 and the collection as a whole. Given its final position, some have naturally assigned Psalm 83 the role of the collection's conclusion.[70] Supporting this view is not merely the psalm's location. More importantly, they point to the linguistic, thematic, and theological links it shares with other psalms in the collection. Some of the most significant perspectives that Psalm 83 shares with the preceding psalms are outlined below.[71]

First, the perspective of Psalm 83 is communal. This is the dominant perspective in the collection's two major units (74–78; 79–82).[72] Second, the opening verses of Psalm 83 reflect the important perspective found in both units that the nations are God's enemies, not just Israel's.[73] A third, and related, perspective is that the threat of God's enemies has negative implications for God's "name" (שם), while Divine intervention would have positive implications for it (see שם in Pss 74:7, 10, 18, 21; 75:2; 76:2; 79:6, 9; 80:19; 83:5; 83:17, 19). Another concerns the threat of the

---

69. Contra Leuenberger, who we noted saw Ps 77 as something of a "hinge" (*Scharnier*) connecting Pss 73–77 and 78–83.

70. For example, Zenger argues that Ps 83 is a "programmatic conclusion" for this group of Asaph psalms. See Hossfeld and Zenger, *Psalms 2*, 345–6. See also the discussion of the views of Weber and Leuenberger in Chapter 2.

71. Psalm 83 divides neatly into two parts: vv. 1–9 are primarily a lament over an attack threatened (not actually undertaken) by a stereotypical list of Israel's enemies. Verses 10–19 are dominated by petition for Yahweh to judge these enemies. These enemies are making war with Yahweh himself (see vv. 3, 6) and threatening the very existence of Yahweh's people (v. 5).

72. The reader will recall that while Pss 73 and 77 have an individual focus, the community was also in view (see "Israel" in 73:1; the focus on national deliverance in 77:12–21).

73. See "your adversaries" (74:4; 23); "those who rise up against you" (74:23); "nations have come into your inheritance. They have defiled your holy temple" (79:1); the reproach with which they reproach you (79:12); "your enemies," "those who hate you" (83:3); "against you they make a covenant" (83:6).

nations to annihilate or make extinct the people of God: "They say, 'Come, let us annihilate them from being a nation; let the name of Israel be remembered no more'" (83:5). This perspective is reflected most prominently in Psalm 79, especially in the opening lament over the carnage wrought by the enemy in Jerusalem (see vv. 1–4, 7).

Fifth, Psalm 83 shares with the collection (particularly its first major unit) the view that God should act on behalf of his people in the present/future in accordance with his past works of salvation/judgment (see 83:10–13; Pss 74:12–17; 77:12–21[74]). Sixth, the psalm's closing verses reflect the concern found especially in the psalm group of Psalms 79/82 that the nations would recognize Yahweh as the Most High (עליון) over all the earth (Pss 83:19; 82:6, 8). Finally, the opening urgent threefold petition ("Do not keep silence! Do not be silent! Do not be still!") (83:2) reflects the overall perspective of the collection that the community is in urgent need of God's intervention (see Pss 73, 74, 77, 79, 80, 82).

These observations (and others not mentioned) demonstrate clear parallels between Psalm 83 and the rest of the collection. But does it, therefore, follow that Psalm 83 functions as the collection's conclusion? Not necessarily. The strong literary unity of Psalms 74–82, argued extensively in this study, shows that Psalm 83 stands outside of this unit, for *some* reason. This is a significant disjunctive feature not taken into account in previous studies. Not recognizing the literary unity of Psalms 74–82, studies considering Psalm 83 as a conclusion focus almost solely on the literary similarities that Psalm 83 shares with Psalms 74–82, and/or a supposed parallel relationship between Psalms 73–77 and 78–82. But in terms of the latter, if the analysis offered here is sound, those sequences of psalms do not stand in a *deliberate* parallel relationship. Regarding the former, we have seen time and again that indicators of editorial separation (here, the unity of Pss 74–82) are equally important for establishing literary structure. Given these considerations, I would suggest two possible interpretations for Psalm 83 in light of the conclusions reached so far.

Psalm 83 as Conclusion to Psalms 73–82

The first is the most obvious: Psalm 83's position outside of Psalms 74–82 marks it off as the collection's conclusion. This is analogous to the function of the minor break between Psalm 73 and Psalms 74–78 at the beginning of the collection. We have noted how that break set Psalm 73 apart as an introduction. However, in such a case, Psalm 83's concluding role should cohere with the overarching editorial strategy discovered for Psalms 74–82. Keeping this point in mind, the following observation is noteworthy: Psalm 83 would be the only lament in the collection whose appeal does not center on the perception of a severe conflict of faith and

---

74. For the petitionary nature of these verses within Ps 77, see Broyles, *The Conflict of Faith and Experience in the Psalms*, 156.

experience.⁷⁵ While the circumstances lamented are indeed formidable, the community of Psalm 83 nevertheless expresses confident trust that Yahweh will act in accordance with his past behavior (vv. 10–19)—not that he has apparently, or will, enigmatically contradict it.

On this first interpretation, the lament of Psalm 83 concludes the collection by embodying the resolution that each of its constituent groupings has promoted: trust in God's self-revelation (vv. 10–13) amid unchanged circumstances. In this case, the collection would end essentially where it began (see Ps 73:18–28).⁷⁶

Psalm 83 as Appendix to Psalms 73–82

An alternative interpretation is possible: Psalm 83 stands outside of Psalms 74–82 because it is *not* this collection's conclusion. Supporting this view is the collective argument of Chapters 3 through 8: Psalms 74–82 stand on their own as a cohesive and coherent psalm collection; they provide a sustained and coherent response to a singular theological crisis that needs no augmentation from Psalm 83. Thus, on this second view, the editorial strategy uniting Psalms 73–82 does not extend to Psalm 83. Psalm 83 was apparently appended to Psalms 73–82 at some stage of textual development simply due to its superscription (see לאסף) and clear correspondences in content with Psalms 74–82. In the present writer's view, the argument advanced in this study favors this second interpretation.

---

75. The negative petitions opening the psalm (see v. 2) may seem to contradict this claim. But as Broyles notes, given the *non-indicative* nature of negative petitions, we cannot automatically assume they are semantically equivalent to "God-laments" such as the "Why?" and "How long?" interrogatives found in psalms like Pss 74, 77, 79, and 80. See Broyles, *The Conflict of Faith and Experience in the Psalms*, 46. It is therefore by no means clear that such petitions reflect the same underlying severe faith crisis. Supporting such an interpretation of the petitions in the present case is also the fact that the attack lamented has not yet taken place. These petitions are therefore best viewed simply as urgent pleas for deliverance rather than accusations, analogous to the negative petition that the Gibeonites address to Joshua in Josh 10:6.

76. It is worth pointing out in this connection that two of the three occurrences of the verb אבד ("to perish") in the collection come toward the end of Pss 73 and 83 (see 73:27; 83:18). The only other instance of the verb appears in 80:17.

Chapter 9

CONCLUSION

This study has argued that Psalms 73–82 have a deliberate design that may extend to Psalm 83. The unity suggested by the "author" designation לאסף atop these ten/eleven consecutive psalms is not merely formal: this collection reflects a singular concern to address a multidimensional (and severe) collision between "faith" (i.e., various core Israelite beliefs about God) and "experience" (the individual/community's current experience of God) that was precipitated by God's prolonged absence in the Temple's destruction (*c.*586/587 BCE). Each of its four psalm groups (Pss 74–76; 77–78; 79/82; 80–81) focuses on a different dimension of this collision, and its two major units provide complementary vantage points: the first has a temple focus (Pss 74–78); the second broadens the focus to Jerusalem as a whole (79–82). Psalm 73 sits at the collection's head as its programmatic introduction.

Craig Broyles's comments about "God-lament" psalms in particular apply to this collection as a whole: "We see Israel's faith in a position of extremity … when circumstances test that faith with challenge and lead to a critical examination of faith's foundations."[1] Significantly, the study has revealed a sustained concern to *strengthen* those "foundations," which appeared to be crumbling under the weight of one of the most disorienting crises in ancient Israel's national history. The collection's shape resolves this crisis for the reader/singer in a consistent way throughout: its two major units encourage resolute commitment to "the God of Israel's faith"—ultimately the doctrine "God is good to Israel" (73:1)—in the face of circumstances that appeared to severely undermine this Divine profile. And it consistently grounds this commitment in God's self-revelation, both in God's words and works. The overarching theological message that emerges is that God *is* good to Israel—despite conflicting evidence. Consequently, this collection would have served an important function for the original exilic/postexilic communities as they wrestled with the "God of experience."

But while rooted in the sixth-century crisis, the collection's relevance transcends those circumstances; this collection is an enduring resource for the community of faith in all ages. Brevard Childs's comments on the enduring relevance of the Hebrew canon are relevant here:

---

1. Craig C. Broyles, *The Conflict of Faith and Experience in the Psalms: A Form-Critical and Theological Study*, JSOTSup 52 (Sheffield: Sheffield Academic Press, 1989), 222.

> The major task of a canonical analysis of the Hebrew Bible is a descriptive one. It seeks to understand the peculiar shape and special function of these texts which comprise the Hebrew canon. Such an analysis does not assume a particular stance or faith commitment on the part of the reader because the subject of investigation is the literature of Israel's faith, not that of the reader. However, apart from unintentional bias which is always present to some extent, *the religious stance of the modern reader can play a legitimate role after the descriptive task has been accomplished, when the reader chooses whether or not to identify with the perspective of the canonical texts of Israel which he has studied.* (emphasis added)[2]

Modern readers who "choose to identify" with the perspectives reflected in this collection will find it a great source of hope and encouragement when faced with circumstances that, like those facing the exilic/postexilic community, threaten to erode "faith's foundations."

Greater methodological awareness was an important concern in this study. Central in this regard was the focus on establishing the collection's structure. As noted in Chapter 1, such a focus was warranted, indeed deemed essential, given the close relationship between structure and *meaning*. A central argument running throughout Chapters 3–8 was that previous studies had failed to grasp important aspects of the collection's message and purpose because they largely overlooked the two most significant paratextual features related to the collection's design: (1) a deliberate parallel relationship between the opening Psalm 73 and four psalm sequences/pairings that follow (Pss 74–76; 77–78; 79/82; 80–81); and (2) progressive repetition as the organizing principle at work in psalm sequencing—not a linear narrative-like principle, multiple "compositional arcs," and so on. Recognition of these tacit indicators of structure has revealed a clearer

---

2. Brevard S. Childs, *Introduction to the Old Testament as Scripture* (Philadelphia, PA: Fortress, 1979), 72–3. As noted, my suggestion for the continuing significance of this collection is predicated upon the modern reader's "choice to identify with the perspective" reflected in the final form. It is noteworthy that this perspective presents a significant challenge to Walter Brueggemann's thesis that the type of conflict between faith and experience featured in this collection is a "tension that precludes and resists resolution." Walter Brueggemann, *Theology of the Old Testament: Testimony, Dispute, Advocacy* (Minneapolis, MN: Fortress, 1997), 400. As this study has argued at length, the editorial strategy uniting Pss 73–82 aims to do this very thing for the reader. Thus, the collection's final form bears out Childs's general critique of Brueggemann's approach, namely, that Brueggemann "feels free to reconstruct voices on which Israel's authors [and editors] had already rendered judgment. … [W]hen Brueggemann assigns an independent role to such traditions as countertestimony, he is running in the very face of Israel's canonical witness" (emphasis added). Brevard Childs, "Walter Brueggemann's Theology of the Old Testament. Testimony, Dispute, Advocacy," *SJT* 53 (2000): 230–1.

and more definite purpose for the collection, a more hopeful message, and a more positive role for David/Zion theology than previous studies have proposed.

If the conclusions reached are sound, the collection's present configuration has an elegant, though simultaneously ornate, design that bears the marks of intentionality: its two major units and four psalm groupings purposively develop Psalm 73's topic in multiple, complementary, directions and in the definite historical context of the aftermath of the temple's destruction. As discussed briefly in Chapter 6, this observation may provide a window into the formation of the collection's present shape. In my view, the elaborate nature of the literary correspondence that reveals this design, as well as its remarkable overall symmetry, is more compatible with a model that conceives of formation/configuration as a single creative act (in response to the sixth-century crisis) rather than a diachronic process.[3] This conclusion, however, is tentative. As noted earlier, attempting to reconstruct the collection's history from a synchronic analysis of its final shape, rather than actual manuscript evidence, involves considerable speculation.

It is my hope that this study further confirms what the best exemplars of editorial criticism have already shown: "Psalms exegesis" and *Psalterexegese* are not in competition but are complementary. Psalms 73–82 are ten discrete texts, each with its own distinct structure, message, and purpose. *At the same time*, close investigation has suggested that these ten discrete texts are also part of a larger "text" that has its own structure, message, and purpose.[4] And I would suggest that full appreciation of these psalms requires taking into account *both* levels of context.

The study's major conclusions are summarized in Table C.1.

---

3. To reiterate a point made multiple times: such a view does not (necessarily) entail that each individual psalm was created at this time.

4. In this connection, the reader should recall the analogy of the modern volume from Chapter 1.

Table C.1 The Shape and Message of Psalms 73–82

Psalm/ Psalm group	Confrontation with a severe conflict of God's goodness and Israel's experience	Resolution to the conflict of faith and experience	Historical setting	Core Israelite belief challenged/ promoted	Theological message
Programmatic introduction: Psalm 73					
Psalm 73	vv. 1–16	vv. 18–28	-----------	"God is good to Israel"	"God is good to Israel"
The Unit of Psalms 74–82					
Psalms 74–76	Psalm 74	Psalms 75–76	the Temple's destruction	God's status as the Great King	-----------
Psalms 77–78	Psalm 77	Psalm 78	-----------	Exodus 34:6–7	-----------
Psalms 79/82	Psalm 79	Psalm 82	-----------	God's status as a God of justice/ Zion's Defender	-----------
Psalms 80–81	Psalm 80	Psalm 81	-----------	God's status as a God who hears and delivers	-----------

Note: The broken dotted line indicates that the relevant cell agrees with the occupied cell in the same column.

BIBLIOGRAPHY

Books

Alter, Robert. *The Art of Biblical Narrative*. New York: Basic Books, 1981.
Alter, Robert. *The Art of Biblical Poetry*. New York: Basic Books, 1985.
Ballhorn, Egbert. *Zum Telos des Psalters: Der Textzusammenhang des Vierten und Fünften Psalmenbuches (Ps 90–150)*. Bonner Biblische Beiträge 138. Berlin: Philo, 2004.
Barr, James. *Comparative Philology and the Text of the Old Testament*. Winona Lake, IN: Eisenbrauns, 1987.
Berlin, Adele. *Poetics and Interpretation of Biblical Narrative*. Winona Lake, IN: Eisenbrauns, 1983.
Berlin, Adele. *The Dynamics of Biblical Parallelism*. Grand Rapids, MI: Eerdmans, 1994.
Bouzard, W. C., Jr. *We Have Heard with Our Ears, O God*. Society of Biblical Literature Dissertation Series 159. Atlanta, GA: Scholars Press, 1997.
Breck, John. *The Shape of Biblical Language: Chiasmus in the Scriptures and Beyond*. Crestwood, NY: St. Vladimir's Seminary Press, 1994.
Brodersen, Alma. *The End of the Psalter: Psalms 146–150 in the Masoretic Text, the Dead Sea Scrolls, and the Septuagint*. Beihefte zue Zeitschrift für die alttestamentliche Wissenschaft 505. Berlin: De Gruyter, 2017.
Brown, William P. *Seeing the Psalms: A Theology of Metaphor*. Louisville, KY: Westminster John Knox Press, 2002.
Broyles, Craig C. *The Conflict of Faith and Experience in the Psalms: A Form-Critical and Theological Study*. Journal for the Study of the Old Testament Supplement Series 52. Sheffield: Sheffield Academic Press, 1989.
Broyles, Craig C. *Psalms*. New International Bible Commentary. Peabody, MA: Hendrickson, 1999.
Brueggemann, Walter. *The Psalms and the Life of Faith*. Edited by Patrick D. Miller. Minneapolis, MN: Fortress Press, 1995.
Brueggemann, Walter. *Theology of the Old Testament: Testimony, Dispute, Advocacy*. Minneapolis, MN: Fortress Press, 1997.
Brueggemann, Walter, and William H. Bellinger. *Psalms*. New Cambridge Bible Commentary. New York: Cambridge University Press, 2014.
Calvin, John. *Commentary on the Book of Psalms: Psalms 36–92*. Grand Rapids, MI: Baker, 2005.
Childs, Brevard. *Introduction to the Old Testament as Scripture*. Minneapolis, MN: Augsburg Fortress Press, 1979.
Clines, David J. A. *The Dictionary of Classical Hebrew*. 8 vols. Sheffield: Phoenix Press, 1993.
Cole, Robert L. *Psalms 1–2: A Gateway to the Psalter*. Hebrew Bible Monographs 37. Sheffield: Sheffield Phoenix Press, 2011.
Cole, Robert L. *The Shape and Message of Book III (Psalms 73–89)*. Journal for the Study of the Old Testament Supplement Series 307. Sheffield: Sheffield Academic Press, 2000.

Creach, Jerome F. D. *Yahweh as Refuge and the Editing of the Hebrew Psalter*. Journal for the Study of the Old Testament Supplement Series 217. Sheffield: Sheffield Academic Press, 1996.

Dahood, Mitchell. *Psalms II: 51–100*. Anchor Bible Commentary. Garden City, NY: Doubleday, 1968.

Driver, S. R. *A Treatise on the Use of the Tenses in Hebrew and Some Other Syntactical Questions*. Grand Rapids, MI: Eerdmans, 1998.

Efrat, Shimon-Bar. *Narrative in the Bible*. New York: T&T Clark, 2004.

Flesher, LeAnn Snow, Carol J. Dempsey, and Mark J. Boda, eds. *Why … How Long? Studies on Voices of Lamentation Rooted in Biblical Hebrew Poetry*. The Library of Hebrew Bible/Old Testament Studies 552. London: Bloomsbury T&T Clark, 2014.

Fløysvik, Ingvar. *When God Becomes My Enemy: The Theology of the Complaint Psalms*. St. Louis, MO: Concordia Academic Press, 1997.

Fokkelman, J. P. *Reading Biblical Narrative: A Practical Guide*. Translated by Ineke Smit. Tools for Biblical Study 1. Leiden: Deo, 1999.

Foster, L. Robert, and David M. Howard, eds. *My Words Are Lovely: Studies in the Rhetoric of the Psalms*. Library of Hebrew Bible/Old Testament Studies 467. New York: T&T Clark, 2008.

Gärtner, Judith. *Die Geschichtspsalmen: Eine Studie zu den Psalmen 78, 105, 135 und 136 als hermeneutische Schlüsseltexte im Psalter*. Forschungen zum Alten Testament 84. Tübingen: Mohr Siebeck, 2012.

Gentry, P. J. *The Asterisked Materials in the Greek Job*. Society of Biblical Literature Septuagint and Cognate Studies 38. Atlanta, GA: Scholars Press, 1995.

Gentry, P. J. *How to Read & Understand the Biblical Prophets*. Wheaton, IL: Crossway, 2017.

Gerstenberger, Erhard. *Psalms (Part 2) and Lamentations*. The Forms of the Old Testament Literature. Grand Rapids, MI: Eerdmans, 2001.

Goldingay, John. *Psalms 42–89*. Baker Commentary on the Old Testament: Wisdom and Psalms. Grand Rapids, MI: Baker, 2008.

Goldingay, John. *Psalms 90–150*. Baker Commentary on the Old Testament: Wisdom and Psalms. Grand Rapids, MI: Baker, 2008.

Goulder, Michael D. *The Psalms of Asaph and the Pentateuch: Studies in the Psalter, III*. The Library of Hebrew Bible/Old Testament Studies 233. Sheffield: Sheffield Academic Press, 1996.

Goulder, Michael D. *The Psalms of the Sons of Korah*. The Library of Hebrew Bible/Old Testament Studies 20. Sheffield: Sheffield Academic Press, 1983.

Grant, Jamie A. *The King as Exemplar: The Function of Deuteronomy's Kingship Law in the Shaping of the Book of Psalms*. Society of Biblical Literature Academia Biblica Series 17. Atlanta, GA: SBL Press, 2004.

Gunkel, Hermann. *Introduction to Psalms: The Genres of the Religious Lyric of Israel*. Translated by James D. Nogalski. Mercer Library of Biblical Studies. Completed by Joachim Begrich. Macon, GA: Mercer University Press, 1998.

Hensley, Adam D. *Covenant Relationships and the Editing of the Hebrew Psalter*. The Library of Hebrew Bible/Old Testament Studies 666. London: Bloomsbury T&T Clark, 2018.

Ho, Peter C. W. *The Design of the Psalter: A Macrostructural Analysis*. Eugene, OR: Pickwick, 2019.

Hossfeld, Frank L., and Erich Zenger. *Psalms 2: A Commentary on Psalms 51–100*. Translated by Linda M. Maloney. Hermeneia. Minneapolis, MN: Fortress Press, 2005.

Howard, David M., Jr. *The Structure of Psalms 93–100*. Biblical and Judaic Studies 5. Winona Lake, IN: Eisenbrauns, 1997.

Iser, Wolfgang. *The Implied Reader: Patterns of Communication in Prose from Bunyan to Beckett*. London: Johns Hopkins University Press, 1974.

Jacobson, Rolf A. *"Many are Saying": The Function of Direct Discourse in the Hebrew Bible*. The Journal for the Study of the Old Testament Supplement Series 397. New York: T&T Clark, 2004.

Jain, Eva. *Psalmen Oder Psalter: Materielle Rekonstruktion und inhaltliche Untersuchung der Psalmenhandschriften aus der Wüste Juda*. Studies on the Texts of the Desert of Judah 109. Leiden: Brill, 2014.

Klein, Anja. *Geschichte und Gebet. Die Rezeption der biblischen Geschichte in den Psalmen des Alten Testaments*. Forschungen zum Alten Testament 94. Tübingen: Mohr Siebeck, 2014.

Leuenberger, Martin. *Konzeptionen des Königtums Gottes im Psalter: Untersuchungen zu Komposition und Redaktion der theokratischen Bücher IV–V im Psalter*. Abhandlungen zur Theologie des Alten und Neuen Testaments 83. Zürich: Theologischer Verlag, 2004.

Lunn, Nicholas P. *Word-Order Variation in Biblical Hebrew Poetry: Differentiating Pragmatics and Poetics*. Paternoster Biblical Monographs. Milton Keynes: Paternoster Press, 2006.

Mays, James L. *Psalms*. Interpretation. Louisville, KY: Westminster John Knox Press, 1994.

McCann, J. Clinton, ed. *The Shape and Shaping of the Psalter*. Journal for the Study of the Old Testament Supplement Series 159. Sheffield: Sheffield Academic Press, 1993.

McKelvey Michael G. *Moses, David, and the High Kingship of Yahweh: A Canonical Study of Book IV of the Psalter*. Gorgias Biblical Studies 55. Piscataway, NJ: Gorgias Press, 2013.

Millard, Matthias. *Die Komposition des Psalters: Ein formgeschichtlicher Ansatz*. Forschungen zum Alten Testament 9. Tübingen: Mohr Siebeck, 1994.

Miller, Cynthia L. ed. *The Verbless Clause in Biblical Hebrew: Linguistic Approaches*. Linguistic Studies in Ancient West Semitic 1. Winona Lake, IN: Eisenbrauns, 1999.

Mitchell, David C. *The Message of the Psalter: An Eschatological Programme in the Book of Psalms*. Journal for the Study of the Old Testament Supplement Series 252. Sheffield: Sheffield Academic Press, 1997.

Mroczek, Eva. *The Literary Imagination in Jewish Antiquity*. Oxford: Oxford University Press, 2016.

Murphy, Roland E. *The Gift of the Psalms*. Peabody, MA: Hendrickson, 2000.

Nasuti, Harry P. *Defining the Sacred Songs: Genre, Tradition and the Post-Critical Interpretation of the Psalms*. Journal for the Study of the Old Testament Supplement Series 218. Sheffield: Sheffield Academic Press, 1999.

Nasuti, Harry P. *Tradition History and the Psalms of Asaph*. Society of Biblical Literature Dissertation Series 88. Atlanta, GA: Scholars Press, 1988.

Rendsburg, Gary A. *How the Bible Is Written*. Peabody, MA: Hendrickson, 2019.

Rendsburg, Gary A. *Linguistic Evidence for the Northern Origin of Selected Psalms*. Society of Biblical Literature Monograph Series 43. Atlanta, GA: Scholars Press, 1990.

Robertson, Palmer O. *The Flow of the Psalms: Discovering Their Structure and Theology*. Phillipsburg, NJ: P&R, 2015.

Seybold, Klaus, and Erich Zenger. *Neue Wege der Psalmenforschung*. Herders Biblische Studien 1. Freiburg: Herder, 1994.

Snearly, Michael K. *The Return of the King: Messianic Expectation in Book V of the Psalter*. The Library of Hebrew Bible/Old Testament Studies 624. New York: Bloomsbury, 2016.

Tate, Marvin. *Psalms 51–100*. Word Biblical Commentary. Nashville, TN: Thomas Nelson, 1990.
Tov, Emmanuel. *The Text-Critical Use of the Septuagint in Biblical Research*. 3rd ed. Winona Lake, IN: Eisenbrauns, 2015.
Vassar, John S. *Recalling a Story Once Told: An Intertextual Reading of the Psalter and the Pentateuch*. Macon, GA: Mercer University Press, 2007.
Walford, deClaissé Nancy L. *Reading from the Beginning: The Shaping of the Hebrew Psalter*. Macon, GA: Mercer University Press, 1997.
Walford, deClaissé Nancy L., ed. *The Shape and Shaping of the Book of Psalms: The Current State of Scholarship*. Ancient Israel and Its Literature 20. Atlanta, GA: SBL Press, 2014.
Walford, deClaissé Nancy L., Rolf A. Jacobson, and Beth L. Tanner. *The Book of Psalms*. New International Commentary on the Old Testament. Grand Rapids, MI: Eerdmans, 2014.
Wallace, Robert E. *The Narrative Effect of Book IV of the Hebrew Psalter*. Studies in Biblical Literature 112. New York: Peter Lang, 2007.
Waltke, Bruce K. *An Old Testament Theology: An Exegetical, Canonical, and Thematic Approach*. Grand Rapids, MI: Zondervan, 2007.
Waltke Bruce K., and M. O' Connor. *An Introduction to Biblical Hebrew Syntax*. Winona Lake, IN: Eisenbrauns, 1990.
Watson, Wilfred G. E. *Traditional Techniques in Classical Hebrew Verse*. The Journal for the Study of the Old Testament Supplement Series 170. Sheffield: Sheffield Academic Press, 1994.
Weber, Beat. *Psalm 77 und sein Umfeld: Eine poetologische Studie*. Bonner Biblische Beiträge 103. Weinheim: Beltz Athenäum, 1995.
Welch, John W., ed. *Chiasmus in Antiquity: Structures, Analyses, Exegesis*. Hildesheim, Germany: Gerstenberg Verlag, 1981.
Westermann, Claus. *The Psalms: Structure, Content & Message*. Minneapolis, MN: Augsburg Publishing House, 1980.
Whybray, R. N. *Reading the Psalms as a Book*. Journal for the Study of the Old Testament Supplement Series 222. Sheffield: Sheffield Academic Press, 1996.
Willgren, David. *The Formation of the Book of Psalms*. Forschungen zum Alten Testament 2. Reihe 88. Tübingen: Mohr Siebeck, 2016.
Wilson, Gerald H. *The Editing of the Hebrew Psalter*. Society of Biblical Literature Dissertation Series 76. Chico, CA: Scholars Press, 1985.
Zenger, Erich, ed. *The Composition of the Book of Psalms*. Bibliotheca Ephemeridum Theologicarum Lovaniensium 238. Leuven: Uitgeverij Peeters, 2010.

Articles

Allen, Leslie. "Psalm 73: Pilgrimage from Doubt to Faith." *Bulletin for Biblical Research* 7 (1998): 1–10.
Andrason, Alexander. "Making It Sound—The Performative Qatal and Its Explanations." *Journal of Hebrew Scriptures* 12 (2011): 1–65.
Batto. B. "The Sleeping God: An Ancient Near Easter Motif of Divine Sovereignty." *Biblica* 68 (1987): 153–77.

Bellinger, W. H. "The Psalter as Theodicy Writ Large." In *Jewish and Christian Approaches to the Psalter: Conflict and Convergence*, edited by Susan Gillingham, 147–60. Oxford: Oxford University Press, 2013.

Berlin, Adele. "Grammatical Aspects of Biblical Parallelism." *Hebrew Union College Annual* 50 (1979): 17–43.

Birkeland, Harris. "Chief Problems of 73:17ff." *Zeitschrift für die alttestamentliche Wissenschaft* 67 (1955): 99–103.

Boadt, Lawrence. "The Use of 'Panels' in the Structure of Psalms 73–78." *Catholic Biblical Quarterly* 66 (2004): 533–50.

Brodersen, Alma. "Quellen und Intertextualität: Methodische Überlegungen zum Psalterende." In *Intertextualität und die Entstehung des Psalters*. In *Intertextualität und die Entstehung des Psalters: Methodische Reflexionen— Theologiegeschichtliche Perspektiven*, edited by Alma Brodersen, Friederike Neumann and David Willgren, 7–31. Forschungen zum Alten Testament 2. Reihe 114. Tübingen: Mohr Siebeck, 2020.

Childs, Brevard. "Walter Brueggemann's Theology of the Old Testament. Testimony, Dispute, Advocacy." *Scottish Journal of Theology* 53 (2000): 228–33.

Clifford, Richard J. "In Zion and David a New Beginning: An Interpretation of Psalm 78." In *Traditions in Transformation: Turning Points in Biblical Faith*, edited by B. Halpern and Jon Levenson, 121–41. Winona Lake, IN: Eisenbrauns, 1981.

Davies, Andrew, "My God ... 'Why?' Questioning the Action and Inaction of YHWH." In *Why? ... How Long? Studies on Voices of Lamentation Rooted in Biblical Hebrew Poetry*, edited by LeAnn Snow Flesher, Carol J. Dempsey, and Mark J. Boda, 49–67. London: Bloomsbury T&T Clark, 2014.

Efrat, Shimon Bar. "Some Observations on the Analysis of Structure in Biblical Narrative." *Vetus Testamentum* 30 (1980): 154–73.

Fidanzio, Marcello. "Composition des Psaumes 84–88." In *The Composition of the Book of Psalms*, edited by Erich Zenger, 468–83. Bibliotheca Ephemeridum Theologicarum Lovaniensium 238. Leuven: Peeters, 2010.

Gärtner, Judith. "The Historical Psalms. A Study of Psalms 78; 105; 106; 135, and 136 as Key Hermeneutical Texts in the Psalter." *Hebrew Bible and Ancient Israel* 4 (2015): 373–99.

Gentry, Peter J. "The Literary Macrostructures of the Book of Isaiah and Authorial Intent." In *Bind Up the Testimony: Explorations in the Genesis of the Book of Isaiah*, edited by Daniel I. Block and Richard L. Schultz, 227–53. Peabody, MA: Hendrickson, 2015.

Gentry, Peter J. "The Text of the Old Testament." *Journal for the Evangelical Theological Society* 52 (2009): 19–45.

Gerstenberger, Erhard S. "Der Psalter als Buch und als Sammlung." In *Neue Wege Der PsalmenForschung,"* edited by Klaus Seybold and Erich Zenger, 3–13. Herders Biblische Studien 1. Leuven: Peeters, 2010.

Grant, Jamie. "Editorial Criticism." In *Dictionary of the Old Testament: Wisdom, Poetry, & Writings*, edited by Tremper Longman III and Peter Enns, 149–56. Downers Grove, IL: IVP Academic, 2008.

Greenstein, Edward L. "How Does Parallelism Mean?" In *A Sense of Text: The Art of Language in the Study of Biblical Literature*, ed. Stephen A. Geller, Edward L. Greenstein, and Adele Berlin, 41–70. Jewish Quarterly Review Supplement. Winona Lake: Eisenbrauns, 1982.

Grossberg, D. "The Disparate Elements of the Inclusio in Psalms." *Hebrew Annual Review* 6 (1982): 97–104.

Handy, Lowell K. "Sounds, Words, and Meanings in Psalm 82." *Journal for the Study of the Old Testament* 47 (1990): 51–66.
Heiser, Micheal S. "Deuteronomy 32:8 and the Sons of God." *Bibliotheca Sacra* 158 (2001): 52–74.
Heiser, Micheal S. "Divine Council." In *Dictionary of the Old Testament: Wisdom, Poetry, & Writings*, edited by Tremper Longman III and Peter Enns, 112–16. Downers Grove, IL: IVP Academic, 2008.
Hieke, Thomas. "Psalm 80 and Its Neighbors in the Psalter: The Context of the Psalter as Background for Interpreting Psalms." *Biblische Notizen* 86 (1997): 36–43.
Hill, David. " 'Son of Man' in Psalm 80 v. 17." *Novum Testamentum* 15 (1973): 261–9.
Holmstedt, R. D. "The Restrictive Syntax of Genesis i. 1." *Vetus Testamentum* 58 (2008): 59–63.
Howard David M., Jr. "Reading the Psalter as a Unified Book." In *Reading the Psalms Theologically*, edited by David M. Howard Jr. and Andrew J. Schmutzer. Bellingham, WA: Lexham Press, forthcoming.
Jensen, Joseph E. "Psalm 75: Its Poetic Context and Structure." *Catholic Biblical Quarterly* 63 (2001): 416–29.
Kaiser Jr, Walter C. "The Message of Book III: Psalms 73–89." *Bibliotheca Sacra* 174 (2017): 131–40.
Kim, Hee Suk. "A Critique against God? Reading Psalm 80 in the Context of Vindication." In *Why? … How Long? Studies on Voices of Lamentation Rooted in Biblical Hebrew Poetry*, edited by LeAnn Snow Flesher, Carol J. Dempsey, and Mark J. Boda, 100–14. London: Bloomsbury T&T Clark, 2014.
Kselman, J.S. "Psalm 77 and the Book of Exodus." *Journal of the Ancient Near Eastern Society of Columbia University* 15 (1983): 51–8.
Kuntz, Kenneth J. "The Retribution Motif in Psalmic Wisdom." *Zeitschrift für die alttestamentliche Wissenschaft* (1977): 223–33.
McCann, Clinton J. "Books I–III and the Editorial Purpose of the Psalter." In *Shape and Shaping of the Psalter*, edited by J. Clinton McCann, 93–107. The Journal for the Study of the Old Testament Supplement Series 159. Sheffield: JSOT Press, 1993.
Miller, Patrick. "Kingship, Torah Obedience, and Prayer." In *Neue Wege Der PsalmenForschung*," edited by Klaus Seybold and Erich Zenger, 127–42. Herders Biblische Studien 1. Leuven: Peeters, 2010.
Mitchell, David C. "God Will Redeem My Soul from Sheol." *Journal for the Study of the Old Testament* 30 (2006): 365–84.
Nasuti, Harry P. "The Interpretive Significance of Sequence and Selection in the Book of Psalms." In *The Book of Psalms: Composition & Reception*, edited by Peter W. Flint and Patrick D. Miller, 316–21. Supplements to Vetus Testamentum XCIX. Leiden: Brill, 2005.
Pajunen, Mika S. "Perspectives on the Existence of a Particular Authoritative Book of Psalms in the Late Second Temple Period." *Journal for the Study of the Old Testament* 39 (2014): 139–63.
Rendsburg, Gary. "Alliteration in the Exodus Narrative." In *Birkat Shalom: Studies in the Bible, Ancient Near Eastern Literature, and Postbiblical Judaism Presented to Shalom M. Paul on the Occasion of His Seventieth Birthday*, edited by Chaim Cohen, Victor Avigdor Hurowitz, Avi M. Hurvitz, Yochanan Muffs, Baruch J. Schwartz, and Jeffrey H. Tigay, 83–100. Winona Lake: Eisenbrauns, 2008.
Schaper, Joachim. "The Septuagint Psalter." In *The Oxford Handbook of the Psalms*, edited by William P. Brown, 173–84. Oxford: Oxford University Press, 2014.

Sharrock, Graeme E. "Psalm 74: A Literary-Structural Analysis." *Andrews University Seminary Studies* 21 (1983): 211–23.
Smith, Stephen J. "The Shape and Message of Psalms 73–78." *Catholic Biblical Quarterly* 83 (2021): 18–37.
Snaith, N.H. "The Meaning of the Hebrew אָךְ." *Vetus Testamentum* 14 (1964): 221–5.
Spieckermann, Hermann. "From the Psalter Back to the Psalms: Observations and Suggestions." *Zeitschrift für die alttestamentliche Wissenschaft* 132 (2020): 1–22.
Sumpter, Phillip. "The Coherence of Psalms 15–24." *Biblica* 94 (2013): 186–209.
Trotter, James M. "Death of the אלהים in Psalm 82." *Journal of Biblical Literature* 131 (2012): 221–39.
Walford, Nancy L. deClaissé. "The Canonical Approach to Scripture and the Editing of the Hebrew Psalter." In *The Shape and Shaping of the Book of Psalms: The Current State of Scholarship*, edited by Nancy L. deClaissé-Walford, 1–12. Ancient Israel and Its Literature 20. Atlanta, GA: SBL Press, 2014
Walker, A., and N. Lund. "The Literary Structure of the Book of Habakkuk." *Journal of Biblical Literature* 53 (1934): 355–70.
Wallace, Robert E. "The Narrative Effect of Psalms 84–89." *Journal of Hebrew Scriptures* 11 (2011): 2–15.
Waltke, Bruce K. "Supercripts, Postscripts, or Both?" *Journal of Biblical Literature* 114 (1991): 583–96.
Walton, J. H. "Psalms: A Cantata About the Davidic Covenant." *Journal of the Evangelical Theological Society* 34 (1991): 21–31.
Weber, Beat. "Akrostichische Muster in den Asaph-Psalmen." *Biblische Notizen* (2002): 79–94.
Weber, Beat. "Der Asaph Psalter—eine Skizze." In *Prophetie und Psalmen. Festschrift für Klaus Seybold zum 65. Geburtstag*, edited by B. Huwyler, H. P. Mathys, and B. Weber, 135–9. Alter Orient und Altes Testament 280. Münster: Ugarit-Verlag, 2001.
Weber, Beat. "'In Salem wurde sein Versteck …': Psalm 76 im Lichte literischer und historischer Kontexte neu gelesen." *Biblische Notizen* (1999): 85–103.
Weber, Beat. "Psalm 78: Geschichte mit Geschichte deuten," *Theologische Zeitschrift* 56 (2000): 193–214.
Weber, Beat. "Psalm 83 als Einzelpsalm und als Abschluss der Asaph-Psalmen." *Biblische Notizen* (2000): 64–84.
Weber, Beat. "Psalm 78 als 'Mitte' des Psalters?—ein Versuch." *Biblica* 88 (2007): 305–25.
Weber, Beat. "Verbindungslinien von den Psalmen Asaphs (Ps 50; 73–83) zu den Psalmen des Psalterteilbuchs IV (90–106). Erwägungen zu einem asaphitischen Trägerkreis." In *Trägerkreise in den Psalmen*, edited by Frank-Lothar Hossfeld, Johannes Bremer, and Till Magnus Steiner, 97–131. Bonner Biblische Beiträge 178. Göttingen: V&R unipress/ Bon University Press, 2017.
Weber, Beat. "Von der Psaltergenese zur Psaltertheologie: Der nächste Schritt der Psalterexegese?! Einige grundsätzliche Überlegungen zum Psalter als Buch und Kanonteil." In *The Composition of the Book of Psalms*, edited by Erich Zenger, 733–44. Bibliotheca Ephemeridum Theologicarum Lovaniensium 238. Leuven: Peeters, 2010.
Weber, Beat. "Zur Datierung der Asaph-Psalmen 74 und 79." *Biblica* 81 (2000): 521–32.
Willgren, David. "Did David Lay Down His Crown? Reframing Issues of Deliberate Juxtaposition and Interpretive Context in the 'Book' of Psalms with Psalm 147 as a Case in Point." In *Functions of Psalms and Prayers in the Late Second Temple Period*, edited by Mika S. Pajunen and Jeremy Penner, 212–28. Beihefte zur Zeitschrift für die alttestamentliche Wissenschaft 486. Berlin: De Gruyter, 2007.

Willgren, David. "A Teleological Fallacy in Psalms Studies? Decentralizing the 'Masoretic' Psalms Sequence in the Formation of the 'Book' of Psalms." In *Intertextualität und die Entstehung des Psalters: Methodische Reflexionen—Theologiegeschichtliche Perspektiven*, edited by Alma Brodersen, Friederike Neumann and David Willgren, 33-50. Forschungen zum Alten Testament 2. Reihe 114. Tübingen: Mohr Siebeck, 2020.

Willgren, David. "What Could We Agree On? Outlining Five Fundaments in the Research of the 'Book' of Psalms." In *The Formation of the Hebrew Psalter: The Book of Psalms Between Ancient Versions, Material Transmission and Canonical Exegesis. Erich Zenger In Memoriam*, edited by Gianni Barbiero, Marco Pavan, and Johannes Schnocks. Forschungen zum Alten Testament. Tübingen: Mohr Siebeck, 2021.

Wilson, Gerald H. "Evidence of Editorial Divisions in the Psalter." *Vetus Testamentum* 34 (1984): 337-52.

Wilson, Gerald H. "A First Century C.E. Date for the Closing of the Book of Psalms." *Jewish Bible Quarterly* 28 (2000): 102-10.

Wilson, Gerald H. "King, Messiah, and the Reign of God: Revisiting the Royal Psalms and the Shape of the Psalter." In *The Book of Psalms: Composition & Reception*, edited by Peter W. Flint and Patrick D. Miller, 391-406. Supplements to Vetus Testamentum XCIX. Leiden: Brill, 2005.

Wilson, Gerald H. "The Shape of the Book of Psalms." *Interpretation* 42 (1992): 129-42.

Wilson, Gerald H. "The Structure of the Psalter." In *Interpreting the Psalms: Issues and Approaches*, edited by David Firth and Phillip S. Johnston, 229-46. Downers Grove, IL: IVP Academic, 2005.

Wilson, Gerald H. "Understanding the Purposeful Arrangement of Psalms in the Psalter: Pitfalls and Promises." In *Shape and Shaping of the Psalter*, edited by J. Clinton McCann, 93-107. The Journal for the Study of the Old Testament Supplement Series 159. Sheffield: JSOT Press, 1993.

Wilson, Gerald H. "The Use of Royal Psalms at the 'Seams' of the Hebrew Psalter." *Journal for the Study of the Old Testament* 35 (1986): 85-94.

Yarchin, William. "Is There an Authoritative Shape for the Hebrew Book of Psalms?" *Revue Biblique* 215 (2015): 355-70.

Yarchin, William. "Why the Future of Canonical Hebrew Psalter Exegesis Includes Abandoning Its Own Premise." In *The Formation of the Hebrew Psalter: The Book of Psalms between Ancient Versions, Material Transmission and Canonical Exegesis. Erich Zenger in Memoriam*, edited by Gianni Barbiero, Marco Pavan and Johannes Schnocks. Forschungen zum Alten Testament. Tübingen: Mohr Siebeck, 2021.

Zenger, Erich. "Psalmenexegese und Psalterexegese: Eine Forschungsskizze." In *The Composition of the Book of Psalms*, edited by Erich Zenger, 17-65. Bibliotheca Ephemeridum Theologicarum Lovaniensium 238. Leuven: Peeters, 2010.

Zenger, Erich. "Was wird anders bei kanonischer Psalmenauslegung?." In Ein Gott, eine Offenbarung: Beiträge zur biblischen Exegese, Theologie und Spiritualität, edited by F. V. Reiterer, 397-413. Würzburg, Germany: Echter, 1991.

Dissertations

Brown Jones, Christine Dannette. "The Psalms of Asaph: A Study of the Function of a Psalm Collection." PhD diss., Baylor University, 2009.

Davis, Barry C. "A Contextual Analysis of Psalms 107-118." PhD diss., Trinity Evangelical Divinity School, 1996.

Dunn, Steven. "Wisdom Editing in the Book of Psalms: Vocabulary, Themes, and Structures." PhD diss., Marquette University, 2009.
Heiser, Michael S. "The Divine Council in Late Canonical and Non-Canonical Second Temple Jewish Literature." PhD diss., University of Wisconsin-Madison, 2004.
McCann, Clinton J. "Psalm 73: An Interpretation Emphasizing Rhetorical and Canonical Criticism." PhD diss., Duke University, 1985.

GENERAL INDEX

Aaronic benediction 143
acrostics 62
Allen, Leslie C. 71
Alter, Robert 99
Ancient Near East (ANE), culture of 163
Andrason, Alexander 85
anger and mercy 57
arc of suspense/tension (*Spannungsbogen*) 55
artifactual variations 7–8
Asaph 51
  collection 44, 47
  function 51
  Psalms 46, 50–3, 117
  Psalms 73–83, 45
  Psalter 53, 56
Assyrian crisis 53
author designation 3, 10
author-/editor-oriented approach 14–16
authoritative Psalters 5

Ballhorn, Egbert 14–15
Bar-Efrat, Shimon 24
Batto, B. 165
Bellinger, Bill 61
Berlin, Adele 21–2
biblical parallelism 21–32
Block, Daniel I. 34, 131, 171
Boadt, Lawrence 62–3
Boda, Mark J. 68
Bomberg Rabbinic Bible 9
Book III (MT) 133
Bouzard Jr., W. C. 81
Breck, John 76, 171
Brodersen, Alma 7–8, 16, 27
Brown, William P. 78
Broyles, Craig C. 68, 72, 75, 81–4, 103, 105–6, 143–4, 146, 159, 161, 179, 185
Brueggemann, Walter 61, 105, 186

Cairo Genizah 9
Calvin, John 80
chiasmus 62
Childs, Brevard S. 1, 186
Clifford, Richard J. 106–7, 109–10
Codex Leningradensis 4
Cole, Robert L. 27–8, 41–4, 65, 69–70, 96–7, 102, 121, 150
compositional arc (*Kompositionsbogen*) 46–7, 58
Creach, Jerome F. D. 136
cultic prophet-musicians 50

David 41, 109–10, 122
  dynasty of 49
David as king 45
David/Zion theology 67, 187
Davidic collection (Pss 51–72) 45
Davidic kingship 60
Davidic monarchy, failure of 67
Davidic/Zion covenant theology 41
  failure 40
Davidide 42
Davies, Andrew 68
Davis, Barry C. 139
DeClaissé-Walford, Nancy L. 61, 138
Dempsey, Carol J. 68
deutero-Asaph Psalms 51
diachrony 47
distant parallelism 24, 30; *see also* biblical parallelism
Divine anger and punishment 109
Driver, S. R. 108

editorial-critical hermeneutics 70
enemy quotation 74
Ephraim, tribe of 109

Final Hallel 7–8
Flesher, LeAnn Snow 68
Fløysvik, Ingvar 68

Fokkelman, J. P. 172
Formal correspondence, Psalm 73, 97–100

Gärtner, Judith 14, 56–8, 136
  compositional arcs 58
Gentry, Peter J. 11, 34, 36, 131, 179
God
  absence in the wicked's prosperity 75
  anger 45, 62, 69, 83, 108
    Israel's disobedience 62
  goodness 55, 89, 119
  hiding of his "right hand," 83
  Israelite beliefs about 72–80
  judgment of Judah 53
  kingship 85
  profile as the Great King/Judge 94
  self-revelation 119, 185
  status as Zion's Great King 89
  wrathful rejection 126
God is good to Israel 71–80, 89, 98–100,
    119, 122, 135–6, 154, 179, 185, 188
God of belief 170
God of experience 74
God of Israel's faith 74, 84, 137
God-lament psalms 81, 125–6, 140, 144, 185
Goulder, Michael D. 147
Grant, Jamie. A. 1, 32, 128
Greenstein, Edward 97–8, 118
Gunkel, Hermann 84

Handy, Lowell K. 163
Hebrew Masoretic Psalter (MT-150) 4, 16
Heiser, M. S. 163
Hensley, Adam D. 9, 16, 18, 65
Hieke, Thomas 61, 174
hinge (*Scharnier*) 55
Ho, Peter C. W. 23, 35, 58–60, 63, 102,
    128, 173–4
  Davidic collections 59
  lexemes or motifs 59
  on MT Psalter 58–9
  New Criticism 58
  organizational principles 58
  Rhetorical Criticism 58
  superscriptions 59
Holmstedt, R. D. 148
Hossfeld, Frank-Lothar 33, 47–8, 61, 84–5,
    105–6, 109, 115, 124, 134, 138,
    160, 171

Howard Jr., David M. 1, 25, 59

inter-psalm parallelism 24–6
internal reference systems (*internen
    Verweissystemen*) 14

Jacobson, Rolf A. 61, 83, 86–7, 162
Jain, Eva 10
Jensen, Joseph E. 35, 62, 82
Jerusalem sanctuary 129
Jones, Christine Dannette Brown 44–5,
    64–5, 84, 102, 124
  Asaph collection 44
  Psalm 50's placement 45
Joseph 117
Judah 87, 109
Judean Desert 3, 9–10
  Mas1e 9–11
  Mas1e 83:1, 3
  Mas1f 7

Kim, Hee Suk 144
Korahite collection (Pss 42–49) 45, 46
Kselman, John S. 62, 104–5, 115, 119–20
Kuntz, J. Kenneth 74

Leuenberger, Martin 54–6, 124
  Psalms 73–83, 55
lexical parallels between Psalms 73:4–15
    and 18–28 90
Lund, N. 172
Lunn, Nicholas P. 72

Maloney, Linda M. 160
Maskil of Asaph 127
Masoretic sequence, decentralization 7
Mays, James L. 86
mazkir 50
McCann, J. Clinton 35, 40–1, 44, 61, 67,
    71, 74–8, 90–1, 100
  assessment of Book I–III 40–1
  communal laments 41
  Davidic/Zion covenant theology 40–1
  exilic influence, Book I–III 40
McKelvey, Michael G. 26, 130
Millard, Matthias 46–7, 84, 105, 124
  compositional arc
    (*Kompositionsbogen*) 46
  form-criticism (*Formgeschichte*) 46

General Index

Miller, Cynthia L. 108
Miller, Patrick D. 105
Mitchell, David 50-2, 173
Mroczek, Eva 4, 6
MS B19^A 4, 9-12
  Psalms 73-83 in 11
MT Psalter 2, 11, 39, 51, 110, 126, 128, 130
  Book III 39-40, 61
  Books I-III 40
  literary unity 19
MT-150
  sequence 8
  synchronic analysis of 6

pairs of psalms (*Zwillingspsalmen*) 46
Pajunen, Mika S. 4-6
parallelism 21-32, 62
parallelomania 26
progressive repetition 36-7, 102, 131-3, 136, 143, 175-6, 186
prophetic liturgy 84
Psalm 73 analysis 24, 71-80
  Gattung of 71
  as introduction to Psalms 74-82, 179-81
  main theological message 80
  and Psalms 74-76, semantic Relationship 99
  Psalms 74-78, literary relationship 135-6
Psalm 74, analysis of 81-4, 105, 111
  faith crisis 82
  Psalms 75-76, parallels between 92
  theological message 100-1
Psalm 75, analysis of 84-7
Psalm 76, analysis of 87-8
  Songs of Zion 87
Psalm group of Psalms 77-8
  formal correspondence with Psalm 73, evidence 111-18
    analogous literary progression 111-12
    analogous network of parallels 112-17
    linguistic parallels with Psalm 73, 117-18
  formal correspondence with Psalm 73, interpretation 118-24
    structural implications for Psalms 73-83, 123-4

  theological message 122
Psalm 79, analysis 159-63
  exclusion of 138-41
  Mas1e 9
Psalm group of Psalms 80-1
  deuteronomistic interpretation 155-7
  formal correspondence with Psalm 73, evidence 149-54
    analogous literary progression 149-50
    analogous network of parallels 150-4
  formal correspondence with Psalm 73, interpretation 154-57
Psalm 80, analysis of 143-6
  deuteronomistic interpretation 155-7
Psalm 81, analysis of 146-9
  deuteronomistic interpretation 155-7
Psalms 79/82, the psalm group of
  formal correspondence with Psalm 73, evidence 166-70
    analogous literary progression 166-7
    analogous network of parallels 167-71
  formal correspondence with Psalm 73, interpretation
    Theological message 171
Psalm 82, analysis 163-6
Psalm 83, analysis 181-2
  appendix to Psalms 73-82, 183
  conclusion to Psalms 73-82, 182-3
Psalms 73-8
  editorial strategy for 136-8
Psalms 74-76
  formal correspondence with Psalm 73, evidence 88-97
    analogous literary progression 88-9
    analogous network of parallels 89-96
    linguistic parallels 96-7
  formal correspondence with Psalm 73, interpretation 97-102
    correspondence with Psalm 73
    implications for Psalms 73-83, 101-2
    the psalm group of formal
    theological message 100-1
Psalms 74-82
  editorial strategy for 176-9
Psalms 74-76 and Psalms 77-78 as parallel Psalm groups
  evidence 125-7
  interpretation 127-30

Psalms 79–82
  dual response to the sixth-century crisis 175–6
  unit 171–5
    evidence 171–3
    interpretation 174–5
psalms exegesis 67
Psalms of Asaph 64, 67
Psalms of Ascents 46
Psalms of Solomon, The 5
Psalterexegese (editorial criticism) 1–2, 67, 69
  "artifactual" evidence from Judean Desert 6
  criteria for identifying editorially significant parallels 27–32
  deliberate design and structure 32–5
  doxologies 7
  identification and interpretation 20–1
  incidental language 26–7
  method centering on parallelism 21–32
  methodology 2–37
  paratextual features 35–7
  Psalms exegesis 18–20
  synchronic approach 13–18
  teleological fallacy 6

Qumran 4–5, 10

Ras Shamra 164
Rendsburg, Gary A. 17, 137
Robertson, O. Palmer 48–50, 173

Schultz, Richard L. 131
Sharrock, Graeme E. 81, 95
Shiloh sanctuary 109
Sitz im Leben 13
Smith, Stephen J. 125
Snaith, N. H. 80
Snearly, Michael K. 22–3, 64, 91, 130
Song of Moses 107
Spieckermann, Hermann 19

Tanner, Beth L. 61
Tate, Marvin E. 71, 74, 76, 84, 87–8, 99, 104, 106, 143, 149, 159, 163–4
temple's destruction 136, 185
TR-150 (Textus Receptus-150) 9
  TR Pss 90-106, 18

Vassar, John S. 71
Vorlage 11

Walker, A. 172
Waltke, Bruce K. 23, 25
Weber, Beat 3, 47, 52–4, 81, 104, 116, 123, 134, 136
  on Asaph psalms 52–3
  preexilic Asaph Psalter 53
weisheitspsalm 108
Welch, John W. 171
Whybray, R. N. 68
Willgren, David 3, 6–7, 12, 26–7, 128, 137
Wilson, Gerald H. 1, 4, 20–1, 39–40, 44, 136
  assessment of Book III 39–40
  working hypothesis fallacy 21

Yahweh 60, 87, 89, 143
Yahweh's anger 56–7
Yahweh's anger limiting mercy 57
Yarchin, William 3, 9, 11–12, 18

Zakovich, Yair 91
Zenger, Erich 1–2, 19–20, 33, 47–8, 61, 83–5, 105, 109, 115, 124, 134, 138, 160, 171, 181
zikhron (remembrancing) ritual 51
Zion 41, 43, 84, 93, 95, 107, 109–10, 122, 131
  lion/warrior 87
  psalms 41
  temple 60
  theology 68, 125, 127, 132–3

INDEX OF BIBLICAL REFERENCES

Genesis
2:2 [2×] 78
2:3 78
26:29 73

Exodus
10:3 164
15:1–18 109
21:6 164
22:7–8 164
27 164
33:18 73
34:6–7 30, 73, 105, 109–11, 113, 115, 119, 122, 132, 135

Leviticus
17:7 78
20:5 78
21:23 76

Numbers
14:18 105
14:27 164

Deuteronomy
23:7 73
31:16 78
32:1–3 107
32:1–43 107
32:8–9 163

Joshua
1 116
24:29 116

Judges
2:17 78
8:27 78
14:5 96

1 Kings
18:27 162

2 Kings
25 68

1 Chronicles
16 7
16:4 51, 94
23:30 94
25:3 94
29:13 94

2 Chronicles
5:13 94
7:6 94
30:9 105
31:2 94

Ezra
3:11 94

Nehemiah
9:17 105
12:24 94

Esther
9:12 73
10:3 73

Job
20:8 76
27:20 76
30:24 160
37:4 96

Psalms
1–2 40
2 110
2:4 174
3 162

3:4	149	41:9	117
4:4	149	42–43	49
5:4	149	42–44	40
7:11–14	149	42:3	162
8	30	42:10	162
9:9	85	43:2	126
9–10	46	44:9	94
9/10	162	44:10	126
10	29	44:14	174
10:9	87	44:18	144
10:18	117	44:19	144
11	162	44:24	126
12	114, 162	46	87, 110
12:6	149	48	87, 110
12:8	149	50	12, 45, 50–
14:5–6	149		1, 53, 73
14/53	162	50:1	56
15–24	46	50:15	51
17:6	149	51:6	149
18	29	53:4	144
18:22–33	73	54:6–7	149
19:15	114	55:17–20	149
20–21	46	55:17–24	149
21	29	56:10–12	149
22	162	57:3–4	149
22:8	174	58:11–12	149
22:14	96	59	162
25:3	149	59:9	174
25:5	149	59:11	149
25:8	73	59:17–18	149
25:15	149	60:3	126
27:10	149	60:12	126
28:5	149	61:6	149
31–35	9	61:7	116–17
31:11	116	64	162
31:15	149	64:8–10	149
31:20–2	149	65:12	116
34:9	73	66:7	85
34:15	73	69:19	114
35:6	76	69:37	169
35:8	76	70:6	149
35:16	174	71	162
35:18	94	71–72	66
36:6–7	149	71:3	149
37–39	75	71:5–8	149
38:9	96	71:14	117
38:16	49	71:20	149
40:18	149	72	43
41:2–4	149	72–82	3

Index of Biblical References

72:14	114	74:12–17	144
73	24, 28, 36,	74:12–23	51
	40–1, 44–8, 51,	74:13	126
	61–2, 69, 119	74:13–14	126
73–74	40, 49	74:14	126
73–75	61	74:16	126
73–77	47, 55, 60, 63	74:16–17	94
73–78	33, 62	74:18	48, 94, 126
73–82	185, 188	74:18–21	14
73–83	3–13, 20, 26,	74:19	126
	33, 36, 39, 46–	74:21	48, 94
	7, 50–1, 56, 60,	74:22	48, 126
	66, 77, 94–5,	74:23	126
	114, 116	75	14, 18, 30, 35,
73–89	41		41–3, 45, 51,
73:1	118		53, 56, 58, 62
73:1–16	35, 62, 88, 118	75–76	41, 47, 49, 60
73:4–15	90	75:1	127
73:10	42	75:2	29, 48, 73,
73:15	118		94, 127
73:15–17	42	75:3	30, 42, 48
73:17	62, 69	75:3–4	85
73:17–28	60	75:4	94
73:18	28	75:5	48
73:18–28	35, 62, 90	75:9	48
73:27	78	75:10–11	42
73/74	41	76	14, 18, 41–3,
74	14, 30, 34–5,		45, 51, 58, 110
	39–42, 45,	76–78	53
	47, 51, 53, 58,	76:1	123
	61, 63, 68	76:2	29, 48, 123
74-88	143	76:4	29
74–76	24, 29, 35, 48,	76:8	48
	54, 58, 60,	76:8–10	73
	62–3, 185	76:9–10	14, 48
74–78	31, 130–2, 135	76:10	56
74–79	58	76:10–77:1	9
74:1	48, 56, 126	76:12–13	87
74:1–3	129	77	14, 42–3, 47–8,
74:1–11	100, 131		51, 55, 63
74:2	126, 129	77-78	24
74:3	28, 126, 129	77–78	10, 29, 35,
74:3–4	60, 69		118, 185
74:4	30	77–79	45, 48–9,
74:7	29, 48, 94		57, 134
74:9	117, 126	77:1–11	118
74:10	48, 56, 94, 126	77:2	116
74:11	126	77:2–3	51
74:12	126	77:3	117, 126

77:4	126	78:55	169
77:5	118	78:61	114
77:6	114, 116, 126	78:65	76
77:7	117, 123, 126	78:65–72	111, 125
77:8	117, 126	78:67–72	129
77:8–9	111	78:68	129
77:8–11	111, 118, 132	78:68–72	41
77:8–13	51	78:69	129
77:9	118, 126	78:72	116
77:10	126	79	14, 30, 40–3, 47, 51, 53, 56, 62–3, 68–9
77:11	126		
77:12	114, 126		
77:12–21	41, 118	79–80	40, 46, 48
77:13	114, 126	79–82	60, 63, 135
77:14	126	79:1	160
77:14–21	114	79:1–3	51
77:15	114, 123, 126	79:2	56
77:16	114, 117, 126	79:5	56
77:17	126	79:10	97
77:18	126	79/82	24, 29, 35, 185
77:20	126	80	40–3, 45, 50–1, 53, 56, 61–3
77:21	116, 126		
78	41, 46–8, 51, 53, 56–7, 63	80–81	24, 29, 35, 60, 185
78–83	47, 55, 60, 63	80:2	43, 117
78:1	42, 116	80:6	117
78:1–2	107	80:9	169
78:2	114	80:18	42, 127
78:3	127	81	46, 51, 53, 62
78:4	114, 118, 127	81–82	48
78:6	118, 127	81–83	10
78:6–7	9	81:2–3	9
78:8	118	81:8	51
78:10	117	81:9	43
78:11	114	81:9–15	42
78:12	114	81:9–17	45
78:12–13	114	81:12	43
78:17	117	81:12–13	43
78:14	116	81:12–15	62
78:26	114	81:12–17	41
78:32	114	81:14	43
78:33	116	81:15	127
78:35	114	81:15–16	151
78:36–37	9–10	82	41–3, 46, 51, 53, 61, 73
78:38	111, 127		
78:38–72	12	82:1	3, 10, 164
78:42–55	114	82:4	56
78:45	127	82:8	51
78:53	116		

Index of Biblical References

83	12, 40, 42, 44, 46, 48, 51, 53, 56, 61, 63	107–108	30
		107:1	73
		107:2	114
83:1 of Mas1e	3, 10	108:12	126
83:5	97, 117, 169	109:30	94
83:18	51	109:31	149
84	42, 87	111:1	94
84–88	47	111:4	105
85	40, 42	112:4	105
85:1	41	115	162
86	42	115:2	162
86:5	105, 149	115:14	117
86:6	73	116:5	105
86:7	149	118:1	73
86:15	105	118:29	73
87	87	119:111	169
88	40, 42	120–134	3
88:15	126	120:3	117
89	39–40	122	87
89:1–38/39–52	41	123:4	174
89:39	126	126:5–6	149
89:39–52	41	130:7–8	149
90:4	116	135	56
90:9	116	136	56
90:10	116	136:1	73
90:15	116	137:8	149
93–100	26	139:7–12	149
94	162	140:6–7	149
95:10	116	140:13–14	149
96:10	85	142:6–7	149
96:13	73	143:12	149
98:7–9	73	145:8	105
98:9	85	146–150	6–9, 16
99:4	85	147	7
100:5	73		
102:25	116	Canticles	
102:28	116	4:8	87
103:4	114		
103:8	105	Isaiah	
104:21	96	5:1–7	145
104:22	87	5:29	96
105	56	10:9–10	162
105:17	117	13:9	76
106:1	73, 94	29:7	76
106:7	56	36:18b–20	162
106:10	114	36:22	51
106:39	78	38:18	95
106:44–46	149	47:9	76
107–18	30	47:11	76

48:17–18	73	79:6–7	160
50:5	144, 146	79:8	160
54:14	73	79:9	160
59:13	144, 146	79:13	160
66:17	76		
		Lamentations	
Jeremiah		3:25	73
2:10	78		
2:15	96	Ezekiel	
2:21	145	6:9	78
3:1	78	13:16	73
3:6	78	15:1–8	145
3:8	78	16:15	78
4:7	87	16:35	78
6:14	73	16:41	78
7:33	160	21:7	76
8:12	160	22:25	96
8:15	73	23:3	78
10:25	160	23:19	78
11:10	160	23:30	78
12:10	145	23:43	78
14:13	73	26:21	76
14:16	160		
14:19	73	Hosea	
16:4	160	1:2	78
16:6	160	2:7	78
19:8	160	4:12	78
23:1	160	4:15	78
23:12	76	9:1	78
23:26	164	10:1	145
24:9	160	11:10 (2×)	96
25:30 (3×)	96		
25:38	87	Joel	
26:18	160	2:13	105
29:18	160	2:17	162
33:9	73	3:16	96
33:11	73		
34:20	160	Amos	
38:22	146	1:2	96
42:18	160	3:4	87, 96
44:8	160	3:8	96
44:12	160		
48:10	78, 80	Micah	
50:25	78, 80	1:6	160
51:38	96	3:12	160
51:51	76	6:2	165
79:13	160	7:10	162
79:4	160		

Nahum		Malachi	
1:7	73	3:13–18	73
1:7–8	78		
2:13	87	DSS (Dead Sea Scrolls)	
3:4	78	4Q380	7
		4Q87	9–10
Zephaniah		6Q5	9
1:6	144, 146	11Q6	9–10
1:15	76	11Q8	9–10
3:3	96		

www.ingramcontent.com/pod-product-compliance
Lightning Source LLC
Chambersburg PA
CBHW062226300426
44115CB00012BA/2240